Aethelred II

King of the English
978–1016

Mart
Te

To Janine

AETHELRED II

KING OF THE ENGLISH
978–1016

RYAN LAVELLE

TEMPUS

A NOTE ON SPELLING

Philologists may shudder to remark upon the liberties that I have taken in the use of Old English in this book. I have attempted to normalise Anglo-Saxon characters, ð (*eth*), þ (*thorn*) and æ (*ash*) into *th* (for *eth* and *thorn*) and *ae* respectively. Where I have cited original Old English (with translations), I have cut out the original characters and replaced them with the modern characters. I do this with some trepidation, as I recognise that it removes some of the richness of the language spoken by our linguistic ancestors, but at the same time I hope that it may serve to make the words a little more accessible. On the rare occasions on which I quote original Old Icelandic, I have retained the original characters, as these characters are used in modern Icelandic.

Contemporary spellings of Aethelred's name included *Æðelræd* (amongst other variant spellings), but generations of scholars have normalised his name in different ways: as 'Ethelred', 'Æthelred', 'Ethelraed' and, used here, 'Aethelred'. My separation of the A from the E in the first letter of his name is really a concession to computer cataloguing and a desire to hang onto a semblance of the Old English word. However, I have not attempted to standardise the spelling of his name where I am citing someone else's work.

First published 2002

PUBLISHED IN THE UNITED KINGDOM BY:
Tempus Publishing Ltd
The Mill, Brimscombe Port
Stroud, Gloucestershire GL5 2QG

PUBLISHED IN THE UNITED STATES OF AMERICA BY:
Tempus Publishing Inc.
2 Cumberland Street
Charleston, SC 29401

British Library Cataloguing in Publication Data.
A catalogue record for this book is available from the British Library.

ISBN O 7524 1993 5

Typesetting and origination by Tempus Publishing.
PRINTED AND BOUND IN GREAT BRITAIN.

CONTENTS

FOREWORD

In bringing together an account of the political abilities of one of England's least favourably regarded monarchs, I am very conscious of the achievements of the excellent scholarship of recent decades. This has placed Aethelred's reign into a more realistic context than traditional historiography has assigned him. I hope that the following pages, as well as the endnotes and bibliography, go some way toward reflecting these academic developments.

More specifically, I am very grateful to Barbara Yorke for some useful discussions, which have been instrumental in stimulating my interests in aspects of King Aethelred's reign, and for much specific advice. Other friends and colleagues at King Alfred's College have also provided support and encouragement, as well as useful discourse: especially Chloë Edwards, whose preliminary readings of much of this book and advice on saints' cults have been invaluable; Stephany Leach, for her enthusiasm in undertaking a detailed anthropological analysis of work on the relics of 'King Edward the Martyr' and Andrew Reynolds for encouraging me to write this book and for information on archaeological aspects of later Anglo-Saxon England. Kirstine Då has also been very helpful in her willingness to discuss aspects of Aethelred's reign in relation to Danish archaeology.

My thanks also go to members of undergraduate seminar groups at New College, Southampton and King Alfred's College, Winchester, who I have had the pleasure of teaching while writing this book. Some of their often enthusiastic discussions of aspects of King Aethelred's reign and later Anglo-Saxon kingship have been very useful to me. I am especially grateful to Maria Drummond for drawing my attention to the fact that one of the lawcodes of the reign, I Aethelred, can be elucidated with the aid of a simple flow diagram. Invitations from the Barton-on-Humber branch of the Workers' Education Association, to speak at their weekend school on England 1000 A.D., and from the Winchester Branch of the Historical Association, to deliver an evening lecture, have also allowed me to formulate some of my ideas for this book.

My father, Don Lavelle, has been a great help and a source of inspiration in his provision of a series of excellent colour and black and white illustrations, which he undertook with great enthusiasm. Our co-operation in getting these illustrations together has been a great and enjoyable experience for me and I thank him for it. His contribution to this book more than speaks for itself.

Finally, I am deeply grateful to my partner, Janine Shepherdson. Her editorial skills have been brought to bear on various chapters and many of the photographs in these pages have resulted from her willingness to visit the sites of Anglo-Saxon England with me. Janine's encouragement, support, understanding and patience during the long hours of writing have been much needed and appreciated by me during these past few months. It is to Janine that I wish to dedicate this book.

Winchester, May 2002

INTRODUCTION: REPUTATIONS

At some point around the beginning of the second millennium A.D., an Icelandic poet and warrior crossed the North Sea from Scandinavia and, arriving in the thriving port of London, made his way to the court of the English King. Gunnlaug Serpent-Tongue, whose saga was recorded amongst the books of the Icelanders in the thirteenth century, was a poet of renown who had already gained fame in the court of the King of the Swedes. Both poet and royal patron gained much from this mutually beneficial relationship. Skaldic poetry was an integral part of the courtly life of the kingdoms and principalities of northern Europe and, so it seemed to the writer of *Gunnlaugs Saga Ormstungu*, Aethelred, King of the English, was an entirely fitting patron: no less than 'a good ruler' (*góðr hofðingi*) who later rewarded the poet for his praise verses with a valuable scarlet cloak and employed Gunnlaug as a retainer.[1]

Whether Gunnlaug Serpent-Tongue, or his historical antecedent, really arrived in the English court and delivered a skaldic poem to Aethelred is a question which cannot be safely answered here, although, in its defence, it should be noted that the saga demonstrates a good sense of historicity, and Russell Poole has noted that the so-called *Aðalrádsdrápa* has a ring of authenticity.[2] However, what matters is the acceptance of Aethelred within the same world that the heroes of saga society inhabited. By the thirteenth century, Aethelred was viewed as a perfectly good northern European King, on a par with his Danish, Norwegian and Swedish counterparts.

English and post-Conquest Anglo-Norman vilifications of Aethelred 'Unraed' ('No-counsel' or more usually 'the Unready') have a somewhat greater influence in shaping historical views of the King. However, it is instructive to note that the Skaldic verses, which record the Viking attacks upon England perpetrated by King Swein 'Forkbeard' of Denmark and his son Cnut (later to be, in Denmark at least, Cnut 'the Great'), treat Aethelred as a good King, patron, or at the very least as a worthy opponent or ally.[3] The reasons for such a divergence of opinion between the cross-Channel world of the post-Conquest English sources and the North Sea world of the sagas may have stemmed from a number of points of view: beating a worthy opponent always makes a good story (witness the Allied forces' encounters with the 'Elite Republican Guard' in Iraq and Kuwait in 1991 – very rarely are these recalled as Iraqi conscripts); Charles Plummer's suggestion that such portrayals of Aethelred as a 'good ruler' stem from an admiration of his son King Edward the Confessor may equally hold some weight, but for the fact that Anglo-Norman accounts of Aethelred are similarly full of admiration for Edward, but so much more vitriolic about his father Aethelred.[4] What Margaret Ashdown

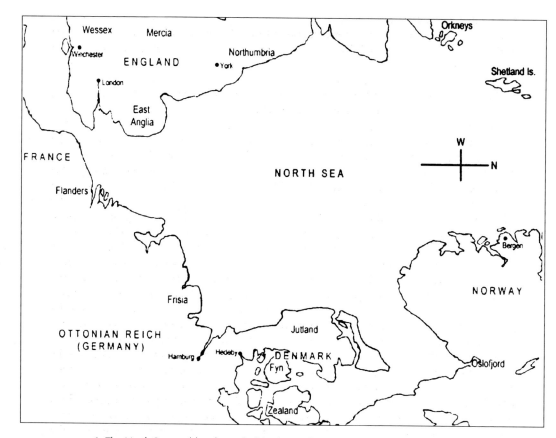

1. The North Sea world at the end of the first millennium, as seen from Scandinavia.

suggested was 'undeserved prestige' for Aethelred may have stemmed from the King's associations with such heroes of later sagas as Olaf Tryggvason.[5] However, the differences of views of King Aethelred may also be a product of the Norman Conquest and the new cross-Channel spheres of influence, which resulted during the later eleventh century. In the later tenth and early eleventh centuries, Anglo-Saxons and Vikings inhabited the same world and shared the same social and political norms; they understood each other.

In contrast to the sagas, but symptomatic of the popular English reputation of King Aethelred, is his brief depiction as the elder brother of Alfred the Great in the eponymously-titled 1969 film. Although one scene in the film is meant to portray Aethelred I, what we get is his namesake, Aethelred II. At the Battle of Ashdown in 871 we are presented with a King Aethelred who owes a great deal to the historical caricature of Aethelred II, then current in schoolbooks. The energetic younger brother Alfred, at that point a prince or *aetheling*, suggests that they lure the Viking hordes down the valley by the use of a decoy in the form of the recumbent King Aethelred: 'I like the plan', replies the King, 'I like it very much. It gives me something to do without doing anything. I always like doing that'.

While Anglo-Saxon history is complicated enough without mixing up our I's and II's, this image of the 'do-nothing king' is one which has prevailed in implicit and explicit criticisms of King Aethelred II. On the one hand, we have William of Malmesbury's twelfth-century indictment of the King who would not raise himself out of the royal bed.[6] In twentieth-century literature, we have J.R.R. Tolkien's picture of the aged King Théoden, deeply under the influence of the evil advisor, Grimer Wormtongue, characters in the *Lord of the Rings* seemingly derived from the traditional image of King Aethelred and his chief advisor Eadric *Streona* (at least, that is, until Tolkien lifts Théodan out of ill-advised peace and into glory).[7] In more academic historical prose, Sir Frank Stenton, in 1943, damned Aethelred with the line that 'historians who see the reign of Æthelred as a time of national degeneracy have good contemporary opinion behind them'.[8]

Judgements on pre-industrial history favour active rulers: rulers who win battles; rulers who instigate sweeping wholesale reform of malevolent corruption within the kingdom; the Alfreds, Williams, Henrys and Richards of the English kingdom. Any *laissez-faire* approach to the administration of a medieval kingdom provides, it seems, a wholly unacceptable historical epitaph. The ninth-century Frankish court writer, Einhard, writing some two centuries before Aethelred's reputation was to be established upon the parchment of the Abingdon manuscript of the Anglo-Saxon Chronicle, set out the damning indictment of the 'do-nothing kings' of later Merovingian Francia in the seventh century. These kings sat in the court, with their beards and locks flowing, meeting ambassadors and parroting the words which their mayoral 'advisors' (the ancestors of Charlemagne himself) had given them.[9] The image of the last Merovingians being pulled around their kingdom in ox-carts as they held this pretence of royal power, which Einhard so graphically describes, is an image that has been held infamous in French history. It appears in nineteenth and twentieth-century school textbooks, and was as well-known in France as those staples of traditional English schoolbooks: Cnut holding back the tide or Alfred burning the cakes.

Was Aethelred similarly inactive? It would seem somewhat disingenuous, therefore, to write a biography of a 'do-nothing' king. This would make historical biography the preserve of the active 'makers' of history, whose actions can be seen to have tangible results. As modern historians have the luxury (or poisoned chalice?) of an embarrassment of private papers, official documents signed and sealed, minute books and diaries, it could even be suggested that intentions are just as important, if impossible to discern. Early medieval historians merely have the *Lives* of a few select kings and it is these, the likes of Charlemagne and Alfred who (perhaps understandably) attract the lions' share of biographical history. For Aethelred, we have no private correspondence (if indeed any royal correspondence could be called 'private' in this period) and no biographies. However, we do have the Abingdon manuscript of the Anglo-Saxon Chronicle (also known as the 'C' manuscript), which does its level best to show the decline of the English kingdom in the face of Aethelred's apparent addiction to bad advice, a tendency which Simon Keynes aptly characterises as 'a dead man writing his own post-mortem'.[10] Written early in Cnut's reign, probably from eastern England rather than Abingdon,[11] Keynes noted that the Abingdon manuscript was a product of the depths of defeat, in which every action and every defeat encompassed part of the apparent masterplan of Danish victory over the English people. In this version of the Anglo-Saxon Chronicle, therefore, we may have an antidote to the somewhat eulogising tendencies of medieval ruler biographies.

This study of King Aethelred 'the Unready', and through him an introduction to the turbulent political life of the tenth and eleventh-century English kingdom, will have an inevitable interest in the operations of the Vikings. That is only natural, given the resurgence of Scandinavian military activity in the latter half of the tenth century, and the fact that the attacks make a fine narrative. However, other chapters that follow consider Aethelred in the context of his kingdom: in terms of his family relations, the composition of the nobility of the kingdom, and King Aethelred's legislative capacities.

It is probably appropriate to conclude this introduction, therefore, not with the negativity of the 'traditional' views of Aethelred's reign, but with some recognition of the King from his own time. Keynes has noted that amongst the heavy criticism propounded by William of Malmesbury, one passage stands out as a possible indication of an alternative tradition, which William, writing in the twelfth century, had heard from his elders: 'as we learn from our forebears', wrote William, King Aethelred was neither 'a great fool nor excessively cowardly'.[12] While there are hints of damnation with faint praise in William's words, it nonetheless seemed to perplex him that the calamities, which he perceived as a character-istic of Aethelred's reign could have happened to such a ruler. Had William been able to separate the contemporary views about the greater part of the reign, from those written about its last years, then perhaps he may have been a little less perplexed.

Similarly relevant is a view from the King's contemporary and distant kinsman, Ealdorman Aethelweard of the south-western provinces, who was engaged in writing a history of the English kings for his German cousin, a certain Matilda. A chapter was planned 'on the reign of King Aethelred and his deeds (*actibus eius*)', but it was never finished.[13] Writing around the late 980s, before the Viking attacks on the English kingdom had taken their bitter hold,[14] we might speculate on what 'deeds' Ealdorman Aethelweard had in mind for the King. Had these been finished, we may have had an entirely different perception of the English King; one which would have been more contemporary with the first decades of his rule rather than the last few years of Viking rampage. Aethelred can be viewed in the light of tenth-century Anglo-Saxon kingship, alongside the reigns of Edward, Athelstan, Edmund and Edgar; those 'deeds of King Aethelred' may thus become far more visible.

1

KINGS, KINGSHIP AND THE KINGDOM OF THE ENGLISH

Aethelred II, youngest son of King Edgar, was arguably the second king (following his half-brother Edward) to ascend to a throne of 'the kingdom of the English' without having to struggle to bring a wider realm together. Did this therefore mean that the unbounded visions and ambitions of his ancestors Alfred, Edward the Elder and Athelstan had finally come to fruition in a wider English kingdom, to which Aethelred was a natural heir? It will be argued in this chapter that this was not so much the case as that the kingdom of England was still very much an artificial creation overseen from the south and while there was a wider sense of 'English' identity, regional and, importantly, kinship group identities were still very much at large within the kingdom.

Much ink has been spilt by scholars in recent years in arguments over the development of the later Anglo-Saxon state, as well as national and regional identities within that state. As part of the development of an overarching government of great sophistication in its administrative abilities, especially its capacity to tax,[1] we can see an important legal and ideological framework which imposed an 'English' identity upon the elite groups of lowland Britain. However, this should not be seen as a West Saxon 'imperialism' imposed simply by right of conquest. Anglo-Saxon kings were more subtle than this, and the ability of Aethelred II to remain on the English throne for nearly four decades suggests that he relied on more than aggression to assert his authority. Academic studies in recent years have shown the importance of the regional identities that survived and even flourished within Anglo-Saxon society. An important aspect of these studies is the growing recognition that these identities could be politically rather than necessarily only 'socially' based.

Above all, the view of the Danelaw as a nearly monolithic 'racially' distinct area has developed into an interpretation of ethnicities which emerged through self-awareness. In our own society, often unsure of its own identities, the idea of 'ethnicity' can take on many forms, not least of which is a synonym for 'racial'. For the tenth and eleventh centuries, by contrast, we should see 'ethnicity' in its broadest sense, not in terms of blood, but an identity implicitly invested with the 'idea' that people belonged to a group. Such regional identities were, by necessity, tied up with those of families and wider kin-groups, as they had been for many hundreds of years.

2. The substantial fortifications at Wareham in Dorset. Wareham was probably fortified during the reign of Alfred the Great in the late ninth century.

3. The defences of the late West-Saxon kingdom, planned so that no part of the kingdom was more than twenty miles from a fortification.

4. Portchester in Hampshire. Portchester was a Roman shore fort refortified in the late ninth century or during the early tenth century when it passed from the Bishop of Winchester into royal hands.

Therefore, when we are looking at the England of the late tenth and early eleventh centuries, we need to rid ourselves of the cultural and emotional baggage of the following centuries. Hastings, Runnymede, Bannockburn, Agincourt, Bosworth, Marston Moor, Culloden, Trafalgar, Alamein, all of the events that succeeding generations have used in the creation of an 'English' identity, were in the future. Despite the political existence of a kingdom of the English for the best part of a century before Aethelred's reign and the ideological influence of Bede's *Gens Anglorum* ('race of the Angles' or 'English') for two and a half centuries, these were still the preserve of intellectual and political discourse.[2] The natural unit for most of those within the English 'regions' was the family and the wider bonds that marriage and kinship could bring into that familial unit. These noble families may have recognised their 'Englishness' at some level but, first and foremost, they defined themselves in terms of their kin. Of course this may hardly be a startling revelation, and is perhaps par for the course in view of the number of studies of Anglo-Saxon society, which emphasise the importance of the family unit for the survival of the individual within that unit, from Dorothy Whitelock's seminal work on the *Beginnings of English Society*, to Richard Fletcher's recent study of *Bloodfeud* in late Anglo-Saxon England. Nonetheless, it needs to be emphasised that an examination of the kingdom of the English should begin by seeing the inhabitants of that kingdom in context, and for this the mental landscape of a *tabula rasa* is necessary. Our area of study is an 'England' which is by all intents and purposes different from the 'England' that we are familiar with. This may, therefore, require a mental adjustment in order to view those 'regions' and at best remove the pre-conceived notions of English 'national' identity from those areas and avoid seeing them as primitive versions of parts of an English whole. Even the idea itself of regional identities is an artificial conception, as it implicitly requires a conscious distinction from the national whole. Ideally, we should begin by seeing the natural unit of early medieval political society as the family group, and its relations with other family groups as the conduits for communication within this society. At the very least, we should acknowledge that

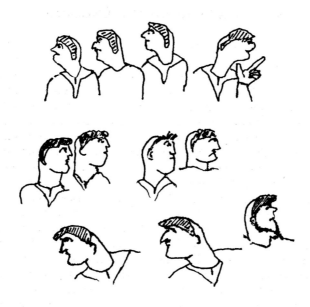

5. The ideal image of the Vikings as the Normans wished to see themselves, portrayed on the Bayeux Tapestry. An Old English letter of the late Anglo-Saxon period berates the addressee for his insistence upon wearing hair that was shaved at the back and long at the front, implying that with a hairstyle they were assuming a Viking (and thus 'pagan') way of life.

the present political geography of England has a great influence upon our understanding of the same area and its inhabitants over a millennium ago. 'Regional' and 'ethnic' identities may be an inevitable product of such social relations, it being more probable that families have relations with other families within their geographical locality (and mutually intelligible languages certainly help), but such regionalism is only a product of the family bonds and not its defining factor.

Recent historiography tracing the families and their patterns of influence and patronage has been instrumental in allowing such interpretations to be followed in the 'regions' of early medieval England.[3] While we can see the creation of an 'English state' as a conscious and even artificial achievement, the fruit of the hard work of many Anglo-Saxon politicians and politically-inclined theologians,[4] we cannot necessarily make a distinction between the 'State' as the product of the kings and his advisors, and 'Region', as the preserve of Mafia-like powerful families who operated independently of the Crown. The royal family had similar interests to the nobility, creating bonds of kinship, extending familial spheres of influence and building up family lands, as opposed to those held on an official basis for their upkeep. When referring to the royal 'house' of Wessex, it must be acknowledged that rather than implying some superior distinction from the average family, the house was indeed the basic unit of the family.[5] The Aethelred who we see here was in so many ways an integral part of such a kin-based society: he was a son, a grandson, a nephew, a brother, a cousin, a husband, a father and father-in-law, an uncle, and a grandfather. It is the products of these bonds with other families and the political power which emerged from these bonds that made the person of King Aethelred II such an important part of this society.

West Saxon Kings and England

Aethelred was born into a long and distinguished line of kings – a line which had emerged – or at least saw itself as having emerged, from Cerdic, the sixth-century pre-Christian founder of the dynasty. Of course, this was not necessarily a direct lineal descent any more than the current royal family could be said to be directly descended from William the Conqueror, but here that mattered little: the very idea of direct descent was still there, and in the ninth century the West Saxon house was the *Cerdicingas*, the people of Cerdic, implying a very special kinship bond with the founder of the dynasty whose position was semi-mythical. This lineage, by the time of the compilation of the 'official' West Saxon version of the Anglo-Saxon Chronicle for the court of King Alfred, had also come to include no less than the pagan god Woden, Old Testament figures and Christ.[6] Again, such a descent may not have been literally believed within the House of Cerdic or by those who dealt with it, but the spirit was there, nonetheless. This was dynastic continuity over a long period, or so it seemed, and by the tenth century the sense of 'great' West Saxon kings was still evident within the royal family. The south-western Ealdorman Aethelweard, related to the king by degrees, like so many of the nobles in late Anglo-Saxon England, produced a Chronicle of the events up to the middle of the tenth century, which was a eulogy of the achievements of King Alfred the Great and his successors in creating an English kingdom.

Even by the late tenth century, then, Alfred the Great was still very much alive in the hearts of the West Saxon royal family; his foundations of the New Minster in Winchester, Shaftesbury in Dorset, and, to a lesser extent, on the island of Athelney in Somerset, were still patronised by kings and their families, no less in the case of Aethelred, whose donation of a tower to the New Minster in the early years of his reign was recorded with some pride.[7] The burden of the past and the achievement of generations, weighed heavily upon Aethelred's shoulders, perhaps more heavily as he grew up quickly as king and the only survivor of this direct line. It is from Aethelred's great-great-grandfather, Alfred, that we can see tangible signs of the emergence of a West Saxon kingship with energy and a vision for rule over all the 'Anglo-Saxons', not just 'overlordship' in the sense of pre-Viking England. It was, however, the politics of the realisation of this vision that were to determine the course of history in the English kingdom over the following centuries. In the tenth century at least, this 'England' seems to have been superimposed upon a network of regional polities and the spheres of influence of noble families, which, *mutatis mutandis*, were still present, even if the Viking activities of the ninth century had been very successful in eliminating ruling families in Mercia, East Anglia and the Deiran part of Northumbria.

However, to argue that the pre-Viking kingdoms of Anglo-Saxon England had simply mutated into areas of influence for families, who were the canny survivors of the Viking attacks and simply learnt to speak a Danish version of English and wore Scandinavian-style brooches may be to push the 'continuity' argument in the Danelaw too far. Many of the estates in the Danelaw were presumably taken over by Viking leaders and warriors, which may be what was meant when the Anglo-Saxon Chronicle recorded that, in 876, the Danes 'proceeded to plough and to support themselves', even if the extent and nature of this is still very much under dispute amongst historians and archaeologists alike (as Simon Trafford has recently reminded us, should we really be so obsessed with simple numbers of people, especially as, one might add, estimates of population in pre-census England vary wildly, anyway?[8]). By the tenth century, many of the ruling families of the old kingdoms may have been long gone but the spheres of power and influence within which they operated were still very much evident. The structures and agencies of state power were now focused in the south of England outside the

6. The philosopher king: King Alfred as the Victorians saw him, holding aloft his sword in the form of a cross, showing the virtues of war and wisdom used by a Christian king against pagan invaders. Erected in 1901, the statue looks along Winchester High Street, a reminder of the 'ideals' of rulership. Comparisons between Alfred and Aethelred may be inevitable, but should not be allowed to dominate our views of the latter.

7. The 1801 monument to the sanctuary of the West-Saxon kingdom under Alfred the Great: the island of Athelney in Somerset was Alfred's base during the Viking seizure of the kingdom in 878. By the time Aethelred, the abbey founded here was still favoured and granted land members of the West-Saxon royal house. (Don Lavelle)

16

former kingdoms in which they had once operated, and we should be careful not to consider the ealdormen of the tenth century as regional rulers resurrecting the pre-Viking kingdoms, but rather as agents of the state, whose individual and family interests depended upon political circumstances.[9] However, 'regional' identities of these areas still became very much imbued with the contemporary politics, and it is inevitable that the former areas of influence of pre-Viking rulers should have become the foci of political power.[10] This was not the 'disintegration' of England, as there was yet no integration to speak of; rather, this was then the natural state of political society. The independence of particular families within these regions was still very much in evidence into the reign of Aethelred, and, as we shall see, was one of the major themes of the beginning and the end of his reign, although it should be remembered that political independence of certain groups of people within the kingdom was a continuing feature throughout the tenth century. This may be demonstrated by the presence of the Northumbrian hostage, Aescferth, alongside the men of Byrhtnoth at the Battle of Maldon in 991.[11] Aescferth was not a hostage taken with hostility in the manner assumed by Dorothy Whitelock, nor was he a demonstration of Ealdorman Byrhtnoth's authority over Northumbria, as Eric John has suggested.[12] He is more likely to have personified the English king's distant authority over the Northumbrian families, while also showing Aethelred's position as a benefactor of the care of a hostage – who was also an honoured guest – to one of his foremost ealdormen, Byrhtnoth. It is also worth noting that the hostage's name, Aescferth, is English in contrast to his father, Ecglaf's, Scandinavian name, and this could reflect the 'Anglicization' of a young noble in the care of one of the agents of the king. We could even go so far as to suggest that in the same manner as with the arrival of the Norman Emma, perhaps he received a new name in this 'English' environment. The relationship between the West Saxon south of the kingdom and Northumbria may have been more appropriate to a

8. The line shows the division of political and legal control agreed between King Alfred the Great and the Viking leader, Guthrum, in 878, with Wessex and south-western Mercia under West-Saxon control and the rest of the former Anglo-Saxon kingdoms under the control of the Viking leaders. Regional divisions between the two areas persisted throughout the Anglo-Saxon period and were to have great bearing in later years, but the extent to which this was a result of Scandinavian settlement or simply regional reactions to the extension of power from Wessex is still debated.

tributary authority, then, rather than being the integral part of the English kingdom that Northumbria technically was.

To the southern English, the stereotype of the hard-drinking and hard-living rough northerners was already in existence by the tenth century. In the *Life of St Aethelwold*, dating from around 1000, Wulfstan of Winchester relates one of the saint's miracles as providing a never-ending supply of mead at a feast held for King Eadred, around the middle of the tenth century. A group of guests from Northumbria were with the king at the time and were more than happy with the proceedings. The author did not miss the opportunity to cock a snook at the northerners; although the rest of the diners seem to have enjoyed themselves in equal measure, it is the Northumbrians who, with what we might perceive to be West Saxon disapproval, are singled out for getting drunk, 'as they tend to'.[13]

Although many of the families living in the new 'Danelaw' (the name of the area is not contemporary) were not necessarily descended from the old families, but rather may have been transplanted West Saxon or western Mercian families, during the tenth century they established themselves with impressive efficiency by using the existing spheres of power.[14] Their influence and lines of patronage and authority, therefore, affected the political landscape of the English regions, and English royal government had to operate according to such parameters. This was not political weakness on the part of the kings. It was simply the way things were.

The political stalemate of the ninth century was translated into a West Saxon victory at *Ethandune* by King Alfred in 878. The result was a treaty between the West Saxon king and the Danish leader Guthrum in the same year, a version of which exists in the form of the so-called 'Alfred-Guthrum' treaty.[15] While the frontier set out along the Thames, up the River Lea and up to the Ouse may not have lasted for long after Guthrum's death in 890, the regularised trade and contact between the two polities envisaged by Alfred still effected political division, which perpetuated the inclinations of Wessex and East Anglia towards mutual antagonism, if not outright hostility. It was such feelings that allowed Alfred's nephew, Aethelwold the *aetheling*, to rebel against his cousin King Edward the Elder during the three years from 899–902,[16] in an action that exposed some major weaknesses within the West Saxon royal family.

If Alfred had been the architect of a *Gens Anglo-Saxonum*, however, it was King Edward the Elder and his sons, Kings Athelstan, Edmund and Eadred, who had gone some way to realising this plan. The 'Re-conquest' of England (better conceived as the *conquest* of England) was a West Saxon affair, arguably with the use of a few key Mercian families, which were to be a dominating force in Anglo-Saxon England for the best part of half a century, arguably with repercussions felt well into the eleventh century. In part, it was an ideological battle, especially as Danes and Northmen could be spoken of in the same breath as the original inhabitants of the areas conquered, but the resources of such a conquest could only be stretched so far. By the reign of Athelstan, the idea of 'English' kingship had developed into an 'Imperial', 'British' rulership, a vision which stretched some way in its ambitions, but at the same time it was a tacit acknowledgement of the limitations of West Saxon power. This was a power that could only be imposed by violence and the threat of violence. Therefore, English rulership developed briefly into that of a wider Britain, an overlordship that may have allowed compromise and the participation of all the 'English' in the subjugation of the Britons and foreigners beyond the fringes of civilised lowland society. It could be argued that it was an inevitable part of the Christian ruler ideology used by the Anglo-Saxon kings, and whether or not this may have been successful, this was still to continue as a policy and an ideal for the kings of England.

By the end of the tenth century, therefore, we can see that the political inheritance of Aethelred was a kingdom with hegemony over a number of distant areas, kinship connec-

9. Hovingham Church, North Yorkshire, in the Northumbrian Danelaw. The church tower dates from the late Anglo-Saxon period, perhaps around the mid-eleventh century.

10. View of Edington (Wilts.), formerly *Ethandune*: site of Alfred the Great's famous victory over the Danish army in 878. The royal estate of Edington remained important to the West Saxon royal family during the tenth century.

tions with a number of disparate, often independently minded families, but yet a state with a strong capacity to tax and take a share of the trade of a strong, controlled economy over which kings arguably played no mean part. It was also a state with ideological ambitions, indeed increasing ideological ambitions as the political reform of the Church took root. Expectations were high.

ENGLAND AND THE WORLD

The kingdom of the English did not exist in isolation in a forgotten corner of Christendom. By the end of the tenth century, politically, culturally and economically, England was 'at the heart of Europe', and it had been for some centuries. English contacts with Scandinavia had been by way of missionary activity in the eighth, ninth and tenth centuries,[17] links were maintained with the noble families of Ottonian Germany, while the north-western coasts of Flanders provided close trading and diplomatic links, as well as monastic connections. While the duchy of Normandy is generally regarded as having been 'Viking' and ever so slightly renegade in its political actions, the area of Neustria, which had become the duchy of the 'Northmen' (hence the name *Normandie*), was hardly alien to the English nor, indeed, was the kingdom of France itself.

The 'London code', known as *IV Aethelred*, a local lawcode dating from the reign of Aethelred, highlights the trade links of the English kingdom or at least those recognized by local government in London.[18] Here, provision was made for trade from much of north-western Europe, and it is with these extensive trade networks in place, a picture augmented by the rich seam of archaeological evidence for economic prosperity from the middle of the tenth century onwards, that we may best see the richness of the English kingdom under Aethelred.[19]

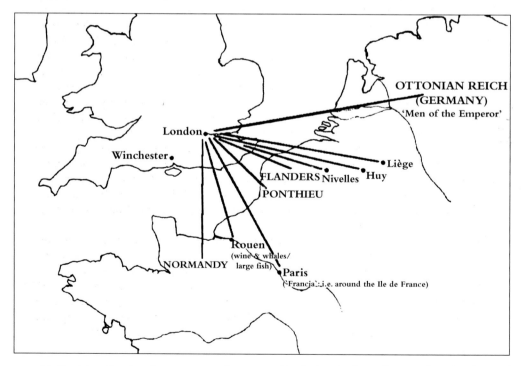

11. The international trading agreements demonstrated by the London lawcode, promulgated in the reign of King Aethelred.

However, links overseas meant more than simply the pursuit of trade and wealth. English political ideology was very much affected by the European presence of Charlemagne and the Carolingians from two centuries earlier. Even if Anglo-Saxon kings were to have wished to turn their backs upon such an influence, this could scarcely have been avoided. Charlemagne was the model for the reforming king, with a court of cultural reform which he had energetically built up around him. Both Alfred and Aethelred's great-uncle, Athelstan, had followed Charlemagne's lead in building up an international court of scholars around them;[20] this lay behind the revival of learning and reform under Edgar and its patronage by Aethelred. Abbo of Fleury's communication with Abbot Aelfric of Cerne is just one example of this climate of cultural exchange, especially between England and Flanders, at the end of the first millennium. From this exchange, Aelfric's portrayal of the martyrdom of St Edmund, the ninth-century East Anglian king, at the hands of Vikings, was part of a pre-millennial fear of the *idea* of Vikings in Western Europe.[21]

The king as a scholar, or at least a patron of learning, was an ideal by which to rule even if that ideal was not always easily pursued. Underlying this picture of Charlemagne as a patron of reform and learning was Charlemagne the Emperor, breathing a new life into the old Roman Empire. *Romanitas*, given some weight by the eighth and ninth-century achievements of Carolingian rulers and in the tenth by Ottonian emperors, was a mode of thought which had some bearing upon the pursuit of kingship in Anglo-Saxon England, a means by which the likes of Athelstan, Edgar and, as we shall see, Aethelred, could pursue the *Imperium* of Britain, fusing political ambitions with a deeper ideology.[22]

While the Ottonians appeared to the English as going from strength to strength,[23] it may also have been salutary for Anglo-Saxon kings to acknowledge the decline of the Carolingian dynasty in the West Frankish kingdom over the course of the tenth century. There is little mention in the English sources of the fate of the Carolingians, even with the death of the French king, Louis V, in 987 and the succession of Hugh Capet, although in defence of the Anglo-Saxon Chronicle, with the disease 'of cattle and men' called *scitte* ravaging the countryside, such insularity might be excused. Nevertheless, to imagine that the extensive trade and cultural links between Francia and Anglo-Saxon England did not extend to acknowledging the death of one of the heirs of Charlemagne would be to stretch the point of insularity too far. From the French side of the Channel, the provincial but hardly uninformed writer, Rodulfus Glaber, recorded King Aethelred among a list of the rulers neighbouring the kingdom of Robert II 'the Pious' (996-1031) who 'sent [Robert] presents and begged his aid'. To consider Aethelred's relationship with the king of the western Franks to have been one-way might be an exaggeration (although aid from France may have been welcome against Normandy[24] or in the later years of Aethelred's reign), but Glaber was placing Aethelred among the important rulers of Robert's day. We may safely consider that diplomatic relations existed between the Kings of England and France at the end of the first millennium.

However, to return briefly to 987, while there may have been no realisation yet that the new ruler, the first of what was to be the unbroken dynasty of the Capetians, would have such significance for the consolidation of the French kingdom, the revival of the Carolingian dynasty in view of a lack of heirs must have seemed somewhat impossible.[25] To Aethelred, by then in his twenties and certainly politically sentient, the significance of the end of a dynasty due to the death of a king without heirs must have been very apparent indeed, and here at least, continental European politics had a very real resonance.

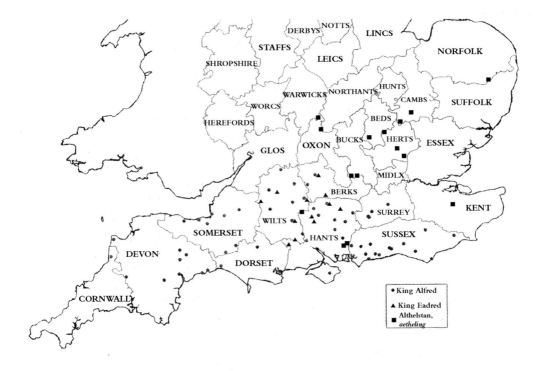

12. Lands bequeathed by members of the West Saxon royal family in surviving wills, from King Alfred (late ninth century), King Eadred (mid-tenth century) and the *aetheling* Aethelstan (1014) respectively. These lands appear to have been 'disposable' family lands, held by charter, although family interests may have made sure that the lands were kept within familial control.

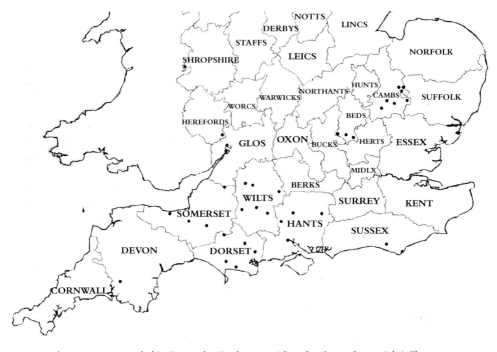

13. Lands in Wessex recorded in Domesday Book as providing the 'farm of one night'. These appear to have formed a corpus of 'inalienable' lands providing support for the royal family in their 'official' capacity – perhaps an Anglo-Saxon equivalent of the Crown lands.

14. Grants of land made by King Aethelred, from 978 to 1016 (after Stafford, 'Reign of Aethelred II'). Many of the grants were made in Wessex during the early part of the reign, but in later years, many of these were in the Thames Valley and north of England.

Royal resources

The wealth at the command of late Anglo-Saxon kings was enormous. Not only could kings command massive levels of taxation through the reminting of coins on a five-yearly basis, but Aethelred was also able to implement a direct taxation in the form of the *heregeld* (the 'army-tax', often mistakenly known as the 'Dane-geld', made infamous through a poem by Rudyard Kipling). The rights and wrongs of this form of taxation and its uses are discussed below, but it must suffice to say that the potential for the king's access to the wealth of the kingdom was impressive. Technically speaking, neither direct or indirect taxation were forms of 'royal resources' as the king himself did not appear to have had direct command over their implementation. The processes of peace-making and geld appear to have been decided by both the king and his advisors, which the Anglo-Saxon Chronicle is keen to point out (although it must be noted that this adds to the Abingdon manuscript's picture of a king 'led astray' by bad advisors). However, to ignore the position of the king in the decision-making processes of the fiscal state would be to ignore the nature of royal power, even if it was power held by consent. The symbols and images on each face of late Anglo-Saxon coins, with very rare exceptions, were those of Christ and the king respectively. The command to render unto Caesar those which are Caesar's held strong resonance indeed with the royal pursuit of governance.

Nonetheless, despite the obvious riches which Anglo-Saxon kings and their families held for themselves,[26] the wealth of the West Saxon royal family rested upon the command of agricultural produce from royal lands, held both on a personal basis, which the king and his

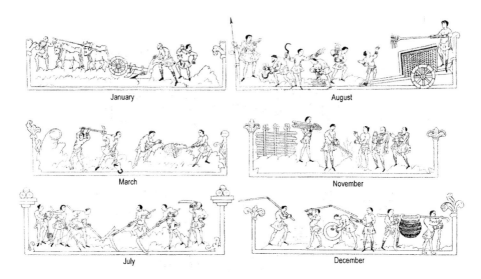

15. Anglo-Saxon peasants at work, after an eleventh-century calendar illustration. November and December were times for rebuilding fences and winnowing.

family held in a manner similar to the lands of any other Anglo-Saxon family,[27] and on an official basis, for the support of the family themselves while they undertook their royal duties within the late Anglo-Saxon kingdom.[28] These lands can really only be identified through the absence of evidence: the surviving wills of Anglo-Saxon kings – that of Alfred and the mid-tenth-century will of King Eadred – set out only the intended disposition of a limited number of lands to the family group, and those churches and people close to the king. This left a large body of lands in Wessex which can be identified as being under royal control. These royal 'official' lands, recorded in Domesday Book as providing the 'farm of one night', were effectively inalienable. The provision of money and render in kind to the king and his family from such lands was closely controlled by the councillors of the kingdom, as happened with the lands around Hurstbourne Tarrant in northern Hampshire at the beginning of the reign of Edward the Martyr.

The other lands were more conventional in the sense in which late Anglo-Saxon noble families held 'booklands', which were not dependent upon whether the royal family held the crown (although of course the king's position of power may have helped). These lands were, as both Patrick Wormald and Simon Keynes have shown, assets which the king had the power to dispose of freely, held 'by book' (i.e. through charters).[29] As is human nature, the kings generally wished to dispose of them among their close kin. The booklands held by an Anglo-Saxon king might vary considerably, but judging by the number of grants made by King Aethelred, he had a good number of privately held and family lands at his disposal, or which could at least provide a relatively steady income for himself.

Such a situation for royal landholding was typical of the way in which the royal family in Anglo-Saxon England operated on two levels. On the one level, they were a noble family just like any other, albeit somewhat richer, and operated on the basis of providing the long-standing survival and wealth of the Wessex-based kindred, while, on another level, they held 'official' positions through consecrated kingship and an unparalleled control of government. This sometimes conflicting doublethink was a development in the emergence of an 'English' kingdom in the tenth century. However, as Pauline Stafford observed from the Domesday

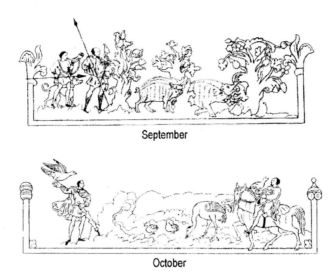

September

October

16. Hunting and hawking, the *raison d'être* of the Anglo-Saxon nobility, as depicted in the Cotton Julius calendar for September and October.

17. The sites of meetings of the witan and royal activities during the reign of King Aethelred.

evidence, the royal lands were mainly concentrated in the area of the former kingdom of Wessex and south-western Mercia.[30] This provided an uncertain basis for the exploitation of royal power any further north than the Midlands and probably reflects the personal interests of tenth-century kings remaining in Wessex. While the lands providing the 'Farm of one Night' may have formed an institution held for the official functions of the king and royal family, their focus remained West Saxon and southern English.

The accumulation of wealth from royal estates was an intricate process. The peasants on the calendar from the British Library Cotton manuscript Julius A.vi shown here (figure 15) are an excellent illustration of the work in the fields which provided the wealth of later Anglo-Saxon England. The manuscript illustrations reflect the minutiae of working and managing large estates. Kings could hardly take an active role in the day-to-day running of their estates, so the administration was delegated to reeves, who could either exploit the land directly or collect the dues from areas which were leased out. Either way, we might expect royal estates to have been amongst the most well-stocked and equipped in an area. An early medieval estate may not necessarily have been a single cohesive unit; although by the tenth century the trend in manorial holding seems to have been heading in that direction, the various elements which made up the estate could be many miles apart. Nonetheless, there was a high art in exploiting the lands to the best of the reeves' abilities. Surviving ecclesiastical documents, such as *Gerefa* (or, more properly, *Bege Sceadwisan Gerefan* – 'on the sagacious reeve') and *Rectitudines Singularum Personarum* (known as the 'rights and ranks of people'), both dating from the late tenth or early eleventh century, show the importance of attention to detail for the 'ideal' estate manager.[31] A charter recording the render of manorial dues at Hurstbourne Priors in Hampshire, datable to the ninth century, perhaps reflects an increase in the efficiency of the exploitation of royal land under King Alfred the Great a legacy, which seems to have lasted through to the tenth and eleventh centuries.[32] Obviously not every manor was run to an 'ideal' standard, but those of a large landowner stood a better chance than most.

Therefore, a direct relationship existed between the power of the king and the exploitation of his estates. Kings were not remote from their lands and the people in them; the 'official' lands of the 'Farm of one Night' may well have preserved some of the lands or at least the spirit of the early Anglo-Saxon rulers, who travelled around their realm eating and feeding their followers from the tributes given to them (indeed, the term 'farm' originates from the Old English *feorm*, which has implications of care, hospitality and entertainment[33]). Late Anglo-Saxon kings such as Aethelred may no longer have needed to move around the kingdom in order to rule in the same manner as early kings, but their itineraries still brought them into contact with their subjects, cementing their relationships with them. The charters of King Aethelred do not record the royal itineraries with the same degree of detail as do those of his energetic grandfather, King Athelstan, but they still show that the king was moving around his kingdom, or at least the southern part of it, staying on both his 'official' and 'private' estates, and presumably hunting and meeting his nobility there.[34] It is here that we can see the inherent indignity with which Viking attacks on royal estates could have been perceived – they were strikes against the very heart, body and soul of the kingdom, a point which will become apparent in later chapters.

This meant that late Anglo-Saxon kingship as practised by King Aethelred was very much a part of the landscape and was closely involved with the people in that landscape. The king was the father of the people and was *of* the people, a point which was still an ideal in the attempt to assert 'English' identity over the disparate kin-groups of lowland Britain. King Hrothgar, portrayed in the verses of *Beowulf* as a good lord, benefactor and kinsman, providing food, drink and treasure, was still 'a good king' in Aethelred's day.

2

THE YOUNG *AETHELING* AND HIS FAMILY

On the occasion of the death of Aethelred's father, King Edgar, in 975, the writer of the Abingdon manuscript of the Anglo-Saxon Chronicle decided that some lines of poetic verse would be more appropriate to the occasion. It was of a sort, commented Dorothy Whitelock, that made one 'glad that the chroniclers mainly used prose'.[1] The quality of the poetic eulogy in the 'D' manuscript has won a little more critical acclaim, but it is not this that is of concern here, so much as the fact that the poems show a strength of feeling for the dead king and his former glories. These were the first poetic epitaphs for a dead king in the Anglo-Saxon Chronicle (the next was to be for Edward 'the Confessor') and in their own way they were worthy commentaries.

So, as the English kingdom stood at the beginning of a new reign in July 975, it looked back wistfully at the age of Edgar 'the Peaceable' and a golden age for England. Of course, history is full of such golden ages (some more golden than others), and that is why we need to look back at the reign of Edgar, his treatment of his family and his understanding of his kingship, in order to understand why the subsequent years were to progress as they did.

Even by the mid-tenth century, the concept of 'England' as a political and cultural unity was hardly an inevitability and, when Edgar came of age in 955, it may have seemed the only natural solution for the youthful Edgar and his elder brother, King Eadwig, to have respectively ruled parallel kingdoms – dividing a kingdom was a perfectly reasonable decision in early medieval Europe, and there was probably a great deal more precedent for this than for England's continuing unity. We may search in vain for evidence of rivalry between the brothers, and indeed violence on the part of Edgar in his take-over of his brother's southern half of the kingdom. After all, while the division of the kingdom is naturally seen as a 'bad thing' in terms of English unity, it should be remembered that the kingdom had only been an 'English' kingdom within the living memory of half a century.

However, Edgar's reign over the kingdom of England became a triumph of achievement. The elder brother, Eadwig, died of natural causes in 959 and, as a result, Edgar succeeded peacefully to a unified kingdom, and although the 'English' people were something of a political creation, this could have been interpreted as the bringing of one people back together.[2] This unification process was consolidated in different ways, which were to have great long-term effects for the reign of the later king, Aethelred. Although not solely an achievement of Edgar himself, the first action was the reform of monastic orders, which heralded sweeping changes within the churches of the kingdom, under the influence of his radical bishops. The most spectacular manifestation was the replacement of secular priests with monks at such institutions as the Old Minster, Winchester, Milton Abbas in Dorset, and Chertsey in Surrey. Aelfric's *Life of St Aethelwold* describes secular, married clerics expelled by Bishop Aethelwold from his diocesan seat at the Old Minster, Winchester, who had been such 'victims of pride, insolence and riotous living' that they even refused to celebrate Mass.[3] This was a period of the revival of the Benedictine rule in the English kingdom: under such conditions of religious fervour (with very tangible aims), we could question how realistic the claims of wantonness, gluttony, drunkenness and lascivious behaviour really were, or whether this was just rhetoric in order to further the monastic reform movement. Nonetheless, there was great strength of feeling, and this was *the* great ideological movement of the tenth century.

King Edgar himself was actively involved in this process, as the various *Lives* of reforming churchmen – St Oswald, Archbishop of York and Bishop of Worcester, St Aethelwold, Bishop of Winchester and St Dunstan, Archbishop of Canterbury – as well as a brief Old English document known as *King Edgar's Establishment of Monasteries* recorded Edgar's reign as a period of monastic dynamism and revival.[4] The king was a protector of the Church and a defender of the Christian faith but, at the same time, he was also empowered by the Church; Edgar's legitimacy as the Christian king became inextricably bound up with the relationship which he held with the Church.

18. King Edgar with Dunstan, Archbishop of Canterbury and Aethelwold, Bishop of Winchester, two of the main architects of ecclesiastical reform in the tenth century: influential figures in the politics of the later tenth century, Dunstan and Aethelwold both remained important into the early years of Aethelred's reign.

A document from around 973, the *Regularis Concordia* (sometimes known as *The Monastic Agreement*), which survives in a number of eleventh-century manuscripts, was intended as a rulebook and liturgical guide for English monks and nuns, but it was also a bold statement of the relationship between God, the king and a Christian people. The king and queen were seen as protectors of monks and nuns in the temporal world, while, in return, the souls of the West Saxon royal family were protected with prayers by the same monks and nuns.[5] The positions of the king and queen were therefore inextricably linked with the survival of Christianity in the kingdom. This was part of a process of legitimising royal power to an extent that was hitherto unparalleled in Anglo-Saxon England. The king had become part of the ecclesiastical order in a coronation ceremony that made him God's representative on earth. The original meaning of Christ's name, *Christus* meant 'the anointed [king]', and the inauguration of Edgar used an *ordo* (an order of service) that put Edgar at a similar level – directly anointed by God.[6] The monastic reform movement gave this a new impetus, to such an extent that King Edgar could go through such a royal inauguration for a second time.

While we do not know where Edgar had first been crowned, the second – and more elaborate – occasion was at Bath in 973. This took place in Edgar's thirtieth year, the age of Episcopal ordination (so perhaps stressing the king's position as the embodiment of a Christian people). The remains of the imperial Roman city of Bath had been a site of fascination for Anglo-Saxons – the elegiac description of the crumbling buildings, 'the works of giants' in the early Old English poem *The Ruin* probably refers to Bath.[7] We could take from this that Edgar was undertaking an act of renewal for the great imperial city. The use of the natural Roman springs at Bath echoed the hot springs at Aachen that

19. Bath, the great Roman city of western England, nestling among seven hills, like the eternal city. Bath was the site of the second coronation ceremony of King Edgar, using the symbolism of imperial Rome.

20. Wherwell, in western Hampshire. Founded in the tenth century, the nunnery at Wherwell was associated by legend with Aelfthryth making restitution for the murder of her first husband. While murder is unlikely to have been the real motive, Aelfthryth's position as the driving force behind the nunnery's foundation, or at least development, is possible.

Charlemagne made so famous and which were then being used in the Ottonian *Reich*. The Anglo-Saxon Chronicle's unique use of the name *Acemannesceaster* here for Bath in place of the more usual *Bað* at once recalls the Latin name *Aquae Sulis* and the name of the Carolingian palace of Aachen. Edgar was therefore very much a king of his time, and this was reflected in the use of Roman, Carolingian, Ottonian, as well as Anglo-Saxon and 'British' imagery.

At Bath, Edgar displayed the legitimate position of the West Saxon royal family, and it was this coronation ceremony that indicated that things had changed. Although Janet Nelson has argued that Aelfflaed, second wife of Edward the Elder, was made an anointed queen early in the tenth century,[8] the coronation at Bath in 973 raised the importance of the king's wife to near-equality, making her consecration an integral part of the entire ceremony.[9] However, as Pauline Stafford has remarked, it was at Winchester in 966 where the all-new West Saxon dynasty were brought out in a great display of familial harmony in the New Minster, the basilica built for the souls of the West Saxon royal family: Edgar, the king, Queen Eadgifu, his grandmother, Aelfthryth, his wife, and a new son, born to the reigning king.[10] Edgar, the serial monogamist, had renounced his previous relationship with a certain Wulfthryth and so with his new wife he had two sons. The first of these was called Edmund, presumably in honour of King Edgar's father, while the second, Aethelred, was given a name which had not been used in the West Saxon dynasty since the reign of the predecessor of Alfred the Great. The ninth-century question of succession between the brothers Aethelred I and Alfred had resulted in virtual civil war after the death of Alfred because the eldest son of Aethelred I, as a certain Aethelwold *aetheling* had attempted to take

21. A detail of Mary depicted as the Queen of Heaven, after an illustration in the *Benedictional of St Aethelwold*, which dates from a period between the last years of the reign of Edgar and the first few years of Aethelred's reign. In view of the close relationship between Queen Aelfthryth and the patron of the original artwork, Bishop Aethelwold of Winchester, the connection of the depiction of Aelfthryth as a Marian representative and mother of the royal house on earth is evident.

the throne or at least a good chunk of the kingdom for himself.[11] Therefore the name of Aethelred was probably not one which was safe to use for some time among the kindred of Alfred: the kindred of Aethelred I remained a comparatively powerful group of nobles through much of the tenth century. Given our hindsight, we could question the wisdom of this choice of name, but Edgar presumably felt confident enough about the security of the royal family to call his youngest son after the middle son of King Aethelwulf from a more turbulent period a century earlier.

Edgar was therefore a king with ambition and a real sense of his rights and duties as a Christian king, as well as an understanding of his position in the West Saxon royal dynasty. But Edgar was more than royal: he was also imperial. The traditional picture of Edgar (one remarked upon in so many old schoolbooks) is of a king rowed down the River Dee by all the other kings of Britain. This was a move that recalled the actions of his great-uncle Athelstan, the successful ruler of Britain, but it was also an English parallel to the tenth-century coronation of the Holy Roman Emperor, Otto of Germany, in which the stem-dukes had undertaken the task of feeding the emperor.[12]

If the events on the River Dee had happened in the manner in which the twelfth-century writer, John of Worcester, recorded them, they would indicate Edgar's aspirations as high indeed, encompassing the *Orbis Britanniae* – the 'world' of Britain.[13] However, some doubt has recently been cast upon the truth of the account: Julia Barrow, for one, has reinterpreted the event as a possible act of peacemaking with the other kings of Britain, as the River Dee was conveniently located as a territorially neutral site on the edge of the Irish Sea, an action which accords well with Edgar's separate treatment of the

22. Coin of King Edgar: one of the first of the 'reformed' coins of the Anglo-Saxon kingdom; the re-minting of the entire coinage on a regular basis instigated by King Edgar was to be an important feature of Aethelred's reign.

legal status of the Danelaw in his lawcode *IV Edgar*.[14] Barrow's contention is that the Anglo-Saxon Chronicle's version of events is somewhat different from the later recensions, and she has a point. A meeting on board a ship, which was a common means of meeting in the early Middle Ages, could easily have been reinterpreted by later generations, who saw Edgar as subordinating the other kings of Britain.[15] Such an interpretation can be understood easily, and we can see how, in the light of Aethelred's apparent failures, his father's reign may have been interpreted by twelfth-century historians as one of boundless imperial ambitions.

However, in the terms of tenth-century southern England from where this was viewed and where it was remembered, what mattered here was the *perception* of Edgar's triumphal peacemaking; it is difficult to see that Edgar's contemporaries would not have seen Edgar's actions in such a triumphal light. Peacemaking within a vertical (i.e. subordinate) relationship invariably reflected that relationship. If Edgar was making peace with eight other kings of Britain, then he could hardly allow himself to be seen by his own people as a mere equal in that process, even if in reality concessions had to be made. In our own era, plenty of peace negotiations end with both sides declaring success to their respective populations. This very human trait suggests that we should not overlook the possibility that Edgar, the anointed King of England, would have seized his opportunity with both hands. With a Christian right to rule and a sense of 'Britain', King Edgar was therefore invoking peacemaking and imperial ambition in the manner in which Carolingian and Ottonian rulers suborned their neighbours. It also recalled a more traditional view of the enforcement of overlordship of the sort described in Bede's *Ecclesiastical History*. In the context of tenth-century English kingship, it is difficult to see how it could have been anything else.

Edgar's ability to realise his imperial ambitions is also given some grounding by the tantalisingly brief record of the suicide of a 'King Sigeferth' who, the Anglo-Saxon Chronicle records, was buried at Wimborne (presumably the Minster) in 962. Like so

23. A famous medieval depiction of a comet, on the eleventh-century Bayeux Tapestry, depicting events of 1066. A comet was seen in the sky in 975 for some three months after the death of King Edgar; such an astronomical event could be interpreted as heralding a major change.

much history of this period, there is little to go on, apart from an attestation of a certain 'Sigeferth' between a sub-king Morgan and two other 'Welsh'-named witnesses, Owain and Jacob, in a charter purporting to be from the reign of Edgar's uncle, King Eadred.[16] Dorothy Whitelock suggested that the two records of Sigeferth referred to the same person and that, as Sigeferth was a Scandinavian name, he may have been a ruler in the Northern Isles subject to Edgar's authority.[17] Here then, we might be able to glimpse the reality of Edgar's imperial rule: far from his own kingdom, Sigeferth's only option was perhaps the most honourable. In the Germanic world, this could be perceived as a form of defiance,[18] but if suicide was the only option available to him, it serves only to highlight the extent of Edgar's power.

The achievements of Edgar's reign also included the reform of the coinage of the kingdom, a move that meant a great deal for the kingdom's wealth and, later, for Aethelred's ability to pay large sums of money. Edgar introduced a system of monetary *Renovatio* (renewal), requiring a five-year cycle of reform of all coins minted in the kingdom.[19] Apart from ensuring that the quantity of silver minted in coins remained consistent, this was also an implicit form of indirect taxation; if all coins had to be returned to licensed mints across the kingdom (the protection of these was to be an important feature for Aethelred's reign), then the number of new coins given back could be deliberately limited, in order to retain some silver as tax. The late Anglo-Saxon state may have been sophisticated, but inevitably underlying these advances was the omnipresent spectre of taxation.

Despite any possible complaints about taxation, we get none here from Edgar's reign; perhaps there was no need for complaint. In the 970s, there was every reason for monastic commentators to be satisfied. However, Edgar was not immune from criticism. Potential problems did exist in the kingdom; to contemporaries the main complaint was Edgar's entertainment of 'foreigners', presumably meaning their use in the defence force of the kingdom – a mercenary navy. As recent research by Shashi Jayakumar has observed, these were Scandinavians in the service of the state[20] and it is possible that this could have placed weaknesses in the defence of the kingdom. However, a problem that we can only see with hindsight was the use of 'English' identity as a part of the imposition of the state upon the English kingdom, a continuing feature of the tenth century, which in turn failed to redress the continuing influence of individual families within the kingdom (presumably this was an issue beyond the capabilities of even Edgar?), a matter which was to have great significance in the years that followed.

A CRISIS OF SUCCESSION: FRATERNAL RIVALRIES

We return to Edgar's death in 975. A sense of foreboding may have emerged, as the Chronicle manuscripts juxtapose Edgar's death with the appearance of a comet in the autumn sky. In the manner in which the Bayeux Tapestry so graphically illustrates with its depiction of a crowd of frightened observers viewing a comet a century later, this could be a sign of terrible events to come. Like the appearance of Halley's comet in 1066 and in 989, this was a major astronomical event, seen throughout Europe, the Middle East and in China and Japan;[21] the comet of 975 could be seen in the sky for some three months, a time at which, as we shall see, the *witan* (the 'wise men') of the kingdom decided upon who would be the next king. A comet did not necessarily have to be interpreted as a dreadful portent, so much as representing change. Nonetheless, there was still a sense of awe and wonder; if the king had died and his death was followed by the appearance of a fireball in the skies for night after night, then the atmosphere which this could have produced within the kingdom must have been portentous.

It could be speculated that had Edmund – the elder of Edgar's 'legitimate' sons – not died in 971, succession to the throne may have been somewhat less disputable, as this would have made Edmund a more suitable candidate, of a close age to the adolescent Edward the Martyr. However deeply the regret for Edmund's death may have been held in the breasts of the Anglo-Saxon nobility, this did not alter the reality that there were only two candidates for the throne in 975. While Edgar's reign had been a successful one, with years of comparative peace backed up by a strong rule of law, a sense of legitimate Christian rule and English *imperium*, factions had developed beneath this. While these were not all the same factions that were to rear their heads later in Aethelred's reign, they nonetheless influenced the conduct of affairs in Aethelred's early years, and were major factors in the succession crisis of 975 and the terrible events of 978.

Upon one side, Edgar's widowed queen, Aelfthryth, was in alliance with Bishop Aethelwold of Winchester and Ealdorman Aelfhere of Mercia. These people were bound together by bonds of kinship and friendship[22] and promoted the young Aethelred as a candidate for the throne. Behind Edward, the elder son, stood Archbishop Dunstan of

24. King Edgar with Mary and St Peter: detail after the New Minster re-foundation charter, drawn up in 966 for King Edgar. The importance of the King is reflected by the fact that he is depicted at the same level as Mary and St Peter.

Canterbury and Ealdormen Aethelwine of East Anglia and Byrhtnoth of Essex. It is debatable as to how far the young teenager Edward and the child Aethelred (probably then no more than ten years old) could have influenced events themselves; they probably were no more than figureheads, but to say that they were affected by the events would be an understatement. Three disturbed years later, in 978, the elder brother had been murdered and the young Aethelred was king.

It is difficult to believe that a king with such a strong sense of legitimacy as Edgar would not have had some concern for the succession. We need to look at previous decades to understand why this became such a problem. Although pre-Viking England was notorious for its series of regicides resulting from disputable succession, such matters were still not fixed in the later Anglo-Saxon period. However, accepted features were beginning to emerge for succession to the throne, making it less easy to justify passing over an elder son. Edward, however, had many factors which counted against his worthiness for the throne. Keynes has pointed out that a century later, his legitimacy was questioned, in Osbern's post-Conquest *Life of St Dunstan*, suggesting that Edward was not the son of a legitimate wife at all, but simply the son of a nun of Wilton Abbey.[23] This is unlikely – more probably it is a confusion of the story leading to Edgar's marriage with Wulfthryth and the birth of the 'illegitimate' daughter who became St Edith of Wilton[24] – but in view of the way in which Edgar had favoured his third wife and anointed queen, Aelfthryth, it does not require too much of a stretch of the imagination to see how Edward's mother became viewed.

As we have seen above, the re-foundation charter for the New Minster at Winchester, presented to the church by King Edgar with the piety of the reborn in 966, had held up the royal family as the model of Christian virtue. In the charter, the queen was not just referred to as a wife, but a '*legitimate* wife of the king' (legitima… *regis conjuncx* – my emphases). This seems to imply, even if it does not boldly state, that Edgar's previous marriages were not legitimate, or at least suggests that Edgar's new marriage was the only one which counted. These were not the later Middle Ages, a time of papal authority in which divorce was impossible: although divorce may have been frowned upon by ecclesiastical authorities, even such a model of reforming piety as Edgar could justify re-marriage and it could be suggested that Edgar had divorced Wulfthryth in favour of a more politically expedient relationship with Aelfthryth.[25]

Additionally, Simon Keynes has observed that Edgar and Aelfthryth's newly born son Edmund was placed higher up within the charter's witness list than Edward, the elder son. Edmund was said to have witnessed the charter and to have 'signed' his name with a cross. The priority given to the 'legitimate' offspring was a policy which was to continue in further charters, and as Aethelred was born, we witness the appearance of his name on charter witness lists after Edmund, but again ahead of that of the half-brother Edward. Such bold statements obviously favoured the new marriage, a trait amongst human beings which can be easily understood. It was as if Edward had been sidelined in favour of Edmund, Edgar's elder son by Aelfthryth. Again, although the younger son, Edmund, was referred to as a 'legitimate son', Edward, by contrast, was merely just another offspring – a 'procreated' son.[26] Here again the statement seems to imply that Edgar's previous wives had not been legitimate. If, as Keynes argues, the witness lists of charters can be trusted as a useful indication of the relative importance of individuals at the royal court,[27] then we can hardly have a clearer indication of Edgar's intentions for the succession to the throne. This may have been following a Byzantine policy of giving legitimacy to (and recognizing the claim to the throne of) the son who had been born to the reigning king.[28] This may be an explanation if Edward was born before Edgar became king of the English in 959, which would have made Edward at least sixteen in 975; while it is possible that Edward was this old in 975, we could suspect that a disputed succession between a sixteen-year-old Edward and a nine-year-old Aethelred would have ruled out Aethelred entirely, however.[29] Therefore, this was not so much a question of real legitimacy, but rather a more usual process of favouring the sons of the current marriage.

A sense of family idealism imposed by the father and the disputes within families were a matter of royal policy and a manifestation of the relations within the state. Such a marriage as Edgar's to Aelfthryth had been a result of the shifting political allegiances within the late Anglo-Saxon state. As a result, the kindred of Aelfhere of Mercia, including his brother, Aelfheah of eastern Wessex, were in the ascendant through Edgar's favour, whereas that of the East Anglian ealdorman was in less favour. Keynes has also observed that in the will of Aelfheah, Ealdorman of eastern Wessex, made around 970, Edmund had been referred to as 'the elder *aetheling*, and king's son'; Aethelred was 'the younger [*aetheling?*]'. The ealdorman made no mention of Edward, and as well as being a deliberate favouring of the offspring of Aelfheah's close friend, Aelfthryth, this could be interpreted as having been a deliberate snub of the less important elder son.

However, accusations of base and illegitimate birth could be commonplace in the early medieval court. This was symptomatic of the way in which political alliances shifted with favours and fortune. Issues of legitimacy and questions of constitutional right were hardly the root causes of disputed succession: such problems grew up from factional rivalries. The rivalries between the kindred of Aelfhere of Mercia and the sons of Athelstan 'Half king' of East Anglia were longstanding, the product of the expansion of West Saxon royal power into the Midlands and East Anglia earlier in the tenth century, which had led to the growth in power of ealdormanries. The support given by Aethelwine and Aelfhere to Edward and Aethelred respectively and the questions of legitimacy accorded to Edward were manifestations of these rivalries, not their root cause. The most famous bastard of the medieval west was no less than Duke William of Normandy, whose legitimacy was only an issue in the dangerous early days of his rule, and once he had become established as Duke of Normandy and later, King of England, this was not an issue.[30]

And what of Edward's character? Advocating Edward for the throne was a political move that may have had nothing to do with his suitability for rule. Byrhtferth's 'anonymous' *Life of St Oswald* is somewhat critical of Edward's character, casting doubt upon his ability to rule: Edward was no less than an unpleasant youth, with a tendency to hit his own followers. This is a strange point to make in a text which was written at the time of the promotion of the royal martyr, and under such conditions we might suspect that there must have been some foundation for stating this.[31] If this part of the account can be trusted,[32] Byrhtferth may reveal something of the pubescent political inabilities of a moody teenager in power, who perhaps alienated potential support from himself during the succession dispute. An ideal of Anglo-Saxon kingship was for the king to look after his immediate followers, ply them with food and drink, and to make sure that they were well rewarded for military service. Unnecessary chastisement was not included in this and, although Keynes has observed that Byrhtferth juxtaposes the disputed succession alongside the account of the young king's death,[33] we might equally note the unfavourable observations on Edward's character which precede the king's death. By comparison, Aethelred was said to be 'mild', a description which is hardly surprising in view of the young *aetheling*'s tender age (and in view that Byrhtferth was writing in Aethelred's reign), but in terms of personality, this cannot have been a bad thing. As we shall see from events later in the king's life, a bi-polar mixture of sensitivity and severity may have characterised Aethelred's reign, so Byrhtferth's judgement here may have been an accurate one.[34]

This was nothing to do with character or throne-worthiness. The rivalry of the sub-rulers of eastern England, Aethelwine, Ealdorman of East Anglia, and Byrthnoth of Essex against the ealdormanry of Mercia resulted in political violence in the period following Edgar's death. The familial rivalries with local and regional interests were making themselves known. In this sense, as D.J.V. Fisher recognised in the 1950s, the arguments were not constitutional regarding legitimacy for the throne, nor were they associated with the question of who were 'friends' and who were 'enemies' of monks; this was a 'primarily political dispute'.[35] The ecclesiastical support which promoted the parties of Edward and Aethelred were also manifestations of these noble families' regional politics. The East Anglian group may have been attempting to recover its former position in which large areas of territory had been controlled,[36] and advocating Edward for the throne was a sensible means by which this could be undertaken.

We can hardly ignore the political interests of the English primate, Dunstan, Archbishop of Canterbury, either. Dunstan was a statesman of some standing, as affairs of Church and state were not mutually exclusive, and Dunstan had his own familial interests to pursue; his biographers do not fight shy of ignoring the archbishop's statecraft.[37] As it was only the Archbishop of Canterbury (or, on rare occasions, the Archbishop of York – who, in any case, also supported Edward) who could consecrate the king's rule with the unguent of kingship, this was an important factor in deciding who would be the king. In addition, as has been seen, while Aethelred can have been no more than nine years old in 975, his elder half brother may have been of an age at which he could have potentially had his own political ideas or a crude desire for power. In this point, at least, the choice of Edward may have been logical.

With two large and powerful factions facing each other, the death of Edgar meant that these could no longer be held in check. The *Life of St Oswald*'s descriptions suggest that the kingdom was in a state of near civil war, and it is only after this that the leading men of the kingdom were to come to an agreement. Here, however, we might address the chronology of events, as the *Life of St Oswald*, uses the occasion of Edgar's death to wander back onto the more usual preoccupation of the fate of the monasteries, specifically such local interests as Peterborough and Ramsey. The sequence of events which our best source, that of Byrhtferth's *Life of St Oswald*, uses here is clear: Edgar, the royal reformer and protector of monasteries had died, and so the kingdom is plunged into anarchy; Abbot Germanus is expelled from Winchcombe, and Ealdorman Aelfhere is portrayed as active in 'appropriating enormous revenues' from the monasteries in his territories.[38] It is only with a council (*synod*) guided by the Ealdorman Aethelwine and the hero-to-be Byrhtnoth that peace is restored to the kingdom. Such a chronology implies that there was an interregnum in England between the death of Edgar and the coronation of Edward, a point to which Byrhtferth gives some weight by stating that two years passed between Edward's election and his death, thus suggesting that he was not crowned until March 976, some eight months after Edgar's death in July 975.[39] This might also be given some weight by an absence of land grants from the first year of Edward's reign – Anglo-Saxon kings would normally grant out large quantities of land to followers in order to bolster their support-base upon succeeding to the kingdom.

However, while such a hypothetical delay between death and succession may have been reasonable in adverse circumstances (the coronation of Edward the Elder had to wait for a similar amount of time to attend to a crisis), even in view of the amount of time which it could take for news to travel and communication to take place in the pre-industrial west, Byrhtferth's chronology suggests that this would have been a long time for the kingdom to

25. Hurstbourne Tarrant, northern Hampshire: a landscape of power. Lands here, along the valley of the Bourne rivulet, formed an important element of the royal holdings in the reigns of Edgar, Edward the Martyr and Aethelred. Hurstbourne was held as part of the resources of the royal office, and, along with Bedwyn in Wiltshire, became part of an important dispute over its control after King Edgar had granted it to the monks of Abingdon. Aethelred's control of such 'lands of the royal sons' represented the reaching of a compromise between the factions of the kingdom.

have been without a king. Such a chronology may be reconciled with the possibility that the election of Edward had taken place *before* his coronation around the March of 976, and thus we need not imagine that the turbulent land seizures took place in a political vacuum. To suggest that the meeting of the *witan* and its election of Edward as king put an end to the disturbances in the kingdom may therefore impose an unnecessary neatness upon the order of events. The chronology of Byrhtferth's account can be reconciled with that of the Anglo-Saxon Chronicle 'D' manuscript, which states that Edward succeeded to the kingdom and, following this, there was a state of unrest in the kingdom; such unrest could have taken place at the same time as the meetings of the *witan*. We need not assume that they were mutually exclusive, but in view of the state of tension which existed, it was a surprisingly brave decision to elect one king, when it was more than possible to split the kingdom. This was presumably Edgar's legacy; the kingdom should remain one.

The great ealdormen of the kingdom may have had mutually hostile intentions, but they could still meet in an official capacity to discuss the succession question. This did not necessarily mean that there was a halt in the violence and land seizures, as peace could exist on one official level, while the petty crimes could take place on another – we can hardly expect the ealdormen themselves to have ridden out against monastic lands. This is more likely to have been the work of their agents, with the rival family members keeping their disputes limited to words at the royal court.

While Byrhtferth's language is necessarily damning of those who 'attacked' monastic lands, the effects for those on the receiving end of attempts to take or recover lands can hardly be underestimated. For those areas in which land disputes took place this was 'civil war', as cattle would have been stolen, farm buildings burnt, fences moved or destroyed, crops stolen, even people killed.[40] We should note that this was not such an ideologically 'anti-monastic' movement as historians thought a few decades ago, however; this was land-feuding typical of early medieval Europe. Ealdorman Aelfhere is generally condemned as an enemy of monks, but the 'anarchy' in the kingdom following Edgar's death may well have simply been the recovery of existing lands in south-eastern Mercia, which Aelfhere considered to have been under the authority of his own family, in any case.[41] Aelfhere's reputation is therefore as a victim of circumstance and, as has since been pointed out, Aelfhere was no more 'anti-monastic' than the East Anglian faction, who were equally willing and able to recover family lands under the same circumstances. Unfortunately for Aelfhere's posthumous reputation, there survives no Mercian equivalent of a Ramsey monk to exonerate him and damn the reputations of the other faction.

However, the strengths of the different factions should not be underestimated here, and it is important to note that the new king was unable to prevent the recovery or taking of lands from monasteries in either Mercia or East Anglia. Although the faction of families supporting Edward the Martyr had 'won' in the sense that they had managed to get their candidate elected to the throne, a compromise had been reached. A charter relating to lands at Hurstbourne Tarrant in Hampshire and Bedwyn in Wiltshire records that the wise men of the kingdom (i.e. the *witan*) were granting the lands of the royal sons to Aethelred, after seizing these particular lands from Abingdon Abbey, which to all intents should not have held them. This was more than a case of who was to hold particular lands: inherent in this decision was one similar to that decided between Alfred and his elder brother, Aethelred I, in the previous century. At some point in 975 or 976, Aethelred II had therefore been chosen as the 'heir apparent'. The throne would not descend to any son of King Edward, and we might even remark from such a fraternal agreement that Edward may have been intended to remain unmarried while on the throne (as perhaps happened with Athelstan and Eadwig). Although, of course, as King Edward could have been little more than

26. Corfe, Dorset: known for its royal castle and hunting ground after the Norman Conquest, Corfe saw the murder of King Edward, Aethelred's half-brother and elder son of the late King Edgar.

nineteen years old at the time of his death (or more likely, seventeen, or even as young as fourteen), intentions had the potential to change over time and who knew whether Edward would have been tempted to renege on any agreement with his younger half-brother? Hindsight at least may show that recognising Aethelred as heir apparent was to be a fateful decision for Edward, but at the time it was a perfectly reasonable one, especially in view of the fact that a powerful faction saw Aethelred's interests as their own and were yet able to pursue those interests.

Edward's reign is only known for tragedy – a famine loomed in the first year of his reign (perhaps exacerbated by the destruction of some of the previous year's crops in land disputes), and in 977 a tragic accident at Calne in Wiltshire may have changed the situation drastically. The Anglo-Saxon Chronicle records that the upper storey of a building collapsed, killing and severely injuring many of the occupants, apart from Archbishop Dunstan, who happened to be standing on a beam. This may provide some commentary on the nascent qualities of two-storey buildings in tenth-century vernacular architecture, as well as the issue that the upper storey was the higher status part of a building, but for the faction which had developed around Edward (or, arguably, shaped him), it may have been a disaster. Although Edward's few charters record the presence of both groups of factions at royal assemblies (the Ealdorman Aelfhere still had to be present, as he was the senior ealdorman), it is likely that the king would still have surrounded himself with those whom he trusted, who may well have outnumbered the 'pro-Aethelred' faction at the royal court. Therefore the fate of those injured in the accident may still have resulted in a *de facto* shift in the balance of power toward the 'pro-Aethelred' faction.

THE DEATH OF A KING

'I cannot escape the conviction on historical, anatomical and surgical grounds that, beyond reasonable doubt, we have here the bones of Saint Edward, King and Martyr.'[42]

In 1963, Thomas Stowell, a forensic pathologist, made a detailed examination of a set of bones which, when they were found in the archaeological excavation of the site of Shaftesbury Abbey in January 1931, caused tremendous excitement. These were, it was claimed by their excavator, John Wilson-Claridge, a local landowner, to be no less than the bones of King Edward the Martyr. Stowell, caught up in a whirlwind of modern-day relic cults, forensic archaeology and historical detective work, agreed with him. It is in Stowell's extraordinary concordance of the evidence of Byrhtferth's *Life of St Oswald* with the bones which he had before him that we can see the magnitude of the death of the young king. Applying techniques more often applied to contemporary criminal pathology than in the examination of thousand-year-old kings, Stowell was able to ascertain the sequence of events in the murder: Byrhtferth, the monk of Ramsey, was, he concluded, telling a wholly accurate story.

Edward's visit to the queen and his younger half-brother Aethelred at Corfe in Dorset was a disaster for the Old English monarchy. According to later accounts, King Edward was hunting in the area and it was during this that the deed took place. Although the death of the king while out hunting may represent something of the judgmental attitudes on the sinful pleasures of Norman kingship (for example, in criticisms of William the Conqueror and the accounts of the death of William Rufus while out hunting in the New Forest),[43] the earliest account of Edward the Martyr's death is from some time before these later criticisms of Norman hunting. It is reasonable to suppose that the area was used for hunting in the pre-Conquest period; in spite of commonly held suppositions, hunting was as much a part of Anglo-Saxon kingship as it was of that of the post-1066 period.[44] King Edmund, grandfather of Edward and Aethelred, had apparently faced death as his horse almost chased a deer over the edge of Cheddar Gorge. While the writer of the *Life of St Dunstan* probably used hunting to emphasise the sinfulness of this king in the face of his disputes with Archbishop Dunstan, it nonetheless shows that hunting played a major part in the lives of Anglo-Saxon kings and, as with so many activities designed to exhibit the manliness of the participants, could be an inherently dangerous business.

Giving our earliest full account of King Edward's visit to Corfe, however, the *Life of St Oswald* plays down any references to hunting. Here, Edward meets his step-mother and half-brother at an unnamed place rather than actually hunting; such references only come later in the Anglo-Saxon period, although we can trust the agreement of the sources with the Anglo-Saxon Chronicle for the reference to Corfe as the site of the crime. As hunting may have played such an important part in the meetings of the Anglo-Saxon great and good,[45] there is little reason to doubt the later accounts in this respect. The death of the youthful King Edward was not a glorious one, however, and hardly compares to King Edmund's death while defending his reeve three decades before. Edward was surrounded by armed men and by a royal cupbearer (the queen? This would at least suggest treachery at a very intimate level). Byrhtferth's account continues: one assailant 'drew him on the right towards him as if he wished to give him a kiss, but another seized roughly his left hand and also wounded him'. The king's reaction, Byrhtferth tells us, was to cry out: '"What are you doing – breaking my right arm?" And suddenly [he] leapt from his horse and died.'

27. Left: St Martin's Church, Wareham, Dorset; close to Corfe and the Isle of Purbeck, the site of this intra-mural church was the resting place of the body of the murdered King Edward for a short time. The nave and chancel of the present building date from late Anglo-Saxon period, and probably represent a later rebuilding.

28. Right: An Anglo-Saxon image of the results of fratricide? Cain enthroned, a detail after the Oxford Bodleian MS Junius II, which illustrated a depiction of Genesis around the beginning of the eleventh century.

29. Below: The altar dedicated to King Edward the Martyr at Shaftesbury Abbey, Dorset, where the sainted King's relics were translated by Ealdorman Aelfhere in 979. The bones of the King await the reconstruction of a shrine suitable for this former foundation of Alfred the Great.

The history of King Edward the Martyr's bones is similarly dramatic, involving archae-ologists, British members of the Russian Orthodox Church, and a court case in which recriminations dragged on throughout the 1980s and 1990s. Stowell's examination may give the account some credibility, although it should be acknowledged that Stowell was working from what he considered to be the authentic account and this may have coloured his interpretation of the damage to the bones: the assailants stabbed Edward and broke both arms in the process. As Edward was pushed back in the saddle, his hip was fractured in the tension, and his left foot forced into the stirrup. The king's horse bolted from the mêlée, and the injured king fell from the right-hand side of the horse, to be dragged along the ground for some yards before the king's foot finally freed itself. It was evidently a dramatic death. Stowell's account was not considered to be the definitive answer, however. Questions have still been raised about the identity of the bones; Stowell's methods of examination may have been better suited to the examination of a recently deceased corpse rather than a skeleton crumbling with age, and many of the traumas visited upon the corpse may have been inflicted after death rather than during a series of accidents.[46] Could it have been an elaborate ploy undertaken by Shaftesbury Abbey in order to promote the cult of their dead king? While the political importance of Edward's cult is considered in a later chapter, here it is sufficient to reiterate a point made by Keynes, that the body examined by Stowell is at least a body which has been revered as the body of the saint since around the turn of the second millennium.[47] This suggests that contemporaries believed in the violent death of the royal martyr, and considered it to have been a terrible event for the kingdom.

The king's body remained without a royal funeral, as it lay in the house of an unknown thegn for a year. Ealdorman Aelfhere of Mercia was later to bury him with full royal honours at Shaftesbury Abbey, an action which may have been interpreted as atonement for the death of Edward.[48] The exoneration by historians of Aelfhere from guilt in the events has developed, based upon the refutation of the previously held view that the conflicts in the kingdom were largely pro- and anti-monastic. Since factionalism along these lines has been shown not to have been the case, should we therefore assume Aelfhere's innocence in the murder? The evidence suggesting his complicity is only circumstantial, but the weight is substantial: Aelfhere's interest in the pro-Aethelred faction, his influence in Queen Aelfthryth's court, at which the murder took place, and his act of translating the royal body. To these, David Rollason added the suggestion of the revival of a saints' cult in East Anglia, around 978-980. In the legend, two young members of the Kentish royal family were killed by their wicked step-mother under what could be perceived as similar circumstances to the murder of Edward. The similarity is such that, Rollason has convincingly argued, this was an attempt on the part of the family of Aethelwine to make a political point against the old rivals in Mercia.[49]

Later accounts vilify the 'wicked step-mother' figure of Queen Aelfthryth,[50] but even in the *Life of St Oswald*, one of the most contemporary of the surviving accounts of the death of the king, the explicit mention of the presence of the queen mother and Aethelred cannot have been a good sign, especially as in later years Aethelred, perhaps through political necessity, did not exact retribution for the murder of his kin. No contemporary accounts were ever to criticise either Aethelred or his mother directly for involvement in the regicide and it should be emphasised that it would have been in the interests of the promotion of Edward the Confessor to later undermine the woman involved in the upbringing of the children of Aethelred's first marriage.[51] However, even if the evidence for the involvement of Aethelred's mother is only circumstantial, the murder of God's anointed could have cast a shadow over her position at court. Whether or not Aelfthryth was directly involved in the action, the fact remained that she benefited politically from the promotion of her son to the throne of the kingdom, and while we might not see her as some Al Capone figure master-minding an intricate operation, and certainly should not believe such later medieval accounts as those that say the queen plunged the fatal dagger herself, we might at least imagine the actions of a particularly diligent group of thegns who believed that they were fulfilling the wishes of the queen-mother and acting in the interests of the kingdom. While there may not be any contemporary parallels for such premeditated regicide, either in Anglo-Saxon England or on the European continent, the actions of the three knights in Canterbury Cathedral following the long-suffering exhortations of Henry II to rid himself of a 'turbulent priest' might show us that such actions were perfectly able to take place in the politics of medieval society.

In the final analysis, it would be too much for us to expect to be able to see the full motivations behind the murder of the king a millennium later – the idea of the conspiracy theory is a product of a post-modern society with the extensive use of communication, but we should recognise that a pre-industrial society was more than capable of developing intricate theories about its own development. Suspicions and counter-suspicions may have been rife, and in this light a modern exoneration of Queen Aelfthryth may perhaps be far too rational; though probably technically innocent, to be suspicious of the queen was perfectly in keeping with the spirit of the times and this heady mixture of political intrigue and ecclesiastical interests provided a fertile ground for the cultivation of a late Anglo-Saxon royal saint.

THE CHILD KING

The same parties who had put Aethelred forward for the English kingship were those who effectively ruled the kingdom on his behalf for the first few years of his reign. King Aethelred's mother, Aelfthyrth, remained the dominant force at the royal court during the king's youth, and it is notable that the witness lists to charters place her in a high position at the beginning of Aethelred's reign. Reservations have been made against this argument by Keynes, who noted that Aelfthryth's relative position amongst the witnesses of charters was similarly high in the last years of Edgar's reign.[52] However, important though Aelfthryth may have been in Edgar's reign, that does not undermine the fact that during Edward's short reign, she did not appear in *any* of the surviving charters' witness lists, and so may not have had little influence at her step-son's court. Therefore, it is only natural to see the political prominence of Aelfthryth during the early years of Aethelred's reign as a sign of her triumphal return to power: she was a queen once more, in the same manner as she had been five years earlier, when crowned alongside her husband at Bath.

Additionally, Bishop Aethelwold of Winchester and Ealdorman Aelfhere may have proved important influences in the circle of royal advisors, as they had been uppermost in the promotion of Aethelred for the throne. Keynes has noted that the prominence of royal advisors in royal government in the first few years, the 'period of tutelage' which he assigns to the years of 978–84. There is no reason to overturn this chronology. From the surviving corpus of charters, Keynes has noted that Bishop Aethelwold was the first of the recipients of favour through land grants after the royal coronation.[53] Although Aelfhere's influence as a friend of both bishop and queen was presumably significant, it is also possible that this was tempered by the questions surrounding his involvement in the murder of Edward the Martyr: whether or not Aelfhere was guilty of involvement in the regicide, the death of the candidate whom Aelfhere had opposed was hardly something which could be brushed off lightly.

Under more auspicious circumstances, the first years of an Anglo-Saxon king's reign would be a flurry of activity, as the benefices of rule were handed out in order to secure the favours of the nobility. However, unfortunately for the new King Aethelred, it was possibly difficult to disturb the *status quo* of lands and patronage too much. The order of prominence and lists of names in charter witness lists, as Keynes has noted, look very much like those of King Edward, which in turn look like those of the last years of Edgar's reign. The ealdormanries of Sussex, eastern Wessex and the Western Provinces, which had fallen absent by the end of Edgar's reign, were already distributed, possibly to extend the circle of patronage for Edward the Martyr's followers.[54]

In a seminal paper, Pauline Stafford asked why Aethelred did not simply get rid of these advisors and stamp his identity upon the kingship? The answer, it seems, comes from the fact that early medieval kingship was a series of compromises between the aims and wishes of the king and his nobility – centuries before the constitutional monarchy of early modern England was to institutionalise this relationship. For Aethelred, it was a result of the 'limitations of royal power'.[55] Consequently, the early years of Aethelred's reign were still a product of the factional interests that had dogged the short unfortunate reign of Edward the Martyr. There was one fundamental difference, however, in the fact that during Edward's reign there had been two possible candidates for the throne, whereas for Aethelred there were no other options. The only conceivable alternative was Aethelweard 'the Chronicler', ealdorman of south-western England, now better known for his achievement in producing a Latin version of the Anglo-Saxon Chronicle and raising the profile of lay literacy in the early Middle Ages. Ealdorman Aethelweard's potential claim to the throne would be an obscure one, going back to the previous century, as he was related to the descendants of Alfred's elder brother, whose claim to the throne had brought about civil war at the beginning of the tenth century (in view of Aethelweard's tenuous claim, it is interesting that he was diplomatic enough not to mention his ancestor's rebellion).[56] Civil war was unwanted now, so the rule of Aethelred and thus the hegemony of the family of Aelfhere of Mercia may have been accepted by the English nobility, although the brooding presence of Archbishop Dunstan remained a feature in the court of Aethelred's early reign, just as he had been for much of the tenth century.[57] As we shall see, there were to be Viking raids upon the coasts of the English kingdom during the 980s, but for the most part, government was more than able to function. Assemblies took place, lands were granted to nobles and clergy (that part of royal life of which we tend to see so much), and the machinery of government ground on relentlessly.

POLITICAL INDEPENDENCE?

If we consider that the king was about twelve years old when he came to the throne in 978, then it would have been another three years before he was of effective political age in physical maturity, if not ability. In fact, it was to be after another six years, when two of the main parties in the royal court died in 984, that Aethelred found himself able to emerge as a ruler without the influence of this key group of advisors around him. Bishop Aethelwold and Ealdorman Aelfhere were both dead, and Aethelred's mother, Queen Aelfthryth, appears to have been relegated to a comparatively minor position at court. Keynes notes that she no longer appeared in charter witness lists; instead, Ealdorman Aelfric of Hampshire and Bishop Wulfgar of Ramsbury, amongst others, may have been prominent in 'misleading' the king. In this period, there was apparently a reduction in the rights of Abingdon Abbey, a place which had been an important reformed foundation during the reign of Edgar, as well as Aethelred's connivance at the seizure of lands from Glastonbury.[58] Divine intervention may have emerged victorious in the latter case – William of Malmesbury reported in his version of the *Life of St Dunstan* that as the body of the covetous noble concerned was being transported for burial in Glastonbury, it was devoured by a rogue pack of foxes.[59]

Vulpine revenge aside, Stafford has questioned the extent to which Aethelred was guilty of such actions. Aethelred was not acting against the Church as a 'monolithic institution', as this was not how the individual churches of late Anglo-Saxon England were perceived, but rather these recorded occasions are 'products of specific political situations'.[60] It could be added that Keynes's instances of royal misdemeanour are evidenced not from the time, but from Aethelred's apparent contrition in making recompense. Such statements in charters could be seen in the context of Aethelred as a very pious king who was emerging in the mid 990s and perhaps emphasising the extent to which he was a sinner who needed to make contrition, because that was what was expected of him – it was what a good Christian king did.

In the meantime, during the 980s, the king may well have gathered a new group of advisors around himself but we should not see them in the light of the 'bad advice' which was portrayed as emerging from the actions of Ealdorman Eadric during the last years of Aethelred's reign. The most serious event of the period was probably the razing of the diocese of Rochester, during a dispute between the king and the Bishop of Rochester in 986. This was evidently a serious event, but our perspective upon this is very much influenced by Dunstan and eastern England. Rochester fell under the close influence of the archbishopric of Canterbury, and we are told by Osbern that Dunstan was a key player in attempting to bring Aethelred to agreement.[61] To see it from another perspective, we might look beyond the idea that Aethelred was being led astray by a group of advisors. If Dunstan, the senior figure at court, saw King Aethelred as a young upstart, he may have felt that he was able to assert his influence upon him, especially following the deaths of two of the major figures at court, and Aelfthryth's absence from the court may also have been under the archbishop's influence. Therefore, for Aethelred, ravaging territory was a perfectly legitimate exercise in the assertion of royal authority, and herein we may see that this was a battle over spheres of political influence. Dunstan's disapproval did not necessarily stem not from the burning of the lands themselves, but from the fact that Rochester was *his* territory. The archbishop's muttered curses may have been tinged with bitterness; in the later 980s, King Aethelred was advancing his own political agenda and, as from what we can see in Rochester, this was proving successful.

3

THE BEGINNING OF THE SECOND VIKING AGE

The machinations of Anglo-Saxon government may have ground relentlessly on during the first years of the young King Aethelred's reign, but it is in relation to Viking attacks upon the kingdom that he is best remembered. These began in 980, for which year the Peterborough ('E') manuscript of the Anglo-Saxon Chronicle records that 'for the first time' seven ships arrived at the town of Southampton and ravaged it. The word which the Chronicler employs to describe the attack – 'ravage' (*hergoden*) – seems more characteristic of an earlier age in the Anglo-Saxon history and we are left with little doubt that the Vikings had returned. These were the actions of such Vikings as had been the scourge of Wessex in the previous century. The entries in the Abingdon manuscript add to this picture of devastation; most of the citizens (*burhwaru*) of Southampton were either 'killed or taken prisoner', Thanet was also 'ravaged', as was Cheshire, the latter by a 'northern ship army' (*north scipherige*).

The annals in the Abingdon manuscript for the following decade present us with a catalogue of attacks by Viking raiders. The Chronicler's single-minded obsession with such actions has become a hallmark on Aethelred's reign from that first appearance in Southampton to Cnut's accession in 1016. While many of the criticisms regarding the last years of Aethelred's reign may be well-founded, as Simon Keynes noted, the Viking attacks of the 980s merit some re-examination in order to place them in their context.

Keynes observed that the Abingdon manuscript of the Chronicle was mostly written a few years after the events it describes, and that the chronicler knew the English kingdom was close to its end.[1] While we may have little reason to doubt the chronicler's account of many of the period's military and political aspects,[2] there is at least logic in asking why certain matters are emphasised. Every Viking incursion is invested with great significance, even so early as the first decade of Aethelred's reign. The annalistic format of the Chronicle therefore gives us a misleading sense of confidence: before Keynes's re-examination, the Chronicle was believed to have been contemporary with the events that it was describing. While the chronicler himself may have had access to the records of events, the emphasis given to military failure and treachery is not contemporary, but rather is more appropriate to a sense of despondency from a particular viewpoint. By contrast, the relatively contem-

30. Portland in Dorset. Site of the first recorded Viking attack in Western Europe, in 789, as well as one of the first attacks of the so-called 'Second Viking Age', in 982. the area probably included land belonging to the royal family, while it was also close to an important royal estate and the administrative centre of the shire of Dorset, at Dorchester.

31. Viking raids on the English kingdom from 980–88.

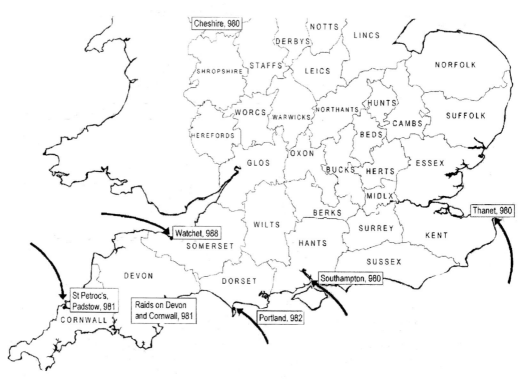

porary Winchester ('Parker' or 'A') manuscript of the Anglo-Saxon Chronicle makes no references to the early Viking raids on the kingdom. By this stage the Winchester manuscript had become a localised set of annals with 'scrappy' entries, the interests of which rarely extended outside Hampshire. As a rejoinder to the picture of relentless assaults upon the English kingdom, it is remarkable that right at its West Saxon heart, Viking attacks – even that on Southampton, some fifteen miles down river – were rarely recorded (with two major exceptions, discussed in chapters 5 and 7) and the life of the church continued to be recorded unabated in the succession of bishops.

So much for the possible intentions of the authors of the different Anglo-Saxon Chronicle recensions. What of the context of the attacks on the English kingdom in the first decade of Aethelred's reign? Here, it must be stressed that the first occasions were only small Viking raids upon the coast. The targets were first Southampton, then Thanet and Cheshire (980), St Petroc's monastery in Padstow and coastal sites in Devon and Cornwall (981), Portland in Dorset (982), and Watchet in Somerset in 988. It has been suggested that the burning of London in 982 was the result of Viking activity,[3] but the Chronicle does not make a direct connection between the presence of Vikings in Dorset and the burning of London, even if the two events may later have been seen in a similarly apocalyptic milieu.

Taken together then, as the chronicler presents them, the activities of the Vikings appear significant, but seven attacks in the space of eight years (most of which took place in 980–2) can hardly compare to the sort of intense Viking raiding which took place in the ninth century and, indeed, later in Aethelred's reign. The raids appear to have been minor ones with few consequences. But for later events showing that the Vikings did prove a major threat, we might even wonder if the events of the 980s would have otherwise warranted much space in the annals of the Anglo-Saxon kingdom.

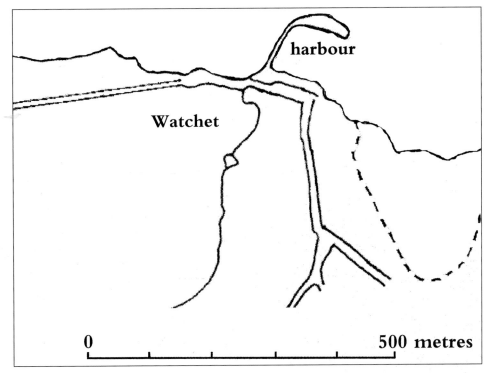

32. The *burh* at Watchet, on the Somerset coast, off the Bristol Channel. From here it was only a short step across the Irish Sea to Dublin, so it was important to provide a strong defence of this royal centre. This resulted in a battle in 988.

The exception to this trend may have been the attack on Watchet in 988, which was also recorded by Byrhtferth in the *Life of St Oswald*. This was significant because a local force of thegns was present to confront the attacking Vikings; presumably this contrasted with earlier raids, in which the Vikings normally moved too quickly for the English to visit any retaliation. However, it must be said that although Byrhtferth records a 'savage battle', the sources' depictions of casualties hardly compare to the long lists of obituaries which the Anglo-Saxon Chronicle musters in the later years of Aethelred's reign. The Chronicle records the death of Goda, a Devonshire thegn (who John of Worcester's twelfth-century version of the Chronicle makes into a *satrap* [ealdorman]), and 'many others with him'. Byrhtferth records the death of a thegn by the name of Streonwold. The death of two thegns or even just one thegn (Goda and Streonwold may even have been one and the same man), shows that this may have been a local battle and that a royal officer or local notable[4] had died in the process. The fact that the 988 encounter appears in the *Life of St Oswald* is not necessarily evidence of this having been a major engagement, as it is sometimes seen,[5] but simply a larger battle than the others of the 980s. The world of government outside the West Country may not have been shaken, but at least it could be said that Viking raiders could be caught and, if we are to believe the *Life of St Oswald's* version of the result, defeated.[6]

The Viking activities of the 980s could almost be seen as a form of 'reconnaissance raids' for later attacks; Eric John hazarded that it 'is almost as though the dismantling of the burghal system were a first object of the Vikings',[7] while Nicholas Higham has also followed a similar line,[8] and it must be admitted that such an interpretation is rather tempting. Certainly, such raiders as those who hit the English kingdom may have returned to Scandinavia with information, but this is unlikely to have been incorporated into some long-term 'master-plan'. There were Scandinavian military activities in England recorded for some twenty-five years of Aethelred's reign and we should not credit disparate groups of Vikings with thinking in terms of such a long-term strategy; to view a long, planned campaign with specific aims from as early as the 980s would be determinist to say the least. The *burhs* of the late Anglo-Saxon kingdom were attacked not as part of a co-ordinated campaign of dismantling defences, but for a very traditional and wholly rational reason: these places were centres of wealth and provided attractive targets and rich pickings for audacious pirates. The Vikings who raided England in the first decade of Aethelred's reign seem to have been only small forces, as the figures which we do have are for three ships in Portland and seven at Southampton, and many of these Vikings probably did not come from the Danish state at all.

THE VIKINGS IN NORTH-WESTERN EUROPE

Many of the attacks on England during the 980s were on the western and southern coasts, and the perpetrators had probably arrived not from Scandinavia but from closer to England – from the Viking kingdoms in Ireland, the Western Isles of Britain and perhaps also from just across the Channel in the duchy of Normandy. Viking activity on the western coast of Britain, mainly western Wales and western Scotland, was a feature of this period.[9] The attacks on Devon, Cornwall and Cheshire might therefore be better understood within a western British context – to Vikings operating in the Irish Sea, these places were certainly fair game.

In Ireland, too, the small kingdoms of the Irish kings were hardly immune from raids launched from the Norse *longphoirt* established at Dublin, Waterford, Cork and Limerick, although in these cases it is difficult to make precise distinctions between straightforward

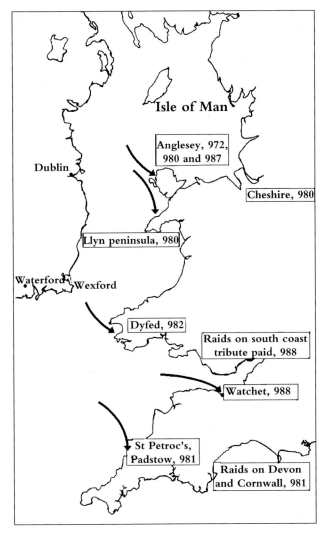

Isle of Man

Anglesey, 972, 980 and 987

Cheshire, 980

Dublin

Llyn peninsula, 980

Waterford Wexford

Dyfed, 982

Raids on south coast tribute paid, 988

Watchet, 988

St Petroc's, Padstow, 981

Raids on Devon and Cornwall, 981

33. 'Viking' activity in the British Isles during the later tenth century.

booty raids and the political machinations of Irish politics, in which the Viking kingdoms had become an inextricable part.[10] Beyond the British Isles, in spite of the partisan claims made by Rodulfus Glaber in his *Five Books of the Histories* that the Normans never fought in the French king's territory except by royal invitation, the French kingdom was nonetheless a victim of Norman interventions in French affairs.[11] Aethelred was well-advised to take heed of the threat posed across the English Channel by a potential 'French Danelaw'. Although at least in the first decade of Aethelred's reign, Viking raids were not necessarily launched by Normans themselves, by 991 the situation was serious enough for Pope John XV to broker a peace between the English king and Norman Duke.[12]

The kingdom of England in the early years of Aethelred's reign had no immunity, however, from a general climate of north-western European pre-millennial turmoil. Such raids were an 'extension of normal Dark Age activity' in the same way as they had emerged in the early ninth century (if Peter Sawyer's famous judgement can be taken so far out of context);[13] for the coasts of England in the 980s this 'normal' activity undertaken by enterprising merchants who were willing to use violence was simply something which was suffered with little demur as a fact of life. This was, as Eric John has intimated, no royal weakness on the part of King Aethelred; through the first decade of his reign, the defences of the kingdom remained effective.[14]

Therefore, it seems unfortunate indeed that Aethelred's reign coincided with this resumption in 'Viking' activity. The reasons as to why large-scale Viking aggression direct from Scandinavia may have remained outside this western corner of Europe for the space of another decade will be examined in the next chapter, but piratical raids may actually have been nothing new for the English kingdom in the tenth century. The will of King Eadred (946–55) records the provision of money for the relief of pagan armies.[15] The years of Eadred's reign are hardly known for Viking raids on southern English soil and, arguably, Eadred may have provided money for a perceived threat rather than an actual one. But this was real money which was to be provided. The Winchester manuscript of the Anglo-Saxon Chronicle does not record Viking attacks upon southern England until 991, despite their appearance in the Abingdon manuscript in seven years of the 980s. This is unlikely to be an indication that these annals were fabricated, instead, it may show that small piratical raids were a feature of the tenth century, to be viewed like disease or famine as something which one endured, the manifestation of God's will, against which little could be done.

King Edgar's relationship with the other kings in the British Isles may have kept Hiberno-Norse Vikings from English shores or arguably even employed them. The comment made by the chronicler Aethelweard during the first decade of King Aethelred's reign that since the Battle of Brunanburh in 937, 'no fleet' (classicus) had 'remained here, having advanced against these shores, except under treaty with the English',[16] does not imply complete safety from attacks after 937; small piratical raids were less the work of 'fleets' than a few ships, but Aethelweard may imply the employment of Viking mercenary fleets under treaty. The blame for the foundations of the second Viking age, therefore, may not necessarily be placed only at the feet of King Aethelred, although it is possible that raids may have become more prevalent due to the probable turmoil of the succession crisis in 975, as ealdormen paid more attention to the politics of royal succession than the defences of their own areas. A charter granted to Ealdorman Aethelweard during the reign of King Edward the Martyr puts the duty of guarding the coast in place of the more normal military obligation of 'bridge-work'.[17] As Aethelweard was in charge of land in the south-west, which was subject to raids by Vikings in the early years of Aethelred's reign, King Edward's grant may perhaps be seen in a similar context.

There is little reason to suspect that these early raids in Aethelred's reign were anything exceptional. Events at Watchet in 988 were recorded with a reasonable level of detail because they were unusual in terms of hit-and-run raiding: an encounter between the local defence force and the Viking attackers. As we shall see in Chapter 6, this seems to have had little effect on the efficient running of government in the shires. Outside the British Isles, however, a very different Viking threat was to emerge.

4

EARLY MEDIEVAL SCANDINAVIA: VIKINGS AND STATES

In the years prior to the Second World War and during the immediate post-war years, the Vikings were largely seen as having only hostile intentions. While the best attempts at historical and archaeological revisionism in the period since the 1960s can hardly expunge the violent achievements of the raiding armies in the ninth century from the historical consciousness, it is worth asking whether there was a 'national' political ambition emergent in the nascent state of Denmark. The discovery of military fortresses in Denmark in the atmosphere of the 1930s could only have been interpreted in the light of the legendary *Jomsvikings* of the *Jomsviking Saga*: the 'warrior monks' who lived an austere life in military barracks, training together, going out on raids and to wars together, and abstaining from the company of women. What could be a better illustration of the virtue of the elite military society and the zenith of the advanced state than their long-standing intentions to invade and conquer England?

In the course of a few generations, Denmark had emerged from consisting of a society of warrior chieftains to being a centralised royal state that identified itself as 'Denmark'[1] and a military power capable of confronting the English kingdom. Although elements of state formation are evident in Denmark from as early as the late eighth or ninth century,[2] the development of a Danish state can be interpreted as a significant feature of the tenth century. What were the causes and consequences of this?

THE CHRISTIAN WEST AND THE JELLING DYNASTY

We must begin with the imperial ambitions of the ruler of the German *Reich*, Otto I, some three decades before the beginning of King Aethelred's reign. Unable to exert influence in the area to the west of the Rhine where an established French kingdom was relatively secure, Otto's interests lay in the Slavs to the east and in the Danes to the north. The paganism of these peoples to the east and the north were reason enough to justify such an extension of Otto's hegemony.

In 948, Otto appointed bishops to three dioceses in Denmark: Schleswig in southern Jutland, Ribe in mid-western Jutland and Århus in the north.[3] It is unlikely, as Niels Lund has suggested, that these bishops ever went to their sees.[4] Adam of Bremen's record of the murder

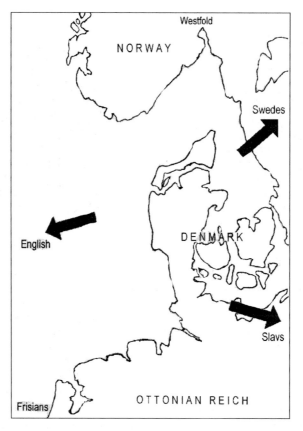

34. The kingdom of Denmark and its neighbours. To the south were the Ottonian Reich of Germany, the Frisians and the Slavic tribes, to the east, the Swedes. The Westfold area of Norway was subject to the political sphere of influence of the Danish king in the tenth century, while the north-eastern coast of the English kingdom was only a few days' sailing across the North Sea.

of Otto's legates at Hedeby, along with 'the whole colony of Saxons',[5] stands as an illustration of the dangers of diplomacy across borders. Even normal diplomatic relations might be dangerous at the best of times, but for foreign bishops to have travelled into hostile territory at the behest of a hostile emperor would have been folly indeed. But in political terms, the physical presence of the bishops was not so important here as Otto's assertion of his authority as a Christian ruler – as Otto demonstrated with his actions amongst the Slav tribes,[6] the message given to the Danes was a simple one: convert or suffer the consequences.

The Danes were not an entirely pagan people by the tenth century, however. St Anskar's missions had not been completely successful in introducing a widespread conversion of the whole ninth-century kingdom, but at the very least, Christian communities were tolerated and in other cases, Christ had become one of the Norse gods. But this was hardly orthodox Christianity and, to Otto, the significant factor was the integration of the Danes, and therefore of their control, within a German Church.

Denmark was more fortunate than the Slavs. In the 950s, it was a politically astute move on the part of King Harald Bluetooth of Denmark, father of the later King Swein Forkbeard, to declare that he had converted the whole kingdom to Christianity; Otto's

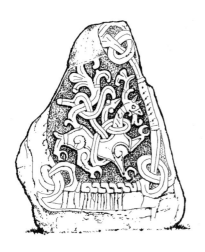 

35. The Jelling Runestone, dating from the mid-tenth century: foundation stone of Danish Christianity, and indeed the foundation stone of King Harald Bluetooth's kingship in the Danish state, this is placed between two burial mounds at Jelling in Jutland. On one side is a dragon motif, while on another the image of Christ's crucifixion. Runes upon a third side (not depicted here) declare the construction of the stone by King Harald in memory of his mother and father, as well as Harald's claim for the credit of the conversion of all Danes and conquest of Norway. (Don Lavelle)

pretext for invasion was thereby removed at a stroke.[7] Christianity was not brought into Denmark by the spear of a proselytizing warlord, then. Here, it was a relatively independent phenomenon, unbounded by foreign imperial ambitions.[8] Even the partisan Adam of Bremen seems to have viewed the independence of King Harald as a given fact. The conversion to Christianity was, Lund notes, recognised outside Denmark: a charter of Otto the Great declares that he relinquished his imperial rights over the Danish dioceses, and the independence of the kingdom was established where it counted.[9]

The 'State conversion' of Denmark to Christianity was also more than just a reaction to the threat from the south. There were inherent political strengths associated with conversion which were useful to King Harald Bluetooth. The Jelling Runestone, which can be seen in a churchyard in Jutland, is a foundation stone of the Danish kingdom, a legacy which has even led to its presence in Danish passports today. The stone declares that King Harald ordered it 'to be made in memory of Gorm, his father, and Thyra, his mother, that [same] Harald who won for himself all Denmark and Norway and made the Danes Christian'. The significance of this stone can hardly be overstated, as this was at the site of the pagan burial mounds of Harald's father and mother; it was, in effect, a declaration that the new religion was being used to augment the royal power of the ruling dynasty.[10]

This was an important issue that had been learnt by Anglo-Saxon kings some centuries before the conversions of Scandinavian kings: a religious worldview which had a pantheon of gods who were often in conflict with one another could not be as effective in a centralised state structure as one which stressed the legitimacy of a single authority through Christ. Previously, Danish kingship may not have been stable in ensuring the succession of a patrimonial dynasty; now, Harald Bluetooth's declaration had boldly showed that through this new religion, he was ensuring the descent of the kingdom through one paternal line.

55

As we have seen with Edgar in England, Christian rule was part and parcel of imperial ambitions. Harald saw himself as a regional player; he made claim to Norway, bastion of pagan chieftains, even if the extent of power held by the Danish king in Norway was limited in reality. In this respect, we can consider the worldview of Danish kings and even see the English and Norwegian territories in the same context; as Norway would continue to be a preoccupation for at least the next century, perhaps even England itself was not beyond imperial ambitions?

It is perhaps indicative of Harald's confidence in his kingship that in 973, following the death of Otto the Great, the Danes attacked the German *Reich* to the south.[11] It was not, it seems, a successful campaign. In a counter-attack by Otto II, the land which Harald claimed was lost, as were parts of Jutland to the north of the *Danevirke*, including the important trading centre at Hedeby, to remain in Otto's hands until Harald seized another opportunity in 983. Unsuccessful though Harald's attack in 973 was to become, it nonetheless showed a great deal of confidence and energy in that the nascent state of Denmark was willing to assert its identity and pursue aggressive policies within its own sphere of influence.

POWER IN THE LANDSCAPE: PUBLIC WORKS

King Harald Bluetooth's statement of newly Christianised power was accompanied by some impressive public works which bolstered his imperial ambitions. A long bridge was built at Ravning Enge to cross the River Vejle and the marshy land leading up to Jelling. In an age of poor communication, this was a major achievement worthy of state power; sets of huge wooden piles of up to four metres in length were driven into the ground at two-metre intervals

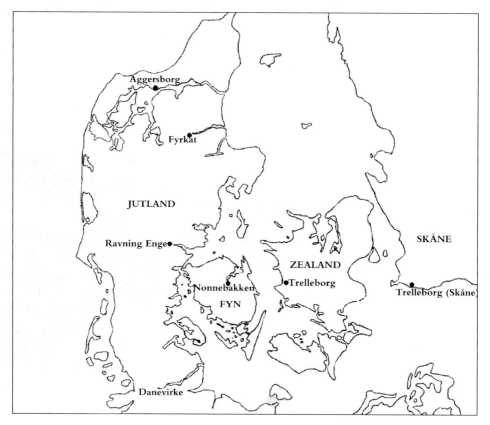

36. The locations of major public works of the Danish state from the tenth century.

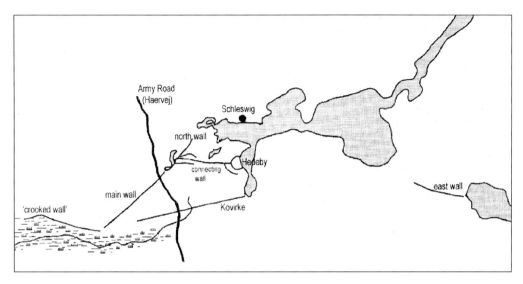

37. The *Danevirke*, a linear defence, originally built in the early eighth century to defend southern Denmark from attacks from the south.

38. A campaign of modernisation was undertaken during the reign of Harald Bluetooth, in order for the *Danevirke* to encompass the important trading centre at Hedeby. (Don Lavelle)

and a wooden bridge rested upon these piles, traversing a length of 700 metres.[12] Built around 978–9, at the same time as Aethelred was coming to the throne in England, Danish royal power was demonstrated in the landscape by this impressive approach to the royal estate at Jelling.

To the south of the Danish kingdom, along the border with the German *Reich*, the independence of Denmark was demonstrated by the continuation of the *Danevirke*. This was a massive twenty-mile (thirty-kilometre) defensive barrier which was first constructed two centuries earlier and, in conjunction with the marshy land and rivers of south-west Jutland, provided protection against incursions from the south.[13] In the 950s, Harald Bluetooth refortified and re-strengthened it, adding a new length to encompass the trading centre at Hedeby in the 960s: a centralised state was consolidating its resources. Static linear defences in the twentieth century tend to be interpreted as a form of strategic weakness; the Maginot Line and the Atlantic Wall in France and the Bar Lev line along the Suez Canal are generally remembered as expensive failures, but linear defences in the early Middle Ages should not be seen in the same light, despite the strength of the German kingdom which stood beyond the *Danevirke*. To refortify such a massive barrier as the *Danevirke* was to make a statement of great strength: it showed that the Danish kingdom had massive human resources to spare

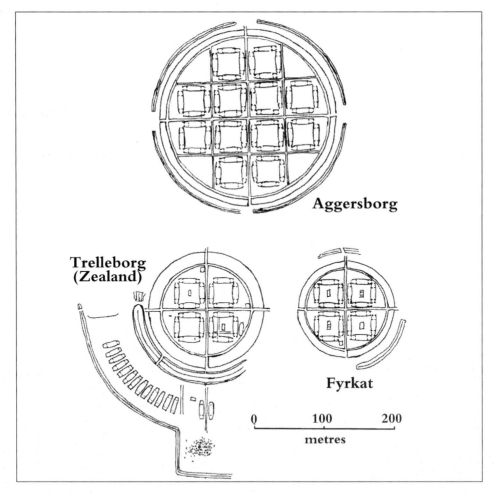

39. Some of the Danish fortresses, built during the reign of King Harald Bluetooth. Sited on the edges of the Danish kingdom, these played an important in the formation of the kingdom under King Harald; they only stood for a short period, which suggests that their purpose was not so much the process of invading England as the consolidation of Danish royal control, including southern Norway and Skåne in Sweden.

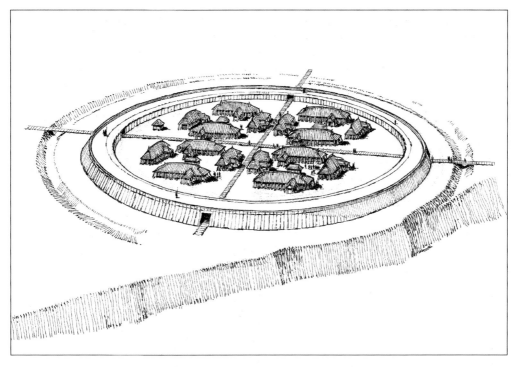

40. Reconstruction of the fortress at Fyrkat. The hall buildings of the fortresses were laid out in regular patterns and surrounded by massive ramparts. (Don Lavelle)

41. Reconstruction of one of the 'bowed' halls from the fortress at Fyrkat, near the town of Hobro in northern Jutland.

and it was emphasising a line of distinction and the status quo between the Danes and their southern neighbours. It was both a fiscal and military barrier, as despite Otto's statement that he no longer claimed imperial hegemony over Denmark, realistically speaking, he still remained the regional superpower. This line of Danish independence remained until the mid-nineteenth century, and while it is perhaps ironic that the area is now in German Schleswig-Holstein, a result of nineteenth-century politics and military campaigning, it is a testament to King Harald Bluetooth that the kingdom should have lasted so long.

However, it is with the five Trelleborg fortresses that the legacy of Harald Bluetooth's Denmark continues to make its greatest contact with the modern world. These massive geometric fortresses stunned the academic world when one was first uncovered at Trelleborg on the main Danish island of Zealand in 1934. As Else Roesdahl has noted, it was considered incredible that the 'barbaric' Vikings could have been capable of undertaking such a complex building operation.[14] Trelleborg was a site laid out to a geometric pattern worthy of Roman engineering. It was not an isolated example, either. Four other similar fortresses were found across Denmark: at Nonnebakken on the island of Fyn, at Fyrkat and Aggersborg in northern Jutland, and at another Trelleborg, in Skåne (now in Sweden). All followed the same geometric pattern: a circular rampart, with multiple groups of four buildings in the centre. Were these the barracks of the legendary *Jomsvikings* of saga tales, the warrior brotherhood who fought for Danish kings with such fearlessness, from their sea-stronghold of Jomsborg, believed to be at the mouth of the River Oder? In the saga of the *Jomsvikings*, the fortress was described in impressive terms. We are told that it encompassed an enclosed harbour for 300 ships, with iron gates preventing entry from the sea and, perhaps more influenced by depictions of Western European and Middle Eastern castle-building of the high Middle Ages than tenth-century Viking warfare, the saga goes on to portray Jomsborg with its own catapults.[15]

Although some of the Danish geometric fortresses were close to coasts and may have been associated with naval power, these were not quite as impregnable as the legendary Jomsborg is supposed to have been. Few scholars have gone as far as to suggest that Jomsborg has been discovered. Nonetheless, the *Jomsvikings* held a strong place in the hearts of the first generation of scholars to confront the geometric fortresses, who suggested that even if these were not the places of the *Jomsvikings* themselves, then perhaps they were communities *like* the *Jomsvikings*.[16] However, what is more important than the possibility of there having been brotherhoods of freebooting mercenaries living by their own codes of honour, is a very palpable sense of royal power inherent in the building of the fortresses. The exact replication of design principles in each suggests not their construction by rebellious independent warlords, but rather that they were all built for the same purpose by a single authority. The fact that not all of the buildings in the Trelleborg fortresses had hearths also seems to suggest that they were not permanent places of occupation – perhaps they might therefore be better understood as marshalling stations for large numbers of fighting men, for a purpose other than freebooting design.

Was that purpose the invasion of England? In the years after the Second World War, when memories of the gathering of thousands of troops within vast dispersal yards across southern England were fresh in many minds, it is understandable that an obsession with the logistics of invasions could have led to such an interpretation. However, there are also other possibilities. It is equally if not more likely that they were built for the unification of the Danish kingdom or the defence of the kingdom against the Germans – a matter that is more important in the long term. Dendrochronological dating of the timbers used in the building of the Trelleborg fortress has shown that the timbers were felled in the winter of 980–81, the best part of a decade before the major attacks on England were launched. A military superpower was being created, which was built upon aggression and which needed to keep feeding that aggression in order to maintain itself;[17] arguably, there was little other choice.

Southern Norway could be a target for 'legitimate' aggression through long-standing claims of overlordship (a preoccupation which Anglo-centric historians would do well to recognise),[18] but the neighbouring state to Denmark's west, the English kingdom, also presented itself as a target for some serious attacks.

Pirates and Silver: Swein Forkbeard

Though ultimately so indirectly important in English history, King Harald Bluetooth is not remembered in relation to the English kingdom. It is the actions of his son, Swein Forkbeard, which are best remembered, and the volatile relationship between the long-reigning father and adult son which manifested itself in the political conditions of the period. This is a common and tragic theme of early medieval kingdoms, not least some two decades later at the end of the reign of King Aethelred (see chapter 11) – a young, politically ambitious son could be a focal point of the groups of disaffected nobles, a matter which became a factor in the relationship between the old father Harald and his younger son. Adam of Bremen's account misses the point by attributing the conflict to a pagan reaction of those 'whom [Harald] had compelled against their will to embrace Christianity'.[19] The political charge and energy of a youthful son chafing against their father's survival upon the throne of a kingdom could easily lead to the attraction of a generation of disaffected nobles. In Denmark, as in Anglo-Saxon England, as in Francia, the nobility of a kingdom only supported a king as far as they wished; an alternative leader could split the factions. Thus, the glorious reign of King Harald Bluetooth ended in 987, with his death from wounds suffered in fighting his son.[20] The dramatic vein may have continued with the exile of Swein himself at the hands of a usurper.

In the tradition of ninth-century Viking raiding, Swein's first attacks on the English king may not have been undertaken with royal licence.[21] Swein may have been, in a traditional sense, a latter-day 'Viking' in the accepted meaning of the word, and as a possible exile, later recovering his patrimony of the kingdom of Denmark from the usurping King Eric of Sweden, Swein's own reputation and position was inextricably linked with the violent politics of Viking behaviour. In later years, even though Swein would be a legitimate Christian king

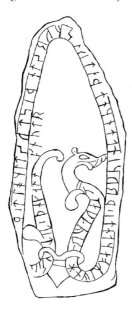

42. Runic inscriptions on a Swedish memorial stone at Yttergärde, in memory of a warrior who had received geld from three men: a certain Tostig, Thorkel, and Cnut. Such stones may show the manner in which Viking mercenaries were willing to fight for different leaders, as necessity and money dictated.

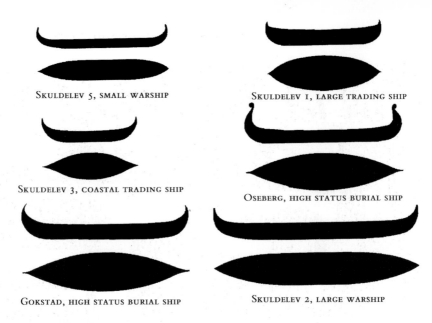

SKULDELEV 5, SMALL WARSHIP

SKULDELEV 1, LARGE TRADING SHIP

SKULDELEV 3, COASTAL TRADING SHIP

OSEBERG, HIGH STATUS BURIAL SHIP

GOKSTAD, HIGH STATUS BURIAL SHIP

SKULDELEV 2, LARGE WARSHIP

43. Comparative diagram of the hulls of Viking ships from the ninth century to the mid-eleventh century. Comparisons can be made between the 'classic' design of the Oseberg and Gokstad ships through to the Skuldelev ships found at Roskilde fjord in Denmark.

undertaking a royal enterprise in full-scale invasions with hundreds of ships upon England, these attacks may still have been fundamentally rooted in the mentalities of Swein as a sea-king in the waters of the North Sea, harnessing the violence of his followers to his own ends. We should also remember that Swein's wars were initially very much focused on the area of the North Sea; attacks on Norway and Saxony[22] were as important as upon England. There was a powerful and deadly combination at large: piratical tendencies and imperial ambitions with the means of royal power at Swein's disposal.

There were good reasons for Swein's ability to recruit Vikings to his cause. While we have seen the piracy of the Vikings around the British Isles coming into play during the 980s, the adventurers and traders of Eastern Europe, the Baltic Vikings who played such an important part in the economic beginnings of Russia, with long lines of river communication to Byzantium, may have been finding that supplies of silver were drying up in the East. The amounts of Arab silver in the form of dinars were severely decreasing by the end of the tenth century. If the easy pickings in trade and piracy that were to be had in the ninth and early tenth centuries were less widely available, as Peter Sawyer has suggested, then it is conceivable that these Vikings were willing to undertake service in the West.[23] A number of runestones in Sweden stand as memorials to Vikings who fought in English campaigns during the reign of Aethelred, showing that the acquisition of silver and fame was an important element of the motivation of the Vikings who fought against Aethelred's kingdom.

LONGSHIPS AND LONG SERPENTS: DEVELOPMENTS IN MARITIME TECHNOLOGY

While the political climate in Denmark and the rest of Scandinavia made it possible for a real Viking threat to re-emerge with attacks taking place as 'private enterprises', the technology that allowed efficient military operations had moved forward. Our picture of the ships of the Viking age is most often influenced by the likes of the 'classic' Norwegian ships discovered at Gokstad and Oseberg, in 1880 and 1904 respectively and, to a lesser extent, by the Danish ship from

44. A post-1066 depiction of the construction of ships from the Bayeux Tapestry. These shipwrights, depicted building the fleet of William the Conqueror, may follow either English or Norman models, depending upon the origins and experiences of the Tapestry designer. In either case, we may be able to see a reflection of the important traditions of Viking shipbuilding.

45. The reconstructed remains of the wreck known as Skuldelev 2, housed at Roskilde Ship Museum, Denmark. Although the wood from which this was built dates to c.1060, it is representative of the sort of longships used by the Viking forces in the invasions of England.

Ladby found in 1935. These vessels followed designs belonging to the ninth century – Oseberg was built in the early ninth century, Gokstad in the late ninth and Ladby in the early tenth century. These have contributed to the picture of the 'classic' design of Viking longship, with sixteen oarports on either side, well rounded proportions and, at least in the cases of the Gokstad and Ladby vessels, high freeboards. Images and reconstructions of these ships are still often used in illustrations of Vikings right up to the eleventh century, and the sleek lines of the Gokstad ship (immortalised by their appearance in the 1958 film *The Vikings*) have come to represent Western society's love-hate affair with Vikings and their activities.

However, although Scandinavian maritime technology was to remain influenced by a basic design principle over the course of half a millennium, the ninth-century vessels were by no means the zenith of this achievement (it has even been argued that the Norwegian vessels were only one branch of this development, suited to the fjords of the Westfold rather than representing Scandinavia as a whole[24]). Ship designs seem have evolved in two ways. The first was a product of the safer shipping lanes in tenth-century Scandinavia, probably due to the protection offered by powerful kings in Denmark and Norway;[25] this allowed specialist trading ships to be developed, such as those excavated at Hedeby in what is now northern Germany and Skuldelev in Denmark (see colour plates 13 and 14). The fat, squat *knarrs*, nearly as broad as they were long, may have seemed nothing like the threatening shape of the dragon ships of the ninth century, but they represent the development of Scandinavian economic power, and such ships may have played a part in keeping lines of communication open between Swein Forkbeard's Denmark and the large armies operating in Aethelred's England.

Although the wealth generated by the squat *knarr* was a product of – and helped to develop – the power of the Danish state, the tangible symbol of the state's military power was the appearance of more substantial longships. No longer crewed by some fifty men, the longships of the later tenth and eleventh centuries were closer to the *drekkar* (dragons) of later saga accounts of Viking warfare and, with up to thirty oarports per side, could carry closer to 100 men.[26] Yet, designed and built with the craftsman's eye to be long, sleek and flexible, they 'snaked' through the waves at speeds which could easily exceed trading craft.

Such ships were largely thought to have been the figments of saga writers' imaginations until the excavation of a group of deliberately-sunk wrecks from Roskilde fjord, Denmark, during the 1960s, found a vessel of some thirty metres in length. This was a ship so long that it was first interpreted as the wrecks of two smaller vessels.[27] Although Skuldelev 2, as it is generally known, can only be dendrochronologically dated to *c*.1060, and is therefore outside the period of this study, we can make a reasonable assumption of the use of such long vessels during the reign of Swein Forkbeard by the existence of a similar ship which can be dated to the later tenth century. This was excavated at Hedeby and had been used as a fire-ship in an assault on the town.[28] It had a freeboard that seems to have been far too low for the ship to have operated outside coastal waters; to have travelled across the North Sea to the British Isles in such a vessel would have been far too dangerous. Nonetheless, the Hedeby ship at least demonstrates the level of the technology of the late tenth century. Excavation in Denmark in 1997 near to the site of the Danish National Ship Museum has added a third long warship to the known group of examples; a vessel that, at thirty-six metres, was even longer than Skuldelev 2. The construction of 'Roskilde 6' is tentatively dated to *c*.1025 and, although reports are not complete, it may be entirely representative of the ships used in the attacks on England.[29]

Ultimately, the technology of the tenth century was more than capable of providing long, fast vessels and, as had happened in the ninth century, the Vikings were once again at the cutting edge of contemporary military technology. What is more, they were ready and willing to make use of it.

1. The city of Winchester, seen from St Giles' Hill, to the east of the city: the layout of the city has remained much the same as it was in the late Anglo-Saxon period. Although London was emerging as a centre of commerce and political power during Aethelred's reign, Winchester still continued to be an important regional centre of power, in terms of both the bishopric of Winchester and the West-Saxon royal family.

2. Corfe Castle, Dorset. It was at the 'Gap of Corfe' that King Edward 'the Martyr', half brother of Aethelred, was murdered in 978.

3. and 4. Ancient landscape: the remains of a trackway on what was probably the former estate of the *aethelings*, later held by King Aethelred's mother, at *Aethelingadene* (now Singleton, Sussex). The importance of the movement to and from summer pasture in creating the wealth of the English kingdom is reflected in such trackways upon the Sussex Downs.

5. and 6. The late Anglo-Saxon church of St Laurence at Bradford-upon-Avon, Wiltshire. This building is richly decorated with pilaster strips. It survives almost intact from its probable foundation in the early eleventh century, perhaps intended by the nuns of Shaftesbury Abbey as a chapel for the relics of St Edward 'the Martyr'.

7. The Old Minster and New Minster at Winchester (Hampshire), as they may have appeared in Aethelred's reign.
(Don Lavelle)

8. Detail of the carvings on the six-storey tower built by Aethelred for the New Minster in the 980s. The New Minster *Liber Vitae* describes the dedications of the different levels: the first level was dedicated to the Virgin Mary, the second to the Holy Trinity, the third to Holy Cross, the fourth to All Saints, the fifth to St Michael and the sixth dedicated to the four evangelists. (Don Lavelle)

ım tranum phanao mœtte þæthéſ tŏðr beánne tá

9. The King in judgement, from an eleventh-century *Old English Hexateuch*. Although dating from at least a decade after Aethelred's reign, the image is useful as a representation of one of the ideals of kingship; the Pharoah of Egypt is interpreted as an Anglo-Saxon king with his wise councillors. The Genesis account depicts Pharoah's decision to hang his baker and to free his cupbearer as an arbitrary one, whereas the Anglo-Saxon artist here depicts the use of counsel, a crucial element of kingship.

10. and 11. Views of the reconstructed ramparts of the later tenth-century Danish fortress at Fyrkat, near Hobro, Jutland. Although the geometrical fortresses may not have operated during the major invasions of England, they still show the intensity of the enterprise in the formation of the Danish state. The white posts are in place to mark out the shape of the excavated hall buildings.

12. The cutting edge of military technology in the second Viking Age: a reconstruction of a large Viking warship in the North Sea. Two examples of such ships have been found in Skuldelev fjord in Denmark and one at Hedeby in Jutland, now in Northern Germany. (Don Lavelle)

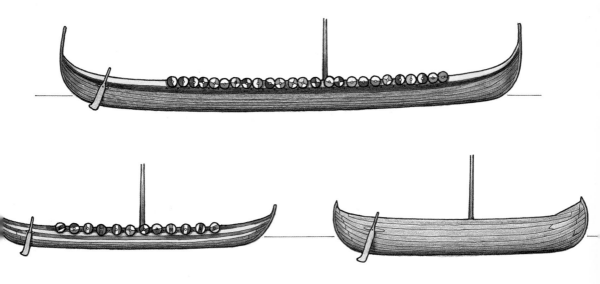

13. Three examples of eleventh-century Viking ship types: reconstructions of the hulls of the Skuldelev wrecks 2, 5, and 1 (large warship, small warship and large cargo ship). (Don Lavelle)

14. The eleventh-century Skuldelev trading ship, wreck 1, as it stands today in the Danish Viking ship museum at Roskilde.

15. Bird's eye view of the Battle of Maldon, 991. The Viking force has beached on Northey Island in the centre of the picture and a ship is just arriving up the estuary. The Anglo-Saxons have mustered by the causeway. The *burh* can be seen in the distance. (Don Lavelle)

16. The landscape of war: a conjectural reconstruction of the Maldon area in 991. The River Blackwater in Essex leads to the *burh* at Maldon.

17. Maldon today: the causeway leading to the English mainland from Northey Island, with a view of the town.
(Barbara Yorke)

18. Lydford, Devon: a steep ravine, incorporated into the defences of the *burh*. Lydford was attacked in 997 by a Viking force; the town probably survived the attack, whereas the Anglo-Saxon Chronicle records that the monastery at nearby Tavistock was burnt down.

19. The barrow of Scutchamer Knob, now in southern Oxfordshire, but formerly in Berkshire. In 1006, a Viking army used the territorial assembly point here to declare that the Anglo-Saxons would not (or could not?) meet them in battle.

Facing Page: 20. Reconstruction of the *burh* at South Cadbury as it was rebuilt during the reign of Aethelred.
(Don Lavelle)

21. The *burh* at South Cadbury (Somerset) as it stands today; the 'Arthurian' hillfort was refortified with stone walls and an impressive entrance way during Aethelred's reign.

22. The minster church at Deerhurst, Gloucestershire and its environs: it was near here, in 1016, that King Edmund and Cnut met to discuss peace terms, and divided the English kingdom between them.

5

ENGLISH AND VIKINGS AT WAR: THE BATTLE OF MALDON

Here stands a noble earl with his troop, who will defend this country,
Aethelred's realm, my lord's folk and land…

Thus some of the greatest lines of early English literature describe the defence of the English kingdom by the greatest noble of the kingdom, Byrhtnoth, Ealdorman of the East Saxons, in 991: the proud statements of defiance by the leader and his *hearthtroop*; the staunch defence made against sea-raiders; the cut and thrust of battle in the shield wall; the tragic death of Byrhtnoth and the ignominious rout of many of his men, apart from his closest companions who prefer to die in battle with their lord. Interpretations of Aethelred's reign so often stem from that year. The Battle of Maldon may even be seen as some great paradigm of Aethelred's reign – the glimmers of hope, the tragedies, the eventual and inevitable fall.

The poem known as *The Battle of Maldon* is one of the most argued-over texts in Old English; only the epic *Beowulf* elicits more critical debate. One argument has swung back and forth as to the degree to which it represented 'real' values in Anglo-Saxon society: would warriors really be willing to die in some blaze of glory after the death of their lord?[1] Another point of contention, which is of some significance here, is the question of the date of the poem: was it written shortly after the events it describes or a long time after, perhaps even at the end of Aethelred's reign or even in the years of Cnut's reign? Both ends of this spectrum have been variously suggested, as have a few dates in between.[2] It can, however, be accepted that some elements of the poem can be seen as a reasonable representation of the events, whereas others may not.[3] To use the poem uncritically as a historical source is to undermine the very nature of historical study, but the poem is just one of a number of texts which relate the events of 991 and the coincidence of the survival of a poem of some length on a subject which is independently supported by other sources is a matter that cannot be ignored.

THE VIKING CAMPAIGN IN EASTERN ENGLAND

It seems quite probable that the force which arrived in Folkestone in Kent in the summer of 991 was a substantial one. Although we cannot be sure whether it was led by the two major Vikings of their day, Swein Forkbeard of Denmark and Olaf Tryggvasson of Norway, as we have seen in the previous chapter there may have been a 'pan-Scandinavian' nature, with Viking adventurers organised through bonds of mutual purpose. The events of 991 were perpetrated by a force organised along similar lines to the pirates who had attacked the coasts of western Britain in the 980s. The difference was that of scale – it was of a size that must have been similar (especially in its impact) to that of the 'Great Army' of the ninth century. The Winchester ('A') manuscript of the Anglo-Saxon Chronicle, in one of its rare entries from Aethelred's reign, records both the size of the fleet – ninety-three ships – and the presence of Olaf Tryggvasson at Maldon. From this, we could at least assume Olaf's role as a leader in England in the summer of 991. However, there is some question as to whether the Winchester chronicler conflated his information from an account of events three years later, which involved Olaf and a similarly sized force, and it may also be remarked that the Maldon poem provides no corroborating evidence of Olaf's presence in 991.[4]

In seeing a possible Viking alliance between Olaf and Swein Forkbeard in 991 (or even a force led only by Swein), Niels Lund suggests that the northern German accounts of Swein's exile in the wilderness during the early 990s are pure fiction and therefore Swein was at Maldon in 991.[5] Although of course, as an exile, Swein may have been equally capable of recruiting Vikings to his command as he would have been able to as king, the presence of Swein seems commensurate with the recorded size of the force which arrived at Folkestone. This suggests that widespread ties of influence and mutual obligation from across Scandinavia had brought it together. In addition, there is a record of possible treachery – that a certain Aethelric of Bocking, in Essex, was planning to receive Swein Forkbeard 'when first he came there with a fleet'.[6] This legal record of the attempt by Aethelric's widow to exonerate her husband's name in the face of possible confiscation may simply have been a misinterpretation, deliberate or otherwise, of Aethelric's failure to appear with the army at Maldon or his retreat from the battlefield, rather than necessarily 'treachery' as such, but it does reflect the probability that Swein was active in Essex in 991 and, therefore, that his Vikings may have formed a substantial portion of the force at Maldon.

In the summer of 991, then, a large army had landed at Folkestone in Kent and, according to the Anglo-Saxon Chronicle, they 'harried outside', presumably implying that Folkestone itself was well defended. However, the Vikings' activity here may signal

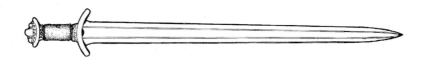

46. Reconstruction of a tenth-century sword, after a weapon recovered from the River Witham, Lincolnshire. (Don Lavelle)

a change in strategy: prior to 991, it was the places which were attacked, presumably for the wealth, which could be seized directly. By comparison, a large fleet of perhaps almost 100 ships, as the Winchester manuscript of the Chronicle records, could do much more than make a simple assault for booty (although the observations made some forty years ago by Peter Sawyer on the size of Viking fleets are still worth bearing in mind, as anyone counting a large fleet could have included smaller boats as well as the large warships[7]). Taking into account reservations regarding the possible conflation of annals discussed above, the Winchester chronicler's report of ninety-three 'ships' seems quite believable, especially if that figure then translates into a force of 2,000 or 3,000 rather than 5,000 or 6,000 men.

However, no matter what the precise statistics are, we should look beyond our modern obsession for reliable numbers; to the inhabitants of eastern England and to those in Winchester who understandably paid some attention the attacks, this was a large Viking army. It was able to sit firm, perhaps safe in the knowledge that it would be difficult for the English to bring to bear an opposing force of a similar size, and so ravaged the surrounding area. From Folkestone, the Vikings went next to Sandwich and then to Ipswich. Evidently, they were making a great nuisance of themselves, a strategy apparent at Maldon. The proclamation by the Viking messenger to Byrthnoth that 'it is better for you to buy this onslaught of spears with tributes than we should come to battle so bitterly' was no poetic hyperbole. The Vikings were prosecuting a campaign along eastern England to extract wealth through destabilising the region.

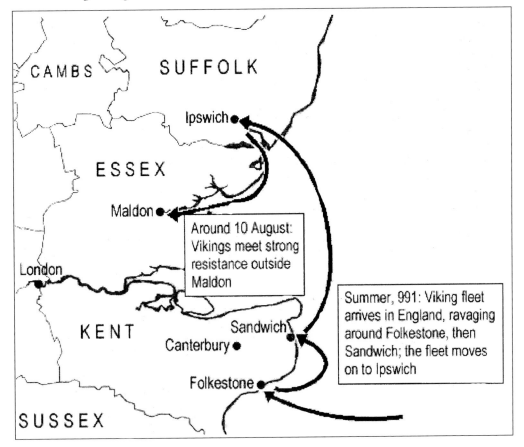

47. Viking activities in eastern England in 991.

BYRHTNOTH'S FINAL BATTLE

The Battle of Maldon was fought just outside the fortified *burh* of Maldon, which now forms part of the modern town. The Vikings had encamped on Northey Island on the estuary of the River Blackwater. Battle was presumably a part of their plans much less than the ravaging of the territory around the *burh*, but they were unable to do so without a fight. The defence employed by Byrhtnoth was the first case of strong resistance against such a large raiding army in England's 'Second Viking Age'. Byrhtnoth's strategy was to make a stand, and the poem's language is resonant with stubborn resistance. He ordered his men to send their horses to the rear and 'advance on foot'. The tactic used against the Vikings was to use a 'shieldwall', with warriors bringing their shields closely together in a stubborn defence against the enemy. The poem is often interpreted as showing that Anglo-Saxon warriors always fought on foot against their enemies, but the circumstances of the battle were such that it was preferable to stand firm, as horseback-mounted troops had the disadvantage of being able to run.[8] The poem emphasises this by depicting Byrhtnoth instructing his men – this was not last-minute training, but a pre-battle exhortation.

Byrhtnoth sent a few of his men to hold the causeway against the Vikings. Today, at low tide, the causeway is still the only means of access between Northey Island and the mainland. As it was a narrow crossing, the presence of a few strong, well-motivated men would have prevented the Vikings from crossing, or would have at least delayed them substantially (a similar situation to the lone warrior defending the crossing at Stamford Bridge in 1066). There were only a few hours between high tides while the causeway was accessible to the Vikings, so they were in a difficult situation.

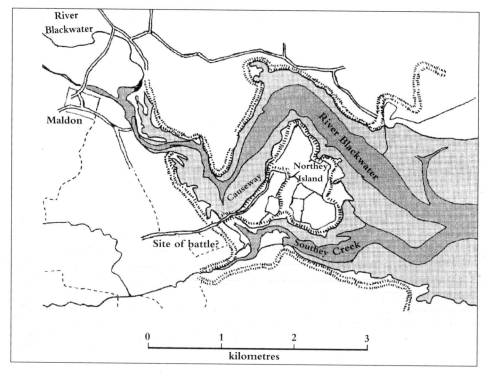

48. The Maldon area in 991: the River Blackwater leading to the *burh* at Maldon. The nearest island is Northey, site of the Viking camp, with its causeway across Southey Creek, known in the Maldon poem as the *Pant*.

49. The causeway at Maldon, seen from the mainland to Northey Island. The causeway can still only be crossed when the tide allows. Ealdorman Byrhtnoth's decision to allow the Viking force across was an action which was to have far-reaching results. (Barbara Yorke)

50. View of the Maldon causeway from Northey Island. (Barbara Yorke)

51. A depiction of an English rout, some seventy years after the defeat at Maldon. Like the Maldon poem, the Bayeux Tapestry is fragmented, and ends with the story incomplete.

However, if Byrhtnoth was to prevent the Vikings from reaching the mainland then he had only fulfilled half of his job. If the Viking force returned to their ships, then what was to stop them from embarking and landing to wreak havoc elsewhere within Ealdorman Byrthnoth's jurisdiction? Byrhtnoth has been criticised, most famously by J.R.R. Tolkien, for his *ofermod* in allowing the Vikings to come unhindered across the causeway: was this a man who whose pride in himself overtook his ability to fight the Vikings?[9] Such a judgement is one that comes from hindsight, knowing that the battle was to be a defeat for the English. As Eric John has observed, the English fully expected to be victorious when Byrhtnoth allowed the Vikings to cross onto the mainland.[10] There was no reason to expect otherwise; Byrhtnoth was the longest-serving English ealdorman, appointed in the early days of the reign of Aethelred's uncle, King Eadwig, and as we have seen in chapter 3, Viking raids during the 980s had been concentrated on the southern and western coasts of England, suggesting that Byrhtnoth's area of responsibility had been well protected. John even goes as far as to suggest that under Aethelred, Byrhtnoth had advanced to become the most powerful regional leader in the kingdom, mostly on the evidence of a Northumbrian hostage who is seen to fight for the ealdorman; this would then suggest that Byrhtnoth's authority stretched north of the River Humber, but an alternative interpretation is that whilst to us the word 'hostage' implies force and the threat of violence, this was not necessarily always the case in Anglo-Saxon England. The care of the children of the nobility between different groups of nobles fell under the authority of the king, who had the power to be given hostages as a matter of course, and to distribute the care and responsibility for them amongst his nobility. The fact that Aescferth, the Northumbrian hostage, is portrayed as shooting with a bow at the Viking enemy could indicate that his position was not one of enforced captivity and that the responsibility for his safety was taken seriously, as he is not among the warriors in the 'shieldwall' (see chapter 1). Though John's suggestions of Byrhtnoth's greatness should not be taken too far, his argument that Byrhtnoth was the kingdom's foremost military leader is a useful one, and shows how the regional delegation of defence was ostensibly a sensible policy. In contrast to the poem's depictions of defiant heroism, Byrhtnoth was not offering a *last* stand against the Vikings, as there was no precedent for this at the time.

But victory was not to be with the English. Following some initial successes after the Vikings crossed the causeway, the ealdorman died at the hands of a Viking who sought to have for himself the glory of killing such a great man, although naturally the poem has Byrhtnoth die only after killing his assailant. The English defence steadily collapsed, as morale plummeted with the death of the leader; men resolved to stay and fight, but more yet fled the field, including some who mistook a man riding Byrthnoth's horse away from the scene for Byrhtnoth himself. Although there are many reasons to dispute the validity of the poem as a historical source which can be taken wholesale as an accurate historical record, such ignominious flight can hardly be subject to glorification, and it is a testament to the utility of the poem to the historian that the individual retreats and routs are recorded by the Maldon poet along with those who conducted themselves bravely.

The poem is incomplete in its surviving form. Like that other famous record of an English defeat, the Bayeux Tapestry, the *Battle of Maldon* breaks off with the English routing. Another record of the battle, surviving independently from the poem in the form of Byrhtferth's *Life of St Oswald* and written only some ten years after the events of 991, refers to the deaths of so many Vikings in the battle that they did not have enough men to crew all their ships.[11] This may be simply a literary motif, as we see this years later in the Anglo-Saxon Chronicle's account of the Battle of Stamford Bridge.[12] However, it is possible that Byrhtnoth's force succeeded in disrupting the Vikings' campaign upon the mainland of eastern England, purely through the attrition of battle. A high price had been paid, and more was yet to be paid in silver and blood, but one of the great nobles of Aethelred's kingdom had made a stand for his lord.

6

RULING THE KINGDOM

Good reputations rarely befall those who live for a long time. Aethelred, as we are seeing, is just one such character. Had he died in the early years of the eleventh century, then we might well remember a king of some competence, whose only problem would have been a lack of an heir of a suitable age – perhaps making Aethelred a king with a reputation similar to that of Edmund or even Edgar. As the reality stands, the relatively successful years of the 990s slide into some historical obscurity beneath those events of the decades that followed. This is a pity, as it was around this period that Aethelred realised some of the major achievements of his reign. We may see the king emerging as a more mature ruler, who may have managed to limit the influence of many of the hereditary ealdormanries within the kingdom or, at least, as Simon Keynes has suggested, was introducing some effective new ealdormen.[1] Aethelred may have been beginning to develop realistic expectations of how he was to exert royal authority. In order to assess Aethelred's reign on its own terms, we need to understand the context of the running of the realm during these middle years of the reign.

PAYING THE DANEGELD

The events of the Battle of Maldon loomed large over the years that followed. Contrary to the words of the *Life of Oswald*, the Vikings may have been down, but they were not out. The Abingdon manuscript of the Anglo-Saxon Chronicle records that in 991, following the defeat at Maldon, money was to be paid as tribute (*gafol*) to the Danes because of 'the great terror which they wrought along the coast'. The use of the word 'terror' (*broga*) which was used here suggests the effectiveness of the Viking policies: presumably they were wreaking damage but the psychological fear which the Vikings brought to the coastal regions may have also contributed to the English decision to make peace.

This was the first payment of what has become known as the 'Danegeld', which, for those raised on a diet of British imperialism, was a word synonymous with surrendering to blackmail or (that very dirty word of the 1930s and '40s) appeasement. This interpretation stems, at least in part, from Rudyard Kipling's famous poem, The Dane-Geld (980–1016), written for a schoolbook on British history: 'For the end of that game is oppression and

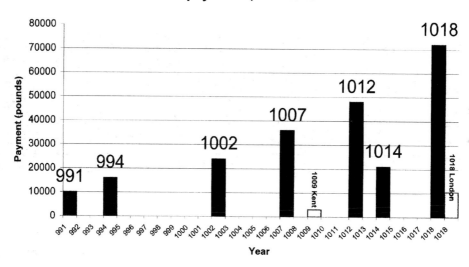

Geld payments, 991-1018

52. Payments of the 'tribute' as recorded by the Anglo-Saxon Chronicle during the years from 991 and 1018. Although the exact figures and the nature of the payments (or taxes) are still debated, they still give a sense of the amount of money spent in the defence of the kingdom.

shame and the nation that plays it is lost'.[2] So is our view of Aethelred's peace-making policies affected by the administration of the British Empire in the early years of the twentieth century: a proud lion standing over its possessions as it tries to warn off the upstarts in the Great Game? Very probably. The historians' extrapolations that have emerged since the nineteenth century have raised many the hackle of a hot-blooded Englishman: £10,000 were paid in 991, £16,000 in 994, £24,000 in 1002, £36,000 in 1006, £21,000 in 1014 and in 1018, £72,000. The payments may have been, as Pauline Stafford has suggested, more localised than the chronicler implies,[3] while in a more controversial series of papers, John Gillingham has argued that the chronicler was simply using a series of calculations to demonstrate the increases in payment.[4] However, whether or not these figures were the products of the imagination of an over-numerate monk, the implication that large sums of money were paid is a fair one: these were genuinely large sums of money, and the survival of charter records of nobles and churchmen selling parts of their estates in order to pay the taxes which they owed, adds to the picture of the massive sums.[5]

There remains a tangible reason for including the infamous 'Danegeld' in a chapter on the royal achievements of King Aethelred. An understanding of the context of the payment of this tribute is worthwhile here, as it allows us to have a more rounded portrait of the government of Aethelred. There are two factors which should be considered. The first is the reinterpretation of the making of peace between Aethelred and the Viking armies, which are better viewed as a making of an agreement between two parties under mutual contracts. Niels Lund has suggested that the peace treaty known as *II Aethelred* is very much

53. A range of some designs of coins of the reign of Aethelred II, showing systematic periodic re-mint-ing of silver bullion under the auspices of the Old English State. From left to right: 'First Small Cross' penny, 'First Hand' penny (*c*.979–85), 'Second Hand' penny (*c*.985–91), 'Crux' penny (*c*.991–97), 'Long Cross' penny (*c*.997–1003), 'Helmet' penny (*c*.1003–9), 'Last Small Cross' penny (*c*.1009–16).

along these lines; less a peace treaty then, than a contract of temporary employment, ensuring that a group of mercenaries would provide effective and trustworthy service for the English king. In this respect, they were not so much a bribe to go away than the payment of money to fight against other Vikings.[6]

For the second factor, we must leap ahead a few decades to the payment of tribute recorded in the Anglo-Saxon Chronicle for 1018. If, by then, Aethelred had been dead for a good two years and a Danish king, Cnut, was on the throne, why should he have been paying this money to himself if he controlled the purse strings, anyway? As other historians have noted, he was surely not threatening to ravage his own kingdom after these years of conquest. For the next few decades, well into the years of Norman rule, this money was extracted from the kingdom,[7] and it is these nation-wide taxations that show us less the fact that these were bribes paid to Vikings to go away, but that they more often were paid to fight other Vikings.

This interpretation becomes a more realistic one when we realise that what have become known to us as this amorphous group known as 'the Vikings' had little sense of overall group identity until after the 'Viking Age' had ended. As we have seen in the introductory chapter, the English were an integral part of the North Sea world which the Scandinavians inhabited, and it was more than possible for one group of Vikings to fight for an English king against another group of Vikings, so long as the price was right. Aethelred knew this well, and was more than capable of playing one group of Vikings off against each other. The huge amounts of money are given a sense of drama by the Abingdon chronicler because they are referred to as payments of 'tribute', implying that the state was under some form of obligation to these pirates – which was clearly not the case.[8] The money payments are more likely to have been those raised across the kingdom in general taxation, some of which were paid directly to Scandinavian pirates who had earlier been attacking parts of the kingdom to go away (hence the chronicler's indignation at this!), to fight for the king, and some of which went towards what we might now call a 'war effort'. This was, after all, a similar strategy to that used by Alfred the Great in the previous century.[9]

The numbers of English coins which have been found in Scandinavia can hardly pass without comment, but it is interesting to note that many of these coins were found in hoards, suggesting that as their owners had seen it prudent to bury them – and, importantly, were evidently unable to return – indicating that these could have been as much a product of unrest in parts of Scandinavia as in England. In addition, English coins continued to make their way into Scandinavia through the reigns of Cnut and his sons, as we might expect, but their number seems to decline after some ten years of the reign of Edward the Confessor.[10] Should we therefore conclude that Viking raiders threatened the kingdom and extracted gelds until about 1051? This is unlikely, and it seems more probable that Edward was simply continuing the policy of his predecessors, just as Aethelred was following his father in employing foreign mercenaries in the service of the state.[11]

The apparently massive payments to Vikings during the reign of Aethelred have also helped to draw attention to another, crucial aspect of the king's rule. An extensive network of state machinery was in place to make sure that the late Anglo-Saxon state was able to produce and control a sufficient number of coins for the economy. It is only in recent decades that the many thousands of coins surviving from the reign of King Aethelred have been able to be studied with a degree of sophistication[12] and, from this, the sequence of issues of coins can be understood with some certainty. As Michael Dolley suggests, there is something inherently impressive in the manner in which coins could be recalled through local mints and new coins reissued from new, royally-licensed dies on a regular (probably six-yearly) basis.[13] As we have seen in chapter 2, this was an innovation introduced by Aethelred's father, King Edgar, but it is remarkable that the system was able to function effectively throughout and after the reign of Aethelred. The reasons behind this efficiency are not fully understood, but the diversity of a network of small regional mints throughout the kingdom may have prevented the system from breaking down. In any case, these sites were in defensible locations, and the state was well geared toward the maintenance of their defences. Numismatic evidence has shown that the system underwent changes throughout Aethelred's reign; at the beginning of the eleventh century, the mint at Wilton (Wiltshire) was moved to a more defensible site at the Iron Age hillfort of Old Sarum, now just outside Salisbury, while the mint at Ilchester (Somerset) was moved around 1009 to an impressively re-fortified hillfort at South Cadbury (see colour plate 20). The same can also be argued for the movement from the Chichester mint to the Iron Age hillfort of Cissbury, near Worthing in Sussex.[14] The degree of planning which evidently went into these so-called 'emergency burhs' may indicate not so much the desperation of the state as the control which was exerted over the issuing of money throughout King Aethelred's reign.

The degrees of success obtained by this policy were mixed, but despite the Abingdon chronicler's attempts to show this as a wholly ill-advised policy over the years of Aethelred's reign, we can follow the use of English money in the defence of the kingdom rather than uniquely as bribes for the Viking armies to depart for Scandinavia. The year 992, following the extraction of £10,000 of geld in 991, saw the gathering of 'all the ships [and their crews] that were any use' in London. In 994, Olaf Tryggvasson was baptised, with King Aethelred standing as his sponsor, at Andover in northern Hampshire. The money paid to Olaf was indirect participation on the part of Aethelred in the politics of southern Scandinavia, as Olaf was involved in the conquest of his own kingdom in Norway. Swein, his erstwhile ally, was out to stop him, and for the next decade Aethelred was affected little by activity on the part of these great Vikings, as most of the money went to exacerbate the enmity between Swein and Olaf and their followers, eventually culminating in the battle of the Svöld in 1000.[15] Divide and rule could be a successful game, and Aethelred knew well how to play it.

THE CHRISTIAN PEACEMAKER

A paper by Theodore Andersson, published in 1989, suggested that some very realistic ambitions manifested themselves through Aethelred's relationship with Olaf in 994.[16] In 994, after a series of attacks on the south coast, the peacemaking involved Olaf leaving his force encamped at Southampton, perhaps outside the city itself, while he was taken by Aethelred to Andover for his confirmation. The Christian ceremony along with the treaty known as *II Aethelred*, resulted in a 'mutually beneficial pact', meaning that through the royal power inherent in Aethelred's relationship with Olaf, this Norwegian pirate could return to Norway with the zeal of the convert as part of his bid for kingship. This, Andersson argued, subsequently released pressure on the English kingdom from pagan raiders.

In the same volume of essays, Peter Sawyer responded to Anderssen's paper with the suggestion that Christianity in Denmark seemed to have done little to pacify Danish attacks on the English kingdom, so why should it have made a difference in the case of Norway?[17] However, rather than presuming from this that Aethelred was simply a Christian peacemaker, naïve or otherwise, one might suggest that sponsorship stood for a more imperial message. By standing as Olaf's sponsor, Aethelred was recalling the role played by early Christian kings of Anglo-Saxon England, and standing as an overlord.[18] Although Sawyer rightly questioned how far this was a practical policy that would have been understood – and, more importantly, accepted – by Olaf and his men, we might also recognize the matter of self-perception for King Aethelred. Aethelred was evidently seeing himself in the role of peacemaker, as an English king with imperial ambitions. The reality may have been marred by the fact that large amounts of money were paid to the Vikings, but the delusion was that Olaf's conquest of southern Norway was undertaken as a virtual sub-king of Aethelred the Unready. This was a useful encroachment by proxy into the orbit of influence of an enemy power, which did achieve some success in playing off one Viking leader against another; in his own terms, therefore, Aethelred was pursuing an entirely sensible policy.

ROYAL JUSTICE? THE KING AND THE LAW

While we have seen the king as a member of his own family, ensuring the continuity of the West Saxon dynasty, we need to consider here the king's position in the state. Patrick Wormald has noted that the lawcodes penned by Archbishop Wulfstan, surviving from the later part of Aethelred's reign, contrast with those of the 980s and 990s; whereas the Wulfstan laws are very ecclesiastical in tone, concerned with the order of English Christian society, those of Aethelred's early reign seem very secular. The apocalyptic influences of the laws and sermons of Archbishop Wulfstan are discussed in chapters 8 and 10, but here we need to address the relationship between the king and his subjects in legal terms – was there anything special about Aethelred's position as the promulgator of God's law within the English kingdom?

The many royal charters which survive from King Aethelred's reign give some indication of the apparent 'unrest' with which the period is synonymous. Generations of undergraduate students of the period may be familiar with the succession of such charters presented by Dorothy Whitelock in *English Historical Documents*, which portray a picture of a landscape ravaged by private disputes in which the king has little influence, fearfully similar to the 'feudal anarchy' said to be raging across the English Channel.[19] At the crucial point at which law came into contact with the society in which it was designed to work, was there a connection between the king's ability to make law and the state's and communities' abilities to enforce it? By addressing the reign of Aethelred and the 990s – the period in which this 'anarchy' is traditionally thought to have emerged – this becomes a very pertinent question. As Keynes has shown, our interpretations of Aethelred's reign may be influenced by the evidence of charters, which during this period are very descriptive, recording the conditions of how certain lands were obtained.[20] Previous Anglo-Saxon kings, Keynes argued, may have been equally concerned with the enforcement of royal authority and may have had similar problems. The achievement of Edgar, by comparison, may only stand out in the tenth century as demonstrating the officiousness, even the oppression of royal reeves in fulfilling the king's will.[21]

Mary Richards has condemned the early laws of Aethelred's reign as 'relatively unexciting except for their depiction of the king's humiliation at the hands of the Vikings'.[22] However, if we look past the apparent 'humiliation' of the treaty known as *II Aethelred*, which, as we have seen above, in its own terms was an effective means of dealing with the Vikings, the lawcodes of the early part of Aethelred's reign represent an effective continuation of the legal policies of his predecessors. The issue of laws from early in Aethelred's reign and, importantly, the fact that a number of laws have survived, suggests that Aethelred's position as a royal lawmaker was taken seriously, and that Aethelred had a sense of national identity in his role as the promulgator of royal laws.

The legal use of the term 'England' (*Engla-lond*) suggests that Aethelred was very conscious of this sense of nascent Englishness. The term was hardly a new one. It had been used by Bede as early as the eighth century to denote the land of the Angles – the area occupied by the non-'British' tribes whom Bede believed had arrived in Britain from northern Germany in the late fifth century. However, here, King Aethelred was using it in a very specific sense to refer to a legally coherent political unit. Therefore, Aethelred was not simply referring to the 'English' (or *Angelcynne*), but was making definite reference to the land in which those people lived. As it is not a consistent term in the Aethelredian sources, this was not necessarily a uniform policy by the king, but nonetheless there is a tangible sense of the legal rights of the king over a kingdom called 'England', rather than over the kingdom of the 'English people'. This is a subtle but important distinction, reflecting the development of royal territorial rights which had taken place during the tenth century, and recognising that there was a 'State' over which the king ruled. Far from letting down the kingdom, if we place the *II Aethelred* peace treaty into its proper context Aethelred's first lawcodes appear to be a consolidation of the achievement of the ninth and tenth centuries. In terms of these first legal codes, while Edgar's economic achievement was to reform the coinage of the kingdom, thus making sure that the state was able to gain what benefits it could from periodic reminting (see chapter 2, above), Aethelred's legal priorities may have been to ensure that guidelines were established within which his father's framework could be fully implemented. Wormald noted an imperial, quasi-Carolingian statement of law made in the *IV Aethelred* code,[23] but Aethelred also ensured that the machinery of state ran as smoothly as possible. The penalty for the striking of false coin seems to have increased from the removal of the forger's hand to death.[24] Neither the increases in severity of punishment or the proclamations of royal peace in the lawcodes show the desperation of Aethelred's state as the king slid into ineffectual despair, as is too often supposed. Instead, these elements of Anglo-Saxon lawmaking show that the state ran efficiently and effectively, and by implementing his royal jurisdiction the king understood this well.

The tightly-controlled 'legalese' of the lawcode promulgated at Woodstock known as *I Aethelred* has been shown by Patrick Wormald to have been a law with every conceivable eventuality catered for; in its operations and the royal vision underlying the law, the Woodstock code was a law that 'commands respect' (see Appendix 4 for an interpretation of its operation).[25] Similarly, royal will was exercised in the Danelaw through other lawcodes, using the local customs.[26] No longer content to simply declare peace across the realm but perhaps recognising that there were limitations in using naked power to exercise royal authority, Aethelred implemented very practical legal means through which the order of the realm could be secured, therefore building upon the work of his predecessors.

It may even be asked, as is often necessary when confronting the issue of the survival of evidence, whether the high number of disputes recorded from the reign of King Aethelred are a product of the development of this legal system and not, as is traditionally thought, a symptom of its ineffectiveness. The legislation did not take place in a vacuum and there is an understanding of the necessity to provide a working written law. To take three of the most well-known and best-recorded examples from the twenty or so charters which Keynes has identified as demonstrating the forfeiture of land from criminals, we can see the operation of the law.[27] In the first, land in Oxfordshire granted by Aethelred to his wronged reeve, Aethelwig, was allowed to stand because King Aethelred was his sponsor, a requirement of the *I Aethelred* lawcode.[28] In the second case, the fulfilment of the will of Aethelric of Bocking was opposed by the accusation that the dead man had supported Swein Forkbeard (see chapter 5); the will stood because the successive Archbishops of Canterbury, Sigeric and Aelfric, were willing to uphold the reputation of Aethelric.[29] From this case, it may be thought that the king had been defeated in the process of law, but it should be noted that King Aethelred had not made the accusation against Aethelric of Bocking himself; rather, he had informed the archbishop of the accusations.

The final case is stated by Whitelock to give a picture 'of the weakness of Ethelred's regime';[30] the crimes of a certain Wulfbald are described in a charter granted to Queen Aelfthryth in 996, as after Wulfbald's theft of his stepmother's land, the king made four judgements against him, finally seizing his possessions at a national council, although he managed to hold on to these until his death. In addition, following Wulfbald's death, his widow and her child (the charter does not say whether the child was Wulfbald's) killed Eadmaer, the king's thegn, who happened to be Wulfbald's nephew ('the son of Wulfbald's father's brother', as the charter describes), along with fifteen companions. Does this imply the impotence of state power against outlaws? To an extent, yes. But, nonetheless, the number of judgements against Wulfbald also indicate royal determination against powerful nobles. Royal justice would get its man, dead or alive. The fact that the charter juxtaposes the placing of Wulfbald 'at the king's mercy, whether to live or die', alongside Wulfbald's untimely death may be a hint that the law reached its final sanction. There is another reason to believe this. As the death of the king's thegn, Eadmaer, follows the death of Wulfbald in the account and the matter that this was upon land at Brabourne in Kent which had previously been seized by Wulfbald, suggests that Wulfbald's widow and child took revenge for the due legal process that had been imposed upon their family.

In the light of royal authority and the intricate workings of the machinery of state, we might see better how the massive geld payments recorded in the Anglo-Saxon Chronicle could have caused a sense of indignation to contemporaries. These were massive taxations of the sort which previous kings had not been able to impose before and which in the king's remoteness from the provinces of the kingdom, must have caused some resentment amongst the nobility and provincial churches. The fact that some of this money went to employ Danish raiders in the service of the state presumably added to the misery for English commentators, but it was not its root cause. So we return once again to that bane of the medieval monarchy and a more traditional maker of reputations – high taxation and a king's willingness and ability to make use of it.[31] It is perhaps here that an interpretation of the mature King Aethelred must rest: not the sluggish incompetent, but the despotic monarch, able to extract every last drop of wealth from his subjects, with a full understanding of his God-given right to do so.

7
FAMILY DYNAMICS

Aethelred has been criticised by some generations of historians for pursuing peace where war could have been a more effective policy, and the 990s are often seen as the beginning of this unfortunate decline in the face of Viking aggression. Much of this criticism has been levelled at Aethelred's supposed inability to lead by example, at the front of his army, a point contrasted with the apparently glorious acts of Aethelred's ancestors, Alfred the Great, Edward the Elder, Athelstan and Edmund, all of whom led armies against their enemies. Why was there such a difference, then? Should we simply accept the traditional judgements of Aethelred's cowardice? Such criticisms stem from hindsight and from a failure to see the running of the kingdom in its own terms. Given the activities later in Aethelred's reign, the charge of cowardice does not appear to be a realistic one.

There are two possible reasons behind such policies, both of which stem from a sense of royal dignity. The first is that we may overestimate the threat of Viking attacks during the 980s and 990s; the defence of the kingdom was a responsibility for the ealdormen, not the king himself. The English state was (potentially, at least) a powerful, well-oiled machine, and the king had an increasing sense of his divine right to stand at the pinnacle of that state – why should he sully his hands by becoming involved in what could be perceived as actions against pirates? Later years would show the importance of the king's role in fighting Viking attacks in London, but the very presence of the king showed that these attacks in later years were a major threat, whereas, by contrast, it is possible that Viking activities during these middle years of Aethelred's rule were not so serious, despite the appearance of Viking raiders in what seemed like every major shire at some point – in any case, what could the king do, if these attacks in the late 990s were simply small-scale raids once more? It is important to recognise that Aethelred's martial abilities did manifest themselves when it was more suitable for a king to give battle – against the rebellious city of Rochester in 986, against the rebels in Lindsey (North Lincolnshire) in 1014, as well as acting against Britons in the north and north-west of the kingdom in 1000.

The other important matter is that, should Aethelred have died, there were no other possible successors to the throne.[1] The potential difficulties faced by the kingdom must be appreciated. As we have seen in chapter 2, the only possible adult claimant to the English Crown (at least the only one known of) was the Ealdorman of the south-west, Aethelweard, whose claim would have been through the brother of Alfred the Great. Presumably there were others with similar elongated claims to the throne, and these must have been known of and the implications understood in the royal household: Aethelred's death had the potential to herald a new era of internal unrest within the kingdom, a matter which must have been well remembered from the period following the death of Edgar, some two decades earlier. 987 had seen the death of the last of the Carolingian kings and the ending of what had appeared to be one of the most established dynasties in Europe – had this fact been known in England (and there is little reason to assume otherwise), the implications to be learnt from this must have been immense.

Aethelred's priority from at least the mid 980s was therefore to make sure that there was a suitable heir to the throne. In the shadow of the many Viking raids which clog up the annals of the Anglo-Saxon Chronicle, this is an aspect of Aethelred's reign which we all too often overlook, and which, when addressed, places the king on an equal footing with the reigns of other medieval rulers. The question of the succession to the kingdom which must have occupied the minds of contemporaries and the birth of some ten children in the space of little more than a dozen years may have been of no little concern for Aethelred's first wife, Aelfgifu, either. Such a large number of potential heirs, nuns and potential sons-in-law was not unprecedented in the West Saxon royal family, but it is nonetheless noteworthy, and shows where the royal concern lay during the years since Aethelred's adolescence, a concern which was to continue into the next century. There was also a sense of dynasty within the West Saxon royal family. While the name of Edward was to be a notable absence until his second marriage, the names of Aethelred's sons read like a regnal list: Athelstan, Ecgbert, Edmund, Eadred, Eadwig, Edgar are all names of West Saxon or English kings from the previous two centuries.[2] Two of the three royal daughters whose names we know are also named after West Saxon royal women: Edith, Aelfgifu and Wulfhild (the latter perhaps named after the saint whom Edgar wished to marry).

THE DEATH OF A QUEEN

Around the turn of the millennium, Aethelred's mother, Queen Aelfthryth, and his wife, Aelfgifu, died. The disappearance of Aethelred's wife from the court circle is less discernible. Aelfgifu never appeared in charters, being merely the king's wife and never the anointed queen. However, we can assume with reasonable certainty that in view of the high number of children born to the royal couple, she had lived up to the turn of the millennium. As with so many of the king's wives (especially first wives) in the Anglo-Saxon period, there is little record of her presence. While we do not know how she died, considering the labour that she endured, it could be assumed that her death was in, or hastened by childbirth,[3] although it should be acknowledged that she may have been repudiated by Aethelred as his wife in favour of a new relationship; as Pauline Stafford has noted, by about 1000–2, the circumstances were favourable for Aethelred to take a new wife.[4] However, had Aethelred separated from Aelfgifu, then we would surely have heard of it from some disapproving account, especially in view of the treatment given to the subject with regard to Aethelred's father Edgar and, later, Cnut's bigamous second marriage.

However, we need not consider that it was only the loss of Aethelred's first wife which had such an impact upon the king's life – such notions of grieving at the loss of a spouse may be distinctly anachronistic for an era of political marriages. What may be more significant is the death of Aethelred's mother around the beginning of the second millennium, and, as we have seen from the events at the beginning of Aethelred's reign, she had been a powerful influence. Her absence from political society was to prove a key factor.

We can only speculate on the psychological influences which Aelfthryth wielded over Aethelred as he grew up. The story in the late eleventh-century *Passio Sancti Edwardi* regarding Aethelred's fear of candlesticks after he was beaten with one by his mother as a child in order to stop his mourning for his dead half-brother is a fiction which gives further substance to the picture of an incompetent king.[5] In such an imagined picture, it then takes only a short step from the fear of candles to the fearful King Aethelred skulking in darkened rooms, a self-imposed exile from the brightness of society, and even also provides a direct contrast with the innovative King Alfred, who, according to Asser, invented a device to prevent his candle from guttering in the wind while studying late at night.[6]

Aelfthryth, however, was a woman with a political will of her own. Powerful women in political society are a longstanding motif of medieval texts, although in such texts, female power is rarely accompanied by virtue. Therefore, by the late eleventh century, with the appearance of the text of the *Passio Sancti Edwardi*, Aelfthryth was seen as utterly culpable in the death of the innocent King Edward the Martyr,[7] and by the twelfth century, she was also held responsible for the death of her luckless first husband, Aethelwold, Ealdorman of East Anglia, who, according to William of Malmesbury's reportage, was killed by a lustful King Edgar, seduced by Aelfthryth's beauty.[8] The death of the ealdorman while hunting in the forest of Wherwell bears a little too much resemblance to the death of King Edward for comfort, and Aelfthryth's pious reasons for the foundation of Wherwell as penance for this are overly dramatic; we should dismiss it (William himself admits to simply relating what 'some people' say) as a rather salutary misogynistic tale.[9]

The power of such a political woman as Aelfthryth did not stem from her apparent beauty and the lust that this inspired, though. Her rivalry with Archbishop Dunstan had been based not upon the apparent conflict between vice and virtue, but upon different spheres of political influence.[10] It is perhaps instructing that while St Aethelwold could be praised as an agent of ecclesiastical reform, even in the most salacious of later medieval texts there had never been a hint of scandal emanating from his close personal relationship with Aelfthryth.[11] The relationship was important, and the image of a crowned queen was promoted by Bishop Aethelwold.[12] Queen Aelfthryth may be seen as a genuinely powerful figure on the late tenth-century political scene.

However, as Pauline Stafford has so importantly indicated, personality was not the only factor in the conduct of affairs at court.[13] To attribute the power of women to strong personality alone would be to underestimate the structure of Anglo-Saxon political society. The presence of an ordained queen was an important factor in the family politics of early medieval England, signalling the institutional change from fraternal to filial (father-son) succession. A powerful woman could make use of this to her own ends and the crowning of a queen did not guarantee her political influence. Aelfthryth's appearance in the coronation of the royal family (see above, chapter 2) was only the first step in a key position. Aelfthryth's position as a close advisor of King Aethelred from 978 onwards presumably had a strong influence on the young king's life, suggested by her consistently high position within charter witness lists, and the titles which she was given. Aelfthryth also held a number of lands, including some which she had received in her own right rather than just from her son. Some of these she presumably also held as a result of the help which she had given to Bishop Aethelwold.

Although Aethelred had perceptibly 'rebelled' against the influence of his coterie of advisors around 983–4, moving towards the influence of a group of younger nobility (see chapter 2 above), the act of 'breaking free', by being a reaction, may itself have been an acknowledgement of Queen Aelfthryth's influence (that is if her absence was not the work of Archbishop Dunstan). The fact that Aethelred's wife was unable to be influential at court between 983 and 993 (or indeed afterwards – there is no indication of a wife on the charter witness lists of the late tenth

54. Land now at Singleton, in western Sussex, on the border with Hampshire: site of a fierce battle between the men of Hampshire and the Vikings in 1001. As *Aethelingadene* ('Valley of the Aethelings'), it was later granted to Wherwell Abbey by Aethelred, fulfilling the wishes of his dead mother, Aelfthryth. This was despite the fact that this was royal land which was not meant to be alienated, and was meant instead for the support of members of the royal family.

55. The lands of an important royal woman: the estates known to have been granted by or granted to Queen Aelfthryth during and immediately after her lifetime.

century) suggests that at the very least, Aelfthryth ensured that even if her absence may have been enforced, no-one could undermine her rightful position as queen. Although her reappearance in charter witness lists around 993 indicates that Aelfthryth was readmitted to the courtly circle of advisors, she was never to regain her important position, as she appeared somewhat lower down on charter witness lists than formerly. Nonetheless, Aelfthryth was the last of the 'old guard' who had advised the young king, which had included Bishop Aethelwold and Ealdorman Aelfhere. Aelfthryth was no longer with her own people but, even in the last years of the tenth century, she appears to have jealously guarded her own position. Although it may have been a usual queen-mother's role to look after the well-being of the eldest sons (Edgar had had a close relationship with his grandmother), Aelfthryth's influence was evident in the life of at least the *aetheling* Athelstan, who, when making his will in 1014, prayed for the soul of his grandmother 'who brought me up'.[14] Aelfthryth evidently had an important position in ensuring the continuity of the dynasty of Cerdic.

As King Aethelred was Aelfthryth's only surviving child (at least the only one whom we know of), her death can be seen as a tremendous force in Aethelred's life. More than the loss of his wife, this provided a massive shift and a perceptible gap. One of Aethelred's major donations in the period which followed the death of his mother was a grant of sixty hides of land at *Aethelingadene* (around Singleton, East and West Dean in Sussex), which she had held 'as long as she possessed a spark of life' (a telling turn of phrase), and had 'kept for her own proper use'.[15] Although this was land of the *aethelings*, Aelfthryth's holding of the land was presumably connected with her important position of looking after the king's sons. For land to have passed out of royal office into the hands of a church was significant indeed,[16] no less so than the fact that *Aethelingadene* had been the site of a battle in 1001, resulting from an attack by Vikings against an important royal estate.[17] Aethelred's donation may have been a hollow gesture, a donation of land with little value,[18] but, for the Vikings, the significance of making their target *Aethelingadene* may not have been lost. Viking attacks were not always simply crude attempts to gain wealth: an attack on Exeter in 1003, a place under the jurisdiction of Aethelred's new wife, was perhaps undertaken in a similar vein. To attack the important site at *Aethelingadene* which had been in the hands of Aethelred's mother was daring indeed as a political act which showed the understanding of events. By granting this land to the church, Aethelred was fulfilling his mother's wishes in an extraordinary year, and to grant such an important estate to a church flew somewhat in the face of strategic sense, as the land at Dean was an important area close to Chichester and the Roman road along the south coast to Southampton.[19] However, strategic considerations were not the only matters which concerned Aethelred, and to have granted this land to a church which was so close to his mother (soon to be thought of as her foundation) was presumably so much more important to him.[20]

SAINT-MAKING AND FAMILY POLITICS

While the death of Queen Aelfthryth presumably brought grief for the king, it also seems to have allowed him to openly acknowledge and promote the cult of his half-brother Edward at Shaftesbury. The cults of saints within early medieval society cannot be underestimated: saints were intercessors between God and Christian people, but the politics of the promotion of the cults of saints, including the collection of relics and the building of churches and monasteries in which to house the relics and worship the saints made them a keystone of the medieval economy.[21] Therefore, the significance of the elevation and promotion of the saintly members of the royal family (two of them in recent years – Edward, and Aethelred's half sister, Edith of Wilton) was everything: it was significant in terms of the integrity of a Christian

56. The River Avon at Bradford-on-Avon (Wiltshire): land here was granted to Shaftesbury Abbey by King Aethelred in 1001, possibly in order to provide a safe place for the relics of St Edward.

English society, economics, family, politics, military strategies, as well as the fundamentally spiritual beliefs in the intercession of saints with God.

While the promotion of Aethelred's half-sister, St Edith, at Wilton may have been controversial enough, as she was a possibly illegitimate daughter of King Edgar, her death was not so politically motivated as that of King Edward the Martyr. The development of her cult after her death in 984 seems to have been somewhat less stifled as the nunnery of Wilton took advantage of her veneration during the 990s. However, the development and promotion of the cult of St Edward is a matter which has generated debate amongst historians in recent years. While it was a couple of decades after the death of Aelfthryth that we see the *official* promotion of the cult of King Edward the Martyr, the initial translation of the body may have been part of or began as a popular cult in Wessex.[22] However, as far as we can see, apart from a late eleventh-century record of Archbishop Sigeric's attempt to persuade King Aethelred to found a monastery at Cholsey (Berkshire) in honour of the saintly king during the 990s,[23] the elevation of St Edward was not undertaken by the royal family until around 1001. In this year, King Aethelred granted land at Bradford-on-Avon in Wiltshire to the nuns of Shaftesbury Abbey, in order to provide a place of refuge for the saint's bones (and when, according to Goscelin, St Edward appeared to a monk in a dream in order to make known his wish to wander). This has been taken to mean that the royal promotion of the cult of St Edward, King and Martyr was part of Aethelred's attempts to boost his own kingship in the face of the increasing Viking onslaught – being associated with a royal saint was no bad thing (and it is noteworthy that the later accounts of Edward's murder make a good show of exonerating the younger Aethelred).[24] By contrast, David Rollason suggested that the cult of St Edward was promoted for political reasons by the enemies of King Aethelred,[25] while Catherine Cubitt has argued that Edward's was a cult whose roots lay purely in popular religious beliefs.[26] However, the coincidence of the royally sanctioned elevation of St Edward with the death of Queen Aelfthryth may also be significant. After all, she managed to make sure that there were no other powerful women at the court of King Aethelred while she was alive as queen-mother; why could she not have prevented Aethelred from promoting his half-brother, too?

The coincidence of naming Aethelred's first son of the new millennium after the king's saintly half-brother should not pass without comment. The *aetheling* Edward (later King Edward the Confessor) was born between 1003 and 1005, following Aethelred's marriage to his new wife, Emma.[27] Edward's biographer, Frank Barlow, as well as Peter Sawyer, have both suggested that the use of the name of Edward within the royal family may simply have been the result of working through the names of the royal house – Aethelred had used up all the names of tenth-century kings, so he was now working backwards.[28] Personal names were immensely significant in such early organised societies as that of late Anglo-Saxon England. Without family surnames, the personal name identified the person themselves *and* their position within their family[29] – hence the importance of the title *Aethel* (noble) within the West Saxon royal family. The choice of name *Ead-weard* (wealthy guardian) had a familial and dynastic significance that brought the generations of the family together: *both* Edward the Elder (899–924) and Edward the Martyr (975–8), but it was the absence of the influence of Queen Aelfthryth from the royal court that allowed King Aethelred to so name his son, thus presumably invoking a lasting memorial to his murdered kinsman that ran parallel to his promotion of the royal saint.

Of course, such interpretations may appear as if they stem from an underlying mistrust of the historical portrait of Queen Aelfthryth – the wicked step-mother of traditional historical writing may have been replaced by the brooding figure of the elderly mother exerting influence upon her adult son, even if it is perhaps an image more suited to a Manhattan-based comedy film of the late twentieth century than the West Saxon-based royal court of the late tenth. However, such uncertainties in interpretation should not be allowed to undermine the issue of Aelfthryth's abilities to mix political interests with familial interests. This had happened during the rest of the tenth century (most notably in Aelfthryth's standing against the promotion of Edward for the throne), so it is only logical to presume that this also had happened in the last two decades of the tenth century – the only difference being that, after 978, King Edward the Martyr's interests had become posthumous interests.

At the beginning of the new millennium, Aethelred was in the difficult position of on the one hand remaining faithful to his mother's memory, while on the other having to be loyal to the memory of his brother, an individual who, in both life and death, had embodied many of the political problems that had faced Queen Aelfthryth. As far as we can see, there is little reason to suspect that Aethelred had been anything but genuinely upset about the death of his half-brother, as the situation of the time – including the presence of his mother, who had ultimately promoted him to the throne – is likely to have prevented anything approximating a real grieving process (the body of Edward lay hidden for the best part of a year). The death of Aelfthryth could therefore have released a mixture of emotions for the king: her absence meant that he could now grieve for the death of his brother. The political value of invoking a powerful royal saint in the defence of the realm against the Vikings was only one strand in a complex web of issues that formed the politics of saint-making; for King Aethelred at the beginning of a new millennium, the memory and sainthood of his dead brother was one means of dealing with the familial issues that faced him and ensuring the continuity of the dynasty of the house of Cerdic.

57. Line drawings of Queen Emma, after her appearences on eleventh-century manuscripts: to the left, as a wife, as portrayed with her second husband, King Cnut, presenting a gold cross to the New Minster at Winchester. Both images are of an experienced political player in post-Aethelred England; the young woman who came to England from Normandy was rather less versed in English politics, but was still ambitious, as her employment of a 'French *ceorl*' at Exeter in 1003 indicates.

EMMA OF NORMANDY: A NEW QUEEN

By the turn of the second millennium, Aethelred was nearing his mid-thirties. This was a mid-life point in terms of a period in which the average life expectancy was low and after twenty-one years on the throne, Aethelred had already ruled for more years than many of his ancestors, including his father, and he was approaching the lengths of reign of the two longer-reigning monarchs of the dynasty – Alfred, who had ruled for almost twenty-nine years, and Edward the Elder, who ruled for twenty-five. In our own times, manifestations of the 'mid-life crisis' famously seem to come in the form of the purchasing of sports cars or a drastic change of career path, but for Aethelred the marriage to a new queen – Emma of Normandy – only a couple of years or less after the death of Aethelred's influential mother, is notable as a coincidence of major life experiences.

Of course, this is hardly to say that Aethelred's new marriage was simply the acquisition of a young trophy second wife as the result of a mid-life crisis. That would be to deny the political and dynastic importance of the contracting of a marriage; Aethelred's marriage with Emma represented the forging of relations with the duchy of Normandy, and there were very real and sensible reasons for this,[30] but the appearance of an anointed queen at Aethelred's side would have added to his sense of royal importance. It may also be signifi-cant that, despite the modern historical preference for referring to Aethelred's second wife as Emma, her name in Anglo-Saxon society was Aelfgifu, the same as that of her predecessor.[31] The renaming of a queen (though perhaps we should not assume that it was entirely involuntary on Emma's part) demonstrates a necessity for historical continuity on the part of the house of Wessex, although we should not rule out the possibility that this nomenclature was effectively a living memorial to Aethelred's dead first wife.

However, the renaming of Emma to suit a more politically expedient identity that made the sister of a Norman duke into an Anglo-Saxon noblewoman did not mean that she was without political acumen. Her actions in Aethelred's final years and in the years that followed the death of Aethelred showed that she knew how to further her own position in terms of the influence of her sons (see chapter 10 and epilogue, below). As we have seen, personal names were politically significant in a very different way to today, signifying part of a group identity, and there was no reason why Emma could not have been known by and, importantly, identified herself by more than one name.[32] Edward the Elder gave the name of Eadgifu to two of his daughters by different marriages, presumably because the first child who had been given that name was no longer alive. Emma's new Anglo-Saxon nomenclature may perhaps be seen in a similar milieu, suggesting a different perception of the individual within a familial context to what might be expected in modern Western society. That said, this in itself does not deny Emma a high degree of political importance in her own right.

From the very start, Emma became a significant figure at court. She appears high in the witness lists of charters from 1002 onwards, and in the same year she was in receipt of an important plot of land in the centre of the city of Winchester, at what is now known as Godbegot House. This was a landed immunity, and was the first recorded such immunity to be granted to a member of the royal house who was not a high-ranking member of the clergy, male or female.[33]

The shift from an old woman to a young woman as the prominent source of female power at court was a massive sea change in political terms, no less significant for Aethelred in that the one old advisor left from the pre-983 era had now died. At least partly through choice but also by the ravages of time, within a generation Aethelred had become surrounded by a new group of people. As has been noted in chapter 2, many Anglo-Saxon kings surrounded themselves with 'new men' from the moment they ascended the throne, whereas Aethelred had more difficulties in asserting this during the first few years of his reign.[34] Partly because Aethelred had been too young in 978, and partly because of the sheer inertia of a group of nobility who were already well entrenched by that time, a 'night of the long knives' had never been possible when he came to the throne. Aethelred's own political creatures had been installed over the years, a group under whom he had been influenced in 983 (see chapter 2). However, the culmination of the process of change was only around the year 1000, with the death of the last of the West Saxon old guard, and the appearance of a new agent of female political power at the court.

The daughter of a foreign duke represented a new move within the Anglo-Saxon political milieu, showing that Aethelred was no longer looking within the ranks of the Anglo-Saxon nobility for his political alliances, even though there were still plenty available (witness Cnut's marriage to Aelfgifu of Northampton); rather, Aethelred was moving onto an international stage. Aethelred and Emma's marriage was the first foreign marriage since that of Aethelwulf of Wessex to Judith, daughter of Charles the Bald, in the mid-ninth century (although most marriages before the tenth century had been to the daughters of other Anglo-Saxon kings, Mercian royal women being especially prominent[35]). The trend of tenth-century royal marriages had been with the daughters of the Anglo-Saxon nobility – not with the royal families of the Celtic kingdoms in Wales or Scotland, nor with Viking powers in northern England. Presumably, marital connections to polities more normally

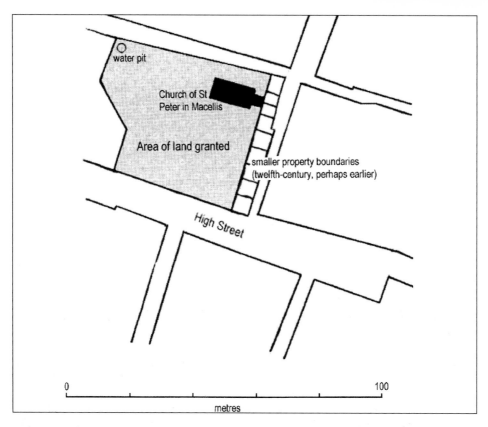

58. The house of Godbegot – 'well begotten' or 'good bargain' – the site of an area of land immune from taxation once held by Queen Emma in the city of Winchester. Here the Queen had a residence, with a small private chapel.

considered as subject to the English king had not been desirable, and up to the end of the tenth century, the Anglo-Saxon kings' interests may have been better served by consolidating relations with the nearer nobility.

When seen alongside the intervention of the Pope in relations between the two Channel powers in 991, as well as the probable English attack on Normandy around 1000, the marriage of Emma to Aethelred represents a serious attempt to ensure that the English kingdom consolidated its international relations. It was not a short term tactic, although it did have its benefits in shoring up relations between the English state and the French duchy, which had been rocked during the course of the tenth century by Viking raids launched from Normandy.[36] Amongst so many other things, Aethelred has received some blame for the loss of Anglo-Saxon independence through sowing the seeds of discontent by his marriage to an outside line, thus allowing a claim to be made by the Normans in 1066.[37] To be fair to his critics, prior to the question of who was to succeed Aethelred's son (some six decades after 1002), succession disputes had at least been kept amongst the English. However, such historical blame as this is wildly anachronistic, dependent upon Norman propaganda of the later eleventh century. If an idea of a pervasive 'French' threat could have existed in the eleventh century, it was more amongst the occasional criticism of Edward the Confessor's clique of friends and allies some four or five decades later. It did not lie with the pitiful mention of the fact that Emma's reeve in Exeter happened to be 'French'. In any case, as Stafford has remarked, the theme of Emma's 'foreign-ness' stems from the perspective of the last three years of Aethelred's reign which the Abingdon chronicler imposes upon the narrative that we read.[38]

8

MILLENNIUM AND APOCALYPSE:
THE POLITICS OF FEAR AND AGGRESSION

While in recent years European reactions to the advent and passing of the year 1000 have played a major part in shaping our interpretations of the Middle Ages as ultimately 'different' and 'superstitious' in comparison to our own scientific age, it should be observed from the outset that the concept of millenarianism was entirely 'rational' within the worldview of the inhabitants of early medieval Europe. Aethelred was, of course, the king of the millennium in an island on which the system of *Ab Incarnatione* dating became standard after Bede used the A.D. system in his *Ecclesiastical History of the English People*. In a theoretical sense, the millennium of Christ's incarnation and the English people were therefore very much intertwined.

In our own times, we have seen a high degree of interest in what the millennium actually *meant* to the people who experienced the first passing of 1,000 years since the, then, accepted year of the birth of Christ. Prior to the advent of 'millennium fever' in the late twentieth century, it seems to have been assumed that the English awaited the second coming of the Lord with a sense of stoic resignation. French historiography, by comparison, had a more established tradition of addressing popular conceptions of millenarianism, at least since Georges Duby's publication of his *L'An Mil* in 1967.[1] In medieval France, the popular millenarian movements proclaimed peace and involved the gathering of large crowds in fields who had consumed mind-altering chemicals. Similarity to the manner in which many have passed the last few years from 1999 to 2000 may be remarked upon, excepting the fact that, in the year 1000, the consumption of mind-altering chemicals with effects similar to LSD was unintentional but was the result of eating bread which had been made from a spoiled crop of rye, infected with ergot.[2] The experience of 'St Antony's fire' was less by the choice of the peasantry than by the necessity of avoiding starvation. In the English countryside, not least because less rye was grown than wheat,[3] there do not appear to be recorded cases of ergotism around this time, but millennial angst was more than a product of chemically induced hallucination. Such a climate was still present in Anglo-Saxon England just as it was in France.

The modern concept of the millennium stems from the idea of a precise period of 1,000 years having passed. However, in an early medieval worldview, this was to do not so much

59. An Anglo-Saxon view of the end of the world: the Last Judgement, redrawn after a mid-eleventh century Anglo-Saxon manuscript.

60. The Cerne Valley, Dorset: writing within view of the famous Cerne Abbas Giant, Abbot Aelfric of Cerne was the author of some of the most well-known apocalyptic literature of the millennium.

with reaching the year 1000, as what happened after it. The Apocalypse meant the arrival of the Anti-Christ, followed by the second coming of Christ, and whether that happened on the first day of the year 1000 (whatever day that might be), the first day of the year 1001 or some years later, what mattered more was that it was imminent.[4] Until quite recently millenarian ideas were generally believed to have been absent in Anglo-Saxon England, but the homiletic writings of Archbishop Wulfstan and Abbot Aelfric fit squarely into this context. Where the movements for the Peace of God in France were concerned with the fighting of the nobility, which affected helpless clergy and peasants alike, the sermons delivered by the leading English theologians of their day were designed as commentaries upon society itself.[5] The ravaging of the Northmen could be very real for their victims, but Viking activities had evolved since the heady days of the ninth century's series of hit-and-run raids.[6] Here it was not so much what the Vikings actually did but the climate of fear itself which they could engender. Although Eric John's suggestion that the Vikings and English were embroiled in a 300 years' war may be something of an exaggeration,[7] parts of Anglo-Saxon England had nonetheless felt the threat of Vikings for the best part of two centuries, so the Vikings were very much an ingrained part of the psyche of English society.[8] While the ninth-century activities of the Great Viking Army had led to the destruction of at least a few churches and monasteries in England and across Europe, Viking attacks of the 990s and immediately after 1000 were designed less to cause destruction than trouble, in order to extract wealth in the form of protection money. As many of the Vikings who attacked the English kingdom were now at least nominally Christian, targeting churches was probably unacceptable, whereas to attack the lands themselves, including the centres of manorial estates, was perfectly acceptable.

In the theological writings of the period, it was not so much the Vikings themselves that provided the fear as what they represented. For Aethelred's military leaders, the Vikings were forces against which local and national defences had to be organised. For his churchmen, the existence of Vikings meant the payment of a tax which was to last well into the reign of Edward the Confessor, but the destruction which they wreaked and, perhaps no less importantly, were capable of wreaking, fitted into a context which had been in existence for some two centuries: they represented the wrath of God. Never mind that many of the Vikings were Christian and their religion had been due in no small part to the activities of English churchmen in Scandinavia, the fear of Northmen was a very real and established one. This was the era of the promotion of St Edmund's gruesome martyrdom at the hands of Vikings in East Anglia from the previous century and, as Malcolm Godden has suggested, Apocalypse was deeply ingrained in the theology of writing at the time. While the accounts of Viking torture are now largely taken to have been exaggeration and are not acceptable as reliable history for the ninth century, the tenth-century interpretation of such history is somewhat more acceptable as representing a real fear and hatred of what these people from the fringes of the civilised world represented.[9]

It is perhaps revealing that the only recorded instance of the martyrdom of a churchman in the traditional manner of the pagan execution of a holy Christian is the death of the Archbishop of Canterbury, Aelfheah, close to the end of the reign of Aethelred. The Anglo-Saxon Chronicle records that in 1012 he was pelted with cattle bones by drunken Vikings and finished off with the back of an axe. Whether or not this happened as the Chronicle describes (it is generally accepted as such), the feeling which lay behind the portrayal of Vikings is real enough: beneath the veneer of civilisation, it took only a few barrels of southern wine to turn these northern men into their true barbarous selves (see chapter 10). However, if such an act can hardly be condoned (perhaps the Danish Earl Thorkell agreed, as he took service with Aethelred later in that year[10]), the truth beneath the layers of piety heaped upon Aelfheah between then and Canterbury's later promotion of a much more up to date saint in the form of Thomas Becket is difficult to bring out. The singular occurrence of a solitary travesty highlights the fact that for the most part, many of the Vikings respected churches and churchmen, and treated them in much the same manner as the castellans of southern Francia did. Thus the lands and people of churches became caught up in the vicissitudes of warfare as it raged across the English kingdom, but this was not deliberate targeting of the Christian churches, not even as sources of plunder, as the Vikings' ninth-century ancestors had done. What mattered here was the perception of a climate of fear. While the actual authority of King Aethelred was undiminished in the face of Viking attacks, the perceived authority at the turn of the millennium may have been in a less than perfect state.

In 989, Halley's Comet had appeared across Europe, an event which is largely ignored by English historians because of the absence of an annal for that year in the Anglo-Saxon Chronicle.[11] Unless we are to assume an unusually cloudy sky for a long period, it is likely that the comet was as visible over the skies of England in 989 as over the rest of Europe. Rodulfus Glaber's account of the comet's trajectory in the Western sky in France for three months from September is suitably dramatic, telling us that it 'lit up the greater part of the sky until it vanished at cock-crow'.[12] This was a natural phenomenon that must have had a tremendous impact. While sober views of the English mentalities prior to the first millennium largely prevailed prior to the 1990s, this may have been at least partly a result of the fact that no living generation of historians has been witness to the appearance of Halley's Comet, the most recent appearance of which in 1986 was somewhat unremarkable, witnessed only by the privileged few with high-powered telescopes. The prevailing sense of possible apocalyptic destruction through the appearance of rogue comets that has emerged in the recent years of the post-Cold War era (at least partly through the release of such films as *Armageddon* and *Deep Impact*) as well as, conversely, the communal excitement concerning the European solar eclipse of August 1999 bring us closer to the early medieval *mentalité* of awe and wonder than we might otherwise have been. Writing some years later of his witnessing of the lightened sky, Glaber admitted a sense of uncertainty: was this a new star 'sent by God', or was it an existing star that God made brighter? In either case, it was an omen.[13] For Glaber in France, the event portended was the destruction of the greatest church of the realm, Mont St Michel, by fire; in England, it was the death of the primate of all England, Archbishop Sigeric, even if the Abingdon chronicler had to shift the chronology somewhat in order to make these events coincide. One might suspect that the death of Sigeric's predecessor, Archbishop Dunstan, in 988 could have been a more spectacular bet and would only have entailed moving the comet's appearance back by one year in order to turn it into a premonition, but such a move would have been entirely inappropriate in terms of the succession of events. As it stands in the Abingdon manuscript of the Chronicle, the appearance of the comet followed by the death of the Archbishop, and subsequently the activities of Vikings in the south-west of England and Kent, in 997 and 999 respectively, seems somewhat more appropriate to a sense of apocalyptic angst.

IMPERIAL AGGRESSION

Although the Viking attacks continued in 997, 998 and 999, these may have been on a lower scale than those perpetrated in the first half of the 990s. For one matter, Niels Lund has noted that although many of the Vikings attacking the south-west of England in 997 may have been the same as those operating in the earlier years of the decade (and Simon Keynes has suggested that they had been those who had formerly kept the peace for the

61. Lydford, Devon – a sunken lane behind the remaining ramparts, which may have provided an artery of communication. The Viking attacks on Lydford in 997 revealed a strategy that saw the undermining of West Saxon power in an unstable region.

62. The *burh* at Lydford, Devon, on the furthest south-western frontiers of Wessex, controlling trade and the flow of silver from Cornwall across Dartmoor.

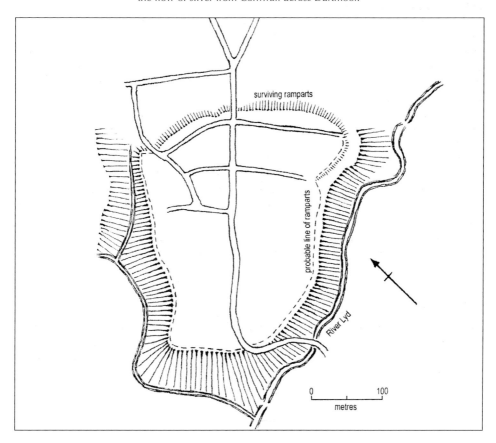

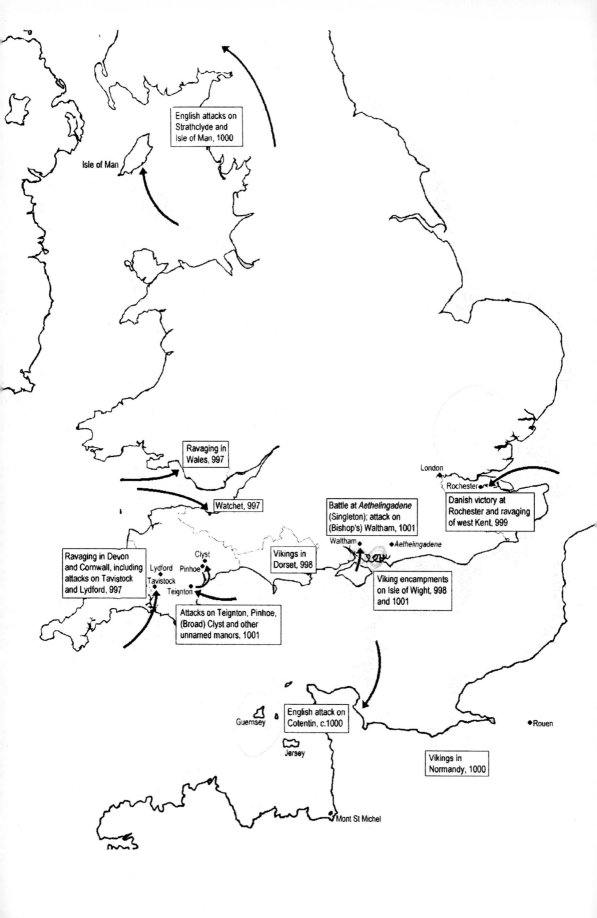

English attacks on Strathclyde and Isle of Man, 1000

Isle of Man

Ravaging in Wales, 997

Watchet, 997

London

Rochester

Danish victory at Rochester and ravaging of west Kent, 999

Battle at *Aethelingadene* (Singleton); attack on (Bishop's) Waltham, 1001

Waltham ◆*Aethelingadene*

Vikings in Dorset, 998

Viking encampments on Isle of Wight, 998 and 1001

Ravaging in Devon and Cornwall, including attacks on Tavistock and Lydford, 997

Clyst
Lydford Pinhoe
Tavistock
Teignton

Attacks on Teignton, Pinhoe, (Broad) Clyst and other unnamed manors, 1001

Guernsey

English attack on Cotentin, c.1000

◆Rouen

Jersey

Vikings in Normandy, 1000

Mont St Michel

English[14]), Swein Forkbeard was otherwise occupied with events in Scandinavia, only being able to put paid to his rival and erstwhile ally, Olaf Tryggvasson, around 1000.[15]

The return of the Vikings to bases in Normandy in 1000 may have given Aethelred an opportunity to take advantage of the new conditions, as the new millennium manifested itself in two ways: attacking both the north and the neighbours to the south. To the north, Aethelred is recorded by the Anglo-Saxon Chronicle as attacking 'Cumbria' (i.e. the kingdom of Strathclyde[16]) and the Isle of Man. This may have been merely an attempt to retrieve lost booty or exact retribution for the raids on the English kingdom, but there was also another side to the English offensives, which reflects upon Aethelred's perception of himself as a king. The Anglo-Saxon Chronicle makes it very clear that the king *himself* was leading the assaults: leading military actions was something which Aethelred was not recorded as doing before 1000, and a king more popularly known for the payment of tribute to Vikings than leading armies against them has come in for criticism from generations of historians for this apparent inactivity.

While, as we have seen, one possible reason for this is the important role which Aethelred had in keeping his dynasty together – until 1000, English military actions were defensive in nature, the work of the ealdormen and local reeves, not the duties of a king (see chapter 7, above). By leading attacks on the kingdom of Strathclyde and probably also against the Isle of Man, Aethelred was invoking an important role in which the English king saw himself – as the 'King [and] Emperor of Britain' (*Rex Imperator Britanniae*). The kingdoms of Strathclyde and Man may well have been seen by the English king as potential subject kingdoms. Aethelred's actions as recorded in the Anglo-Saxon Chronicle for 1000 show that the Vikings were not the overriding concern for his kingdom. Even at this point, when Aethelred is more traditionally thought to have been entirely reactive to Viking initiatives in an unimaginative way, we can get a glimpse of the bigger picture in which the king saw himself. This was an English identity which manifested itself in conquering others, a king over other kings, and this was very much commensurate with the smooth running of government which appears to have continued through these years.[17] To take this suggestion yet further, the attack on the kingdom of Strathclyde was intended to rendezvous with a naval force which had sailed up the coast of western Britain, but it was unable to. Had he succeeded, would we have then seen a submission of the northern kings to Aethelred? John of Worcester adds in his recension of the Anglo-Saxon Chronicle that unfavourable winds were the reason for the naval force's inability to head north, a fact which may be an otherwise unknown record, were John simply adding his own explanation.[18] Whatever the reason for the naval force's inability to meet with Aethelred's land force, this was still an audacious attack by Aethelred and was worthy of the king's aspirations to being 'king of the whole island', as he portrayed himself in a charter of 1001.[19]

Aethelred's conduct around the beginning of the second millennium highlights a little-known incident in the Cotentin region of Normandy, recorded only in the *Deeds of the Norman Dukes* of William of Jumièges, which was effectively a 'Viking' raid in reverse. William records that King Aethelred sent a force of ships across the Channel to raid the Cotentin region: Aethelred's aim, according to the *Gesta's* somewhat excitable account, was no less than the capture of Duke Richard II and to bring him back in bonds to England.[20] This ambitious plan went awry at the hands of the Vicomte of the Cotentin, Nigel I, with a number of knights and levied peasants; the attacking force was reportedly wiped out, to return to England in disarray and shame. This is not least because amongst the Norman peasants were a number of women – thus impugning the masculinity of the English warriors. The exaggerated language for the events described and the fact that William of

Facing: 63. Map of Viking and English activities around the year 1000.

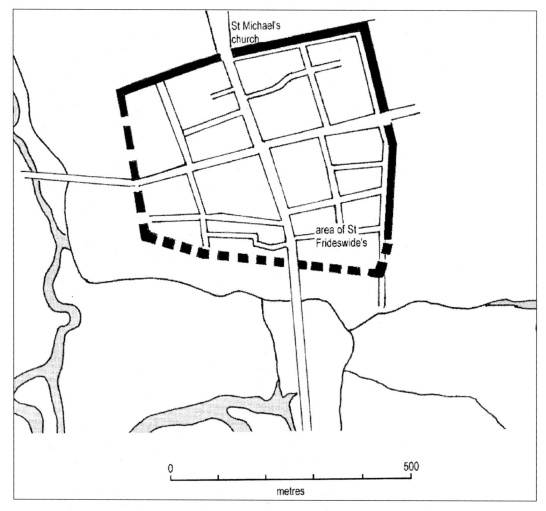

64. The *burh* of Oxford in the Anglo-Saxon period, with the church of St Frideswide, place of the only known massacre of Danes in November 1002, now the site of Christ Church cathedral. As Oxford was one of many regional trading centres across the south of England in the period, we might reasonably expect other communities of Scandanavian traders to have attacked or ejected on or around St Brice's Day, even if the efficiency of the attack was not necessarily as great as has been suggested.

Jumièges's account was written some seventy years after these events were purported to have happened has cast some doubt on the validity of the account: was William simply concocting the story in his head? How could Aethelred have had such relations with Normandy following a peace treaty in 991 and, in 1002, marry the Duke's sister as part of cementing these relations? Above all, why is such a failed attack not recorded in the Abingdon manuscript of the Anglo-Saxon Chronicle? The latter question cannot be answered, but while the marriage to Emma was part of the peace which needed to be made after this English attack upon Normandy,[21] it is possible that the Cotentin region was not fully under the control of the Duke of Normandy, who at that time had a much smaller regional base than he had in 1066; at the beginning of the eleventh century, the Norman Duke held only the territory around the Roman city of Rouen and the Frankish area of Neustria.[22] Writing in the 1070s, in a period of Norman confidence and expansion, one of the aims of the *Gesta* of William of Jumièges was to show a continuity of Norman identity across a consolidated duchy that had been in place ever since the treaty between the Viking leader Rollo and the Frankish ruler Charles the Simple in 911. It would not do William's portrayal of a strong Norman Duke much good if he was to show the factionalism within the Norman territory.

Eric John has commented on Aethelred's aims and success against the influence of the 'French Danelaw' in Normandy through the treaty with Duke Richard made in 991.[23] This suggestion might be advanced further by consideration of Aethelred's actions in the Cotentin around 1000. While the reported aim of the mission as the capture of Richard may have been the result of dramatic exaggeration, there is no valid reason to expect the account of William of Jumièges to have been anything other than correct. Therefore, what we see around the year 1000 is a king who was anything but inactive, pursuing policies which were aggressive, intended to recapture an initiative which Aethelred may have perceived as having been lost.

The St Brice's Day Massacre

In this year the king ordered slain all the Danish men who were in England; this was done on Brice's day; because the king was told that they would faithlessly take his life, and then all his councillors, and possess his kingdom afterwards.
Anglo-Saxon Chronicle (Abingdon MS) for 1002

The feast day of the fourth-century Gaulish bishop, Saint Brice, has entered English history with some infamy: this was either a day of bloody retribution or a massacre of the innocents, depending upon where one's sympathies lie. As historians have drawn attention to the question of the extent of the massacre, this has become no less controversial: was it simply a localised killing, none the less brutal for its scale but still limited, or the bloody manifestation of the efficient state across the shires of 'English' England? The thirteenth-century writer, John of Wallingford, took the story to an extreme in which the Danes, bathing on a Saturday, as was their habit, were taken by surprise; few survived to return to Denmark and inform King Swein that his peaceful subjects as well as his sister, then apparently at the English court, had been cruelly murdered by King Aethelred.[24]

Regarding the somewhat infamous detail of catching the Vikings on their 'bath day' (which was what was meant by the Scandinavian word for Saturday, *Laugar-dagr*[25]), John of Wallingford's story falls. St Brice's Day (13 November) was a Friday in 1002, not a Saturday.[26] John may have been more concerned with showing the Scandinavians' sinfulness in pride but, more fundamentally, we should be careful not to give too much credence to the later medieval sources' tendencies to overemphasise violence and kinly retribution; the idea that revenge was taken by Aethelred against the Danes in 1002 for the apparent duplicity of Pallig, who had been in service with Aethelred but deserted him in 1001, is tempting, but perhaps an oversimplification. Indeed, as with the great theme of so many sagas, the subsequent invasions by Swein were thus seen as an act of revenge and retribution for his sister (Pallig's wife) and they provide some justification for Swein and Cnut's encompassing of the English kingdom within the Danish empire.

Nonetheless, while later sources may have been bursting with exaggeration, another document, a charter from King Aethelred dated to two years later, is inadvertently equally dramatic. It details his order, as the Danes were 'sprouting like cockle amongst the wheat', a reference recalling the words of the Old English version of Matthew 13:24–30 which, Jonathan Wilcox has noted, has apocalyptic overtones.[27] Although the charter's purpose is to record the rebuilding of the church of St Frideswide's, Oxford, and the land granted by Aethelred for this purpose, it also provides some startling details of the sanctuary of a group of Danes in the centre of Oxford who took refuge from an angry mob by barricading the doors of St Frideswide's against them. The defence was presumably sturdy, for the mob was unable to drive the Danes out; instead, 'they set fire to the planks and burnt, as it seems, this church with its ornaments and books'.[28] The lack of remorse for these actions is remarkable and the account is obviously far more concerned with the destruction (and rebuilding) of the church than with the fates of the Danes inside, although we might guess that death awaited them. The Danes who took refuge in the church presumably did so because they were, if not Christians themselves, at least aware of Christianity. These unfortunate Danes in Oxford had not necessarily descended from families who had settled in England through from the ninth century, however. They may instead have been traders from Scandinavia.[29] Being close to the area where Danish law prevailed outside 'English' England meant that Oxford was effectively a frontier town, and archaeologists have noted the extent of possible Scandinavian settlement in the town,[30] although the fact that all the settlers could fit inside one church suggests that it was a relatively small and even elite group of people.

As a kingdom with undisputed material wealth, the extent to which trade took place between different ethnic groups is a feature of late Anglo-Saxon England. The so-called London lawcode, which dates from around this time, reveals a mixture of recorded national legislation and the declaration of local legislation, showing the interaction of people from across north-western Europe (see chapter 1). Danes, however, are absent from this, apart from a reference to the reeves of the 'Danes and the English' when in pursuit of false moneyers, which presumably refers to the reeves in the Danelaw area rather than anyone from Denmark. Their absence seems a surprising omission of what may have been the largest trading group in this period, and especially in view of the care taken to regulate trade between the English territory and the Danelaw in 994. Had there been an active exclusion of trade between the two groups of people, then we might expect this to have been stated in the London code. However, what the London code reflects is different groups of traders from polities and kingdoms with whom Aethelred was on good relations; to have acknowledged trade with the subjects of Swein Forkbeard would have been unlikely. Therefore, while the population of the Danelaw who took part in North-Sea trade had close relations with Scandinavia, in southern England, Scandinavian traders may have been more distinctive and presented a more obvious target; the people in the charter were not a random group of Viking raiders who had entered the town (Aethelred's charter does not even attempt to insinuate this), but they were unfortunate victims of ethnic hatred.

The question remains then as to the extent of the massacre – was this simply an isolated group of traders who were caught up in a localised atrocity at Oxford? John Blair has suggested that some of Cnut's actions in later years were specifically intended to visit revenge upon Oxford for the St Brice's Day Massacre,[31] which would imply that the action took place only in this frontier area between English and Danish law. On the other hand, James Campbell, a historian of the late Old English state, has remarked upon the deadly efficiency with which Aethelred's orders could have been carried out throughout the kingdom at the same time – this was the epitome of the Anglo-Saxon state of which Aethelred was in control.[32] However, the reality of the situation is likely to have been somewhere between the extreme interpretations. Some fifty years ago, Sir Frank Stenton concentrated on the question of how far English authority could have reached into the Danelaw region.[33] Although focused on the question of 'race' according to the ancestry of the inhabitants of such towns as Lincoln and York, Stenton's enquiry still raises valid issues in terms of how far north royal authority could reach. To have perpetrated atrocities against the Danish settlers far north into the area of the Danelaw would have been somewhat more difficult than in the heartland of West Saxon authority. Many of those first-generation settlers of the ninth century may have become essentially 'English' subjects and in the north it could have been impossible to distinguish between those of ninth-century Danish and Norwegian settler families and those who had merely adopted their customs (if, indeed, this is not a rather anachronistic preoccupation; see chapter 1). Therefore, we should look more specifically at what the 1002 Chronicle entry may have meant: atrocities are most likely to have taken place against ethnically-distinct first-generation Danish traders within the area of the east Midlands and southern Mercia, where what was an essentially Wessex-based royal authority encountered regional powerbases. Only one or two sporadic massacres could easily have uprooted small communities from other towns (perhaps, from their size and positions, we might expect the likes of Bristol, Gloucester and London) as news spread quickly across the kingdom. As we have seen in the Balkans in the later years of the twentieth century, the outright destruction of some communities in a few places could lead to fear within others, and the rapid departure of the persecuted minorities as ethnic hatred manifested itself in destruction and killing.

The Oxford charter's account of the massacre makes no mention of the day on which the massacre was to have taken place (although other charters from Aethelred's reign do not specify the days on which events recorded happened), while the Anglo-Saxon Chronicle's account of the order is just that – an account of Aethelred giving the order. Although there is some linguistic ambiguity in the Chronicle entry, it is feasible that not all the massacres took place on the one day of 13 November; instead have been only the *order* itself which was given on St Brice's Day, with the massacres following. Later accounts attribute the drama to just one day, as the Anglo-Saxon Chronicle itself also implies, because it is simply more dramatic. To have given the order to be carried out in secret on a pre-ordained day, as James Campbell suggests,[34] would have meant that it was to be initiated by the royal officials in each town. This is perhaps possible, although it may suggest an organisation more akin to that of Nazi Germany than a regionally divided kingdom. However, what may be significant in suggesting disorganisation in the perpetration of the massacre is the reference in the St Frideswide's charter to the people of the town *and* the suburbs (*urbanos suburbanosque*). While *suburbani* may have been country people here, the term seems far more likely to refer to the extra-mural dwellers who were not under the same level of privilege as those who lived inside the city walls. This could thus have represented a simple social tension between the privileged and under-privileged, the latter seeing the Danish traders reaping the benefits of the Viking campaigns and the massive taxes that resulted.[35]

The question of Danish Christianity is also worth raising here, as it may seem contrary to Biblical teaching to have murdered people who were most probably Christians. Although many Danes had converted to Christianity by the beginning of the second millennium,[36] these belief systems may not have been 'orthodox' in the manner of the reformed Christianity of late tenth-century and early eleventh-century England.[37] Therefore, while English churchmen could deal with Scandinavians as Christians and celebrate the conversion of the heathen in Scandinavia, at another level, it may also have been possible to interpret many of the first-generation Scandinavians in England as being closer to paganism than Christianity. Presumably this was because the long-lasting view of Viking terror stemmed from ninth-century theology. The depiction of cockle amongst the wheat in the St Frideswide's charter has an apocalyptic air of purification, which suggests that there was more than just ethnic hatred. The events on and around St Brice's Day, 1002, correspond with similar developments of persecution in other parts of Europe during the same period;[38] the millenarianism promoted by Archbishop Wulfstan and Abbot Aelfric may have been much more sophisticated than the brutality of the 1002 massacre, but the roots of fear were all too similar.[39]

Therefore, while Aethelred may well have given an order for the massacre of all Danes living in the kingdom, it could be interpreted as not so much a royally executed order but the exploitation of a level of ethnic hatred and popular millenarianism present within the kingdom, over a few days in early winter. A consistent theme of the historical reign of Aethelred is the portrait of a man fearful of those around him, including his councillors and those treacherous nobility. The skulking, fearful king is a dramatic image, and the idea that the king was afraid that he would be deprived of his (rightful) kingdom is entirely commensurate with this. However, the record in the Anglo-Saxon Chronicle's Abingdon manuscript is one which had been developed through hindsight, more suited to the Aethelred of his final years than the active king of the beginning of the second millennium. With the prominence of 'fifth columns' in the modern imagination, it may be easy to understand that there may have been a fear of treachery within, but November was an unsuitable time for a major offensive on the kingdom to begin.

The theme from 1002 is one that is consistent throughout history and it is sadly familiar. Here was a king who was able to hijack a popular mood against a distinct group of people and pin the blame of Viking raids upon them. It did not need the intricate network of the state's agents and agencies in order to carry out the massacre; the links of communication between towns may have been more than enough to inflame mob violence in a few places, and the *fear* of violence amongst Danish communities in other places. This was all too easy but, however reprehensible Aethelred's decisions may have been, St Brice's Day shows a confident, active ruler well aware of national mood, rather than a skulking, fearful king, terrified of treachery, as later historiography has portrayed him.

Overall, the picture which we can construct of Aethelred at the end of the first millennium and the beginning of the second is of a powerful man responding to the issues in the kingdom with a high degree of energy. In hindsight, of course, we may question the wisdom of the actions of the St Brice's Day massacre or the misguided attempts to impose English authority upon northern kingdoms. Given a modern obsession with Viking raids, we may tend to ask why this energy was not directed at providing a strong defence against the Vikings. However, it must be realised that this focus was not a priority in the employment of Anglo-Saxon royal authority. As was the case with so many other late Anglo-Saxon kings, King Aethelred can be seen as concerned with the assertion of the ideals of power, and in the light of the evidence which we have, this seems to have become especially conspicuous at the beginning of the second millennium.

9

DEFEATS, RESISTANCE... AND FAILURE?

The events of 1002 have altered the shape of the political situation in Anglo-Saxon England considerably. Since the cockle had apparently been removed from the wheat, in at least those parts of Anglo-Saxon England in which royal authority could be asserted, Viking activities were now explicitly associated with the presence of Scandinavians within the English kingdom. In some sense, it did not matter exactly how the events of 1002 had proceeded or even the precise number of people who had been killed: what mattered was the *perception* of those events and the growth of that perception.

Therefore William of Jumièges's *Deeds of the Norman Dukes* reflects the development of that myth over the course of two or three generations.[1] William does not pull his punches – women are portrayed as martyred by the attacks of fierce mastiffs upon their breasts and small children are crushed against door-posts. This was a graphic account which anticipates the sensationalism of later depictions of these events. There is little reason to doubt that atrocities could not have taken place against Danes in England, and that Aethelred may well have become associated with these events as they established themselves in the historical consciousness.

In retrospect, the events of 1002 could be seen as a turning point in the relationship between England and Scandinavia, as the Danes became defined not by their activities but by their apparent 'otherness'. However, responses in 1003 were still very much as they were before: the Viking activities in the English kingdom continued as before. The account of William of Jumièges, written some two or three generations later, was to make the politically motivated invasion of 1013 into the direct consequence of the St Brice's Day massacre. This does not necessarily mean that William of Jumièges unwittingly conflated the intervening ten years.[2] The fact that William appears to confuse 1013 with 1003 is often taken to be a reason for dismissing the historicity of his account of events in England, but to take such liberties with the chronology is perfectly appropriate; to William the net result of the events of 1002 was the invasion of England by Viking forces, the supposed ancestors of the inhabitants of Normandy; for one sin perpetrated by an English ruler, the judgement of God was perceived as forthcoming, just as the English people were later seen to be punished by the descendants of Vikings in 1066.

Nonetheless, the Norman explanation of the progress of English destiny between 1002 and 1066 places a rather determinist interpretation upon events in the year following the fateful November of 1002. The situation may have been difficult, even desperate, but in 1002 defeat was hardly inevitable. Attacks were renewed by Swein upon the kingdom of England in 1003. The Anglo-Saxon Chronicle blamed an attack on Exeter on Queen Emma's 'French' reeve, a certain Hugh, who had presumably been one of her party from Normandy. The language of blame and distrust of foreigners in the Chronicle belongs to the world of the last years of the reign of King Aethelred rather than to 1003, as Pauline Stafford suggests,[3] but the record of the destruction of the city is probably reliable.

The Anglo-Saxon Chronicle for 1003 also recorded the burning of the town at Wilton after Aelfric, the Ealdorman of eastern Wessex, failed to lead the *fyrd* of Wessex from Hampshire and Wiltshire against the Vikings. The two armies drew up and were close enough for each side to see each other, but Ealdorman Aelfric 'feigned himself ill and began to retch to vomit, and said that he was sick'. Therefore, the chronicler sensed betrayal once more, citing a now-forgotten proverb: 'When the leader breaks, then all the army will be greatly hindered'.

Wilton was the nunnery of Aethelred's half-sister, St Edith, a saint who was then undergoing an intense campaign of promotion (see chapter 7). As the site of a nunnery with close connections to the royal house of Wessex, the targeting of Wilton by the Vikings was probably a symbolic blow for King Aethelred, even if the attack may have been perpetrated against the lands and the estate centre rather than the church itself. However, comparisons between the military abilities of Ealdorman Aelfric and the doomed hero of Old English literature, Ealdorman Byrhtnoth, are perhaps inevitable. At Maldon in 991, Byrhtnoth held firm; Aelfric, by comparison, acts in a cowardly manner, running away and feigning sickness. As they followed the apparent treachery of the Danes in 1002 and, later, the blame of the French reeve at Exeter, Aelfric's actions, or rather a lack of them, are placed in a similar milieu, but there may be a more believable significance – the early medieval battlefield was a terrifying environment. The tension before a battle could have been unbearable,[4] and the Maldon poem goes only part way to relaying this; it was the leader's job to make sure that his men held firm, to inspire them with courage by his own example, and it is little wonder that real psychologically induced illness could be visited upon a leader who felt unsuitable for the task. This highlights a major weakness of a system which meant that ealdormen were in charge of local defence. While an advantage was that a response could be gathered relatively quickly from the leading men of the shire and decisions could be made on the spot, ealdormen were not necessarily generals. Over the tenth century, the sophistication of the English state had increased significantly,[5] and the ealdorman's place in this had also increased in importance. The ealdorman was expected to be many things: a tax collector and king's representative for justice; it was unfortunate for Aelfric that the king also expected him to be a war leader. As Nicholas Higham has suggested, the responsibilities of an probably ealdorman seemed very different amongst the mud and blood of a battlefield than they had when the ealdormanry was first offered in the warmth of the royal chamber.[6] This was a problem, as the decision to offer Aelfric an ealdormanry may well have been Aethelred's responsibility: he had been one of the first of Aethelred's 'new men'.

LOCAL RESISTANCE

In 1004, however, the strength of local defence was demonstrated in East Anglia by Ulfcetel (also known as Ulfkell Snilling). Simon Keynes has pointed out that Ulfcetel may not have been an ealdorman, as he appears in charter witness lists as *minister* – a 'servant', which is the usual title for a thegn – rather than as *dux*, 'leader', the usual Latin title for an ealdorman.[7] It had been in East Anglia, in the old area of the Viking Guthrum's

65. The city of Durham, a natural citadel of north-eastern England for centuries. Durham was relieved by Uhtred of Bamburgh, in 1006, whose victory against the Scots resulted in a display of the heads of the vanquished upon the city ramparts.

kingdom, that the ealdormanry of Aethelwine had proved troublesome for Aethelred's advisors,[8] and perhaps for this reason, when Ealdorman Aethelwine had died in 992, the ealdormanry of East Anglia was not granted out to a new man. Instead the area of responsibility under Leofsige of Essex had perhaps been extended. Ulfcetel's authority in East Anglia may have stemmed from his kinship to King Aethelred; if we can trust the *Jomsviking* saga, he was married to Wulfhild, one of Aethelred's daughters, although of course this may have taken place after 1004.[9] The marriage of royal daughters was nothing new, but the making of new men through marriage while denying them an official title was perhaps more innovative, as it may have been appropriate to Aethelred's moves to curb the excesses of power held by ealdormen.

The events of 1004 suggest that while Aethelred had made a good choice in Ulfcetel, the lack of any official title could have been a weakness for Ulfcetel's authority, resulting in an inability to lead an army at full strength.[10] The increasingly pessimistic Abingdon chronicler records a ray of hope for 1004. Ulfcetel seems to have stood between a Viking army and

105

66. Ravaging of the countryside, as depicted on the Bayeux Tapestry.

their ships, offering a staunch defence. The Chronicle records that 'many fell on both sides', although 'the flower of the East Anglian people was killed'. In the manner of the Maldon poem, this was a heroic defence of the east coast of the kingdom and, 'if their full strength had been there', it would have been a successful defence; such is the view of hindsight, at least. Tragedy is made all the greater if there is a small hope and it is extinguished. As the Danes said, according to the chronicler, 'they never met worse fighting in England than Ulfcetel dealt to them'. This was the stuff of sagas, and the sagas remembered Ulfcetel with some admiration.[11] *Had* Ulfcetel stopped the Vikings reaching their ships then at least this group of Vikings would never have returned. Such a possibility is naturally worth entertaining. If Ulfcetel did not hold the full authority of the ealdorman of East Anglia, then perhaps this was a reason why he was not able to command the full strength of the province, as the Chronicle suggests.

We may be struck by the irony of the possibility that England's great chance at successfully defending the kingdom against a Viking army could have succeeded had Aethelred only had the foresight to grant the office of ealdorman to Ulfcetel. However, we should see this in the context of the time, rather than judging Aethelred on the basis of the Abingdon chronicler's implicit criticism, whose opinion may have stemmed from an East Anglian perspective, in any case. To gather together a royal army took time, and time was rarely on the side of the English defenders. Ulfcetel's response was presumably so effective precisely because he was able to move quickly and get between the Vikings and their ships; it was just unfortunate that, as a result of this, his force was under strength.

The southern and eastern English perspective of many of the Anglo-Saxon sources also leads us to overlook the fact that the Vikings were not the only threat to Aethelred's kingdom. As we have seen from Aethelred's actions against Strathclyde and the Isle of Man in 1000, the northern frontiers were an important aspect of the integrity of the kingdom.

In this respect, Aethelred dealt with the same issues that faced his predecessors. A lesser-known northern tract, *De Obsessione Dunelmi* ('On the Siege of Durham'), recorded in the chronicle of Simeon of Durham, details a Scots attack on Durham in 1006 and its staunch defence by a hitherto unknown lieutenant of Aethelred, a certain Uhtred. After ravaging Northumbria, perfectly logical opportunism in view of the events taking place in the south of England, the Scots attacked the city of Durham, while Waltheof, Lord of Bamburgh, shut himself up in his fortress. In Waltheof's stead, his son, Uhtred, gathered a force from across Northumbria and managed to defeat the Scots attackers, and in victory he made sure that the local women washed the heads of the corpses before having them hoisted above the stakes of the city on the ends of poles – a mark, perhaps, of crimes against their overlord. Uhtred's reward from King Aethelred was succession to the earldom of Northumbria, an area of control which was larger than the original lordship of Bamburgh.[12]

The tract is useful for a number of reasons, not least because it is the most detailed description of a blood feud that survives from the Anglo-Saxon period; a feud which is described as continuing for most of the eleventh century and results in an inter-generational spiral of violence from the murder of Uhtred in 1016.[13] Understandably, the text dates from the later part of the eleventh century rather than the reign of Aethelred but can largely be trusted.[14] The granting of Uhtred's 'earldom' may simply be poetic licence, similar to the naming of Byrhtnoth as 'earl' in the Maldon poem, or may be the later eleventh-century conventions of title,[15] but the title also reflected the strength of Uhtred's loosely indepen-dent position, somewhat commensurate with his title in the Anglo-Saxon Chronicle (which again, may post-date the development of earldoms from ealdormanries). Was Uhtred made the Earl of Northumbria by Aethelred *after* the siege of 1006, as *De Obsessione* remarks, or was there a more fundamental reason for his success in defending Northumbria against the Scots? The difference may not have been so much that Aethelred conferred the earldom upon Uhtred, but rather that he recognised it.

Uhtred was not simply Aethelred's lieutenant but could be seen in his own right as a regional leader, holding a loosely affiliated English polity by whatever means he saw fit. Uhtred's name suggests that his family affiliations had been 'Scandinavian', but this hardly debarred him from the English court;[16] indeed, Uhtred was later to become Aethelred's son-in-law as he married the king's daughter.[17] Aethelred may have had no choice by the beginning of the eleventh century but to accept such regional independence as Uhtred exercised *de facto*, but in finding a local replacement for the less successful Mercian Aelfhelm as the royal agent in the area, the king's policy was being realistic and effective. This was a good political trade-off, by which Aethelred had ensured the defence of the kingdom for some years yet.

In 1005, the kingdom was offered respite from Viking ravaging, but this was on the basis of famine rather than successful military defence. The Chronicle records that there was a 'great famine throughout England', and as a result the Viking armies had to return to Scandinavia. It is possible that the Vikings had caused famine by their ravaging in 1004, so much that the next year's harvest was a poor one; however, this is unlikely, as the Viking presence during that year had only been in eastern England. Theologically speaking, famine was the same as Viking attacks: they were both vengeance of God, to be prayed for in the same manner.

It is important to recognise that the pressure on the peasantry of the kingdom must have been immense. The last major geld had been taken in 1002 (and whatever we say about the nature or the extent of the payments, they must have been comparatively enormous), but the transfer of people, goods and food to an increasingly militaristic economy was evidently taking its toll. Peasant survival was marginal at the best of times, so bad weather or a poor harvest could tip it over the edge. If there was little food in England, the Viking armies simply had no option but to go home. There must have been great difficulties in keeping an army supplied in the field, and Swein's army seems to have been large by the standards of the early eleventh century.[18] Living off the land, or somewhat less euphemistically, *ravaging*, was a means by which an army could be fed, but it was also unreliable. As John Gillingham has observed in his studies of eleventh and twelfth-century warfare, ravaging could leave an army open to attack. While men were scouring and burning villages, they could be spread out and otherwise occupied, therefore unable to defend themselves properly. Hitting the centres of royal estates was an effective strategy that could guarantee supplies, and seems to have been relied on in the ninth century. English defences of royal estates had improved by the reign of Aethelred.[19]

Therefore, the famine of 1005 can be seen as a dramatic illustration of the problems of ravaging the land for food: by the time of Aethelred's reign, much of the ravaging that took place had other, far more horribly efficient aims than that prosecuted by the Vikings of the ninth century. It was better to make a nuisance of oneself: to burn crops, houses, terrify the peasants, preferably in the lands of an important magnate who could petition the kings to pay tribute – cold, hard, reliable cash was important. With luck, as happened in 994, 998 and in 1006, the king might even feed the Vikings, too.[20]

However, the fact that the Vikings had to leave in 1005 shows the margins of survival in which they found themselves. This may not have been an army with strong lines of communication back to the homelands providing supplies on a constant basis.[21] A combination of ravaging and purchasing would have been needed to maintain a Viking army and their presence could have been a mixed blessing for a local economy. In the winter of 1004–5, we see that the scales became unbalanced.

1006: THE WORLD TURNED UPSIDE DOWN

In the following year, a force of Vikings returned to the English kingdom. The fact that their victorious year of 1006 coincided with various tumultuous events in the English kingdom shows that the Danish leaders were politically astute: the death of an archbishop, the confiscation of the lands of the English noble Wulfgeat, the murder of Ealdorman Aelfhelm of Northumbria and the blinding of his sons. These were events which Keynes has suggested amounted to a palace revolution, perhaps instigated by Eadric Streona, who ensured that many of his brothers were also elevated to the royal court.[22] Again, the order of the English state had shifted. There were probable benefits through such a shift in the officers of state, as we have seen with the abilities of Uhtred of Northumbria, but there were also mixed blessings. News probably travelled quickly between England and Scandinavia.

In 1006, the Vikings ventured far inland. The Anglo-Saxon Chronicle records their appearance at Scutchamer Knob, a barrow in the south of East Hendred parish, Berkshire (now in Oxfordshire), of which 'it was said' that if an invading army came so far, they would never get back to their ships. Regarding this, Guy Halsall has suggested that the making of war could be a 'ritual' process, and gathering at well-known ancient monuments in the landscape such as barrows may have been part of this process, which had been in existence and implicitly understood throughout the Anglo-Saxon period.[23] The 'ritual' elements of war may be overstated here, as this may not have been intended as a battle: rather, the gatherings of Vikings used the pre-battle rituals to make a bold statement of intent with political repercussions for the kingdom.[24] *Cwichelms hlaew* (Cuckhamsley barrow – also known now as Scutchamer Knob) was a meeting point for the shire of Berkshire;[25] its Old English name

67. Scutchamer Knob, also known as Cuckhamsley Barrow, originally in Berkshire but now in southern Oxfordshire. In the Anglo-Saxon period and later, this was the meeting place for the whole of Berkshire. An attacking Viking force reached this site in 1006 and waited for an English force to challenge them.

68. The events of 1006.

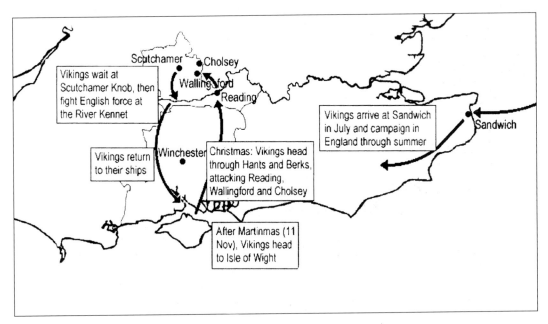

Scutchamer · Cholsey

Vikings wait at Scutchamer Knob, then fight English force at the River Kennet

Wallingford
Reading

Vikings arrive at Sandwich in July and campaign in England through summer

Sandwich

Winchester

Vikings return to their ships

Christmas: Vikings head through Hants and Berks, attacking Reading, Wallingford and Cholsey

After Martinmas (11 Nov), Vikings head to Isle of Wight

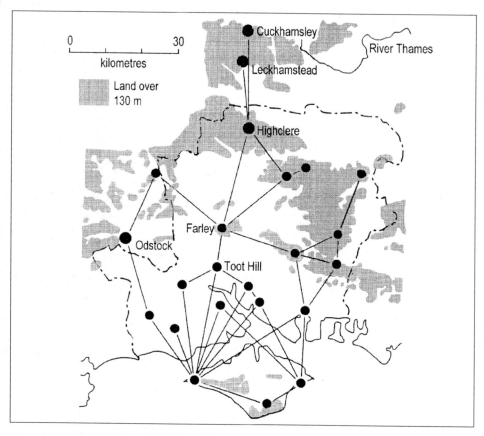

69. and 70. Map of beacons and Silbury Hill, Wiltshire: close to the River Kennet and the Anglo-Saxon
burh at Avebury. Although better known as a prehistoric site, excavations have revealed burnt material
that can be dated to the reign of Aethelred. This, along with its Anglo-Saxon place-name element of
'*burh*' (defended site) would suggest that this was part of a network of siting points and beacons, of the
sort reconstructed for Hampshire.

VENIE·NVNTIVS·AD·WIL
GELMVM·DVCE

Early medieval depictions of rulers upon thrones: 71. from the Bayeux Tapestry (eleventh century).

suggests that it was thought to be the burial place of the king of the West Saxons, Cwichelm, a king infamous in Bede's *Ecclesiastical History* for sending an assassin to the court of the good Christian ruler of Northumbria, King Edwin.[26] It was significant as a place to gather the Viking force. A central point in the West Saxon kingdom was struck at, and the very action impugned the authority of King Aethelred. The Vikings had appropriated that authority for their own purposes. Choosing the place at which the men of the shire would normally meet, and, in pre-Viking times, perhaps muster for battle, was poetry in action; the leading men of the shire were being called to an assembly by their enemies. This was an act of malign authority on the part of the Vikings and may provide an explanation as to why the Vikings encountered none of the men of Wessex at Scutchamer. If the *fyrd* had come there, they would have been obeying that authority which the Vikings had appropriated. It was more advisable for the West Saxons to fight on their own terms and join battle elsewhere. Therefore, this took place at the River Kennet in Wiltshire, although it seems to have done little good; the Chronicle records a Viking victory.

The Anglo-Saxon Chronicle for 1006 uses a great sense of poetry in its description of the events in that year.[27] The Vikings returned to their ships on the south coast, 'lighting

111

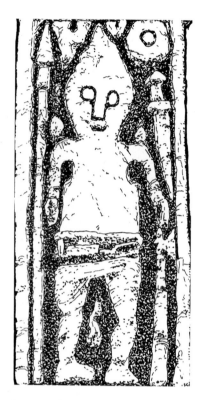

Early medieval depictions of rulers upon thrones: 72. from the Middleton Cross, North Yorkshire (tenth century; drawing by Don Lavelle). Both the Bayeux Tapestry and the Middleton Cross show influences of the Scandinavian idea of rulership.

their beacons as they went'. This was a great use of language, as it reflected the standard use of beacon fires to call out a defensive force, as occasional references among the higher points in the boundary records of Anglo-Saxon charters exemplify an extensive network.[28] However, it was hardly the efficiency of beacon signals that the Anglo-Saxon Chronicle was extolling in its dramatic account: there was no need for this system, as the Vikings were apparently destroying the settlements as they went, and the smoke from burning buildings must have been visible for miles around.

The chronicler's account of the citizens of Winchester being able to see the passing Viking army from their walls is again rather dramatic, suggesting that it was fortunate that the Vikings did not decide to take the city. Winchester had survived through God's grace. However, the Viking activities in southern England must also have alerted the local armies throughout Hampshire as the Vikings were trying to return to their ships as rapidly as possible. Their act of defiance on Scutchamer Knob was a public action by its very nature and any Viking commander would have known that their safest strategy was to return before the southern English gathered their forces. Investing the city of Winchester with a siege was not in the script, as this would have made the Viking force vulnerable to attack from a relieving English army while this took place. By comparison with other assaults on similar towns in the period – Exeter in 1003 and Canterbury in 1012 – it seems to have been the 'treachery' of someone within the city walls who was willing and able to allow in a Viking army (perhaps surrendering?) that was key to their success. Nevertheless, to the citizens of

Winchester, a place which had been at the heart of the kingdom of Wessex for at least a century,[29] the fear of Viking attack was still very real indeed. As they were in a well-fortified town, it was their defences that saved the citizens from any possible Viking onslaught, not providence, but as Roman roads led straight into the city, the appearance of the Viking army as it advanced southwards must have made the citizens feel as if they had experienced a close run thing.

In 1006, the Chronicle also recorded that the Vikings had established a *frithstol* on the Isle of Wight, from which they operated, in turn receiving food from Wessex, while King Aethelred received his own food rents 'across the Thames' in Shropshire. This was very much indeed the world turned upside down. Shropshire can be described in many ways, but 'across the Thames' is something of an understatement; it is much further north than that. For the chronicler, the implication of being 'across the Thames', the traditional boundary of the West Saxon kingdom, was that Aethelred was outside Wessex in the Christmas season. This was a period which was becoming the traditional time for the wearing of the crown in order to demonstrate the king's position in the kingdom. It might therefore be argued that the king would have been better served by an Ottonian-style demonstration of his authority in the westwork of the Old Minster in front of his West Saxon people than by spending a quiet Christmas in the wilds of the Welsh Marches.[30]

It was evidently not a good position, as the Chronicler implies: the Vikings were receiving those food rents (*feorme*) which rightly belonged to the king. The word which the chronicler uses to describe the presence of the Vikings is *frith-stol*, meaning 'peace chair'. Niels Lund, looking beyond the irony of the 1006 Chronicle entry, has suggested that the establishment of this was to set out a contract under which the Vikings could peacefully co-exist with Wessex over the winter period; the term *frith-stol* is therefore one associated with peace set out within a defined time and space.[31] However, there is another implication, of which the chronicler may have been fully aware: that of kingship. A *stol* (or 'gift-stool' – a throne, more elaborate than a simple chair with no back) was what contemporary rulers sat upon, as depictions of a Scandinavian king on the early tenth-century Middleton Cross and, more famously, of the Norman Duke William in the eleventh-century Bayeux Tapestry reflect. This does not mean that the Vikings had established a kingdom on the Isle of Wight, but the chronicler's use of language and imagery hints at a lack of English royal authority in Wessex, even if the reality was a negotiated truce. There is a very strong sense of causation here. The king is implied to have crossed over the Thames outside the kingdom of Wessex *because* of the Vikings. This is the epitome of the motif of Aethelred as a coward: the king is seen to have deserted his kingdom. Perhaps this was understandable in terms of modern 'rational' thought, but this was something which a king was not supposed to do.

However, while the Abingdon manuscript of the Anglo-Saxon Chronicle is condemnatory in its implicit criticism, the Chronicle of John of Worcester, written in the early twelfth century but using an otherwise lost version of the Anglo-Saxon Chronicle, gives the king's actions somewhat more credibility. King Aethelred was described as being merely in Shropshire – not 'across the Thames' – 'at that time'.[32] If any commentators were able to criticise Aethelred 'the Unready' with hindsight, then it was those writing in the twelfth century, far removed from the immediate consequences of the tumultuous events. Here, crucially, John of Worcester was not criticising the king, and it is with this somewhat more sober assessment that we are able to place these actions more realistically within the context of their time.

King Aethelred may not have been in Shropshire as a direct result of Viking activity, although of course considering his later exile to Normandy, his absence may have been politically expedient, and by the time that the Abingdon chronicler was writing, interpreted

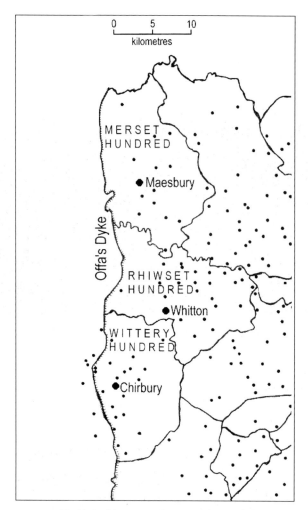

73. Shropshire estates in Domesday Book.

as such – or worse. However, the geography of Shropshire in the early medieval period was more significant than simply being distant from Wessex. Although part of the family lands of the rising star of the kingdom, Ealdorman Eadric[33] – and the relationship between Aethelred and Eadric in the events of 1006 was evident – the area was also part of the Mercian lands close to the Welsh border. These were the borderlands of Offa's Dyke, close to the Welsh kingdom of Powys, and here, throughout the Middle Ages, Anglo–Welsh relations were not always favourable.[34] Shropshire was raided by Gryffydd ap Llywellyn in the 1060s, and Oswestry was to be the site of a Norman castle. As part of a continuum of cultural and political tension, the English king's presence so close to the Welsh kingdoms in 1006 would have been nothing new.

Furthermore, there is a tangible record of the receipt of food rents in the Shropshire lands bordering Powys during the reign of Aethelred. Domesday Book records that the lands of Chirbury, Maesbury and Whittington, all in western Shropshire, provided a 'farm of one night', a unique official form of payment of rent in kind to the royal family.[35]

74. View of the fortifications at South Cadbury, Somerset. Along with Old Sarum in Wiltshire and Cissbury in Sussex, this was made into one of Aethelred's 'emergency' *burhs*, which went some way to sealing his reputation as a failed monarch.

75. As the plan suggests, the former Iron Age and post-Roman hillfort provided an adequate defence for the Somerset mint, which had been moved from Ilchester. Excavations have actually revealed a high standard of construction (see colour plates 20–21).

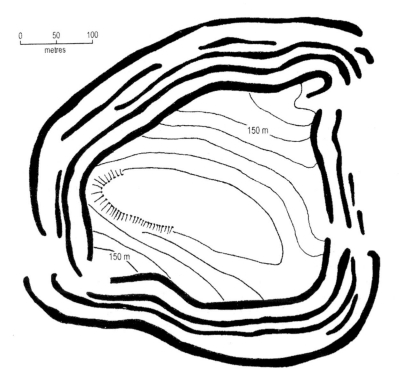

Crucially, however, Domesday specifically records that the payment was made 'at the time of Aethelred, father of King Edward'. This is a rare reference to King Aethelred in Domesday and indeed the only reference to a royal 'farm' in Shropshire, so we should hardly overlook the coincidence of this entry with the Chronicle's record of Aethelred's presence in Shropshire.

This was kingship at the margins of the kingdom then, very much commensurate with 'imperial' Anglo-Saxon kingship as practised by Aethelred's predecessors (see chapters 1 and 2). The food rents given to Aethelred at Christmas 1006 may not have been an alternative to West Saxon food rents, but here they came from the tribute given by a subject people; as an indication of this, Domesday records the importance of Welshmen for these hundreds. Therefore, although the timing was not necessarily appropriate during a particularly successful Viking campaign in Wessex, we should not overlook the evident ambition that lay behind King Aethelred's action.

The presence of Aethelred in the area of the family territory of the ealdorman of Mercia, the now-infamous Eadric *Streona* ('The Acquisitor'), during the winter of 1006–7 cannot have been without political consequence, as, in the following year, Eadric was made 'ealdorman over the Mercian kingdom'. The phrase *Myrcnarice* ('Mercian kingdom') is perhaps significant in the chronicler's eyes: writing around 1016 from an eastern English perspective, which by then perceived a tangible sense of Mercian separatism, we can perhaps see the gravity of the chronicler's choice of words. Eadric's later decisions and actions may have seemed to the chronicler as benefiting Mercia rather than 'the whole nation'. However grave the consequences may later have been, in 1006–7 Aethelred's appointment of Eadric as ealdorman of Mercia was surely a logical one.

The king's Christmas court had another significance, as it decided that peace would be made with the Vikings, so that, as the chronicler dryly remarks, 'this land could be saved before it was utterly destroyed'. The consequence was, we are told, the payment of £36,000 'to the host'. Again, the question can be raised as to whether the payment of geld entirely went to the Viking army or whether there was a higher tax which was also earmarked for other purposes. The order to build ships and make armour (a chainmail corselet and helmet) from every 310 hides of land and eight hides of land respectively, recorded in the Chronicle under the 1008 entry, suggests a wider campaign of rearmament. Richard Abels has calculated from a Domesday figure of 70,000 hides for the kingdom south of the River Tees that this would have allowed 200 ships to be built and 9,000 warriors to be armoured.[36] Of course, as ever, we may question how far north royal authority may have stretched in the practicality of collecting taxes, but nonetheless this would have allowed a formidable army to have been put together, an army presumably entirely mobile in their ships, if we are to accept a round figure of fifty men per ship. In the south of the kingdom, in Sussex and Wessex, we have seen that campaigns of building so-called 'emergency' fortifications from former Iron Age hillforts may have been undertaken during this period: at South Cadbury (Somerset) and Cissbury (Sussex).[37] Archaeological excavations of South Cadbury have revealed a formidable fortification, with faced stone walls and an impressive entrance gateway (see colour plate 20).[38] Naturally, it may be asked whether this was too little too late, but such an observation is only appropriate with the benefit of hindsight. In any case, we can see that the huge taxes extracted were not used simply to pay off the Vikings, as is too readily assumed from the Abingdon chronicler's emphasis: Aethelred's kingdom was preparing, once more, for war.

10
THORKELL'S ARMY

It is during the final years of Aethlred's reign that the widely held views of the much maligned king can be seen to come into their own, and criticisms of royal policy are least tempered. This was the time when the whole system of the late Old English state could be seen to fail; when, according to the Abingdon chronicler's brief but telling verdict on the year 1010, 'no shire would help the next'. The last half dozen years of Aethelred's reign were those which stuck most vehemently in the mind of the Anglo-Saxon chronicler, but even in the dark days, there were still flashes of inspirational kingship and political order. As Simon Keynes has shown, it was through the filter of these final years that that the Abingdon manuscript of the Anglo-Saxon Chronicle had portrayed the previous thirty-two years; in the last years of the reign, the charges of seeming treachery, the cowardice and military failure appear to be very pertinent indeed.

However, there is still a need to separate the actions of the different groups of Vikings in a period which saw two major campaigns. The attacks undertaken with a renewed vigour by Swein Forkbeard and his son, Cnut, from 1013 onwards are discussed in the next chapter; here, we are concerned with the actions of the army of Thorkell 'the Tall'. 1009 saw Thorkell's arrival in the English kingdom. His force, as the Anglo-Saxon Chronicle suggests, was an 'immense raiding army'; even Keynes's rehabilitation of the governing abilities of Aethelred has referred to this as the beginning of the end for Aethelred, in which the millenarian apocalyptic fervour of the previous decades heightened considerably. The laws of 1009, penned by Archbishop Wulfstan when Thorkell's army had actually arrived, advocated barefoot processions to church, strict attendance, public penance, psalms and prayer – the Apocalypse was visited upon the English people.[1] In 1008, another lawcode was issued which declared the renewal of Christianity in the English kingdom, and at the same time a special coin was struck which showed the religious fervour with which this law was undertaken. With a typical sense of Old English wordplay, the place of issue of the lawcode was Enham, in northern Hampshire; in the vernacular, *Ean-ham* meant 'place of the lambs', and, as M.K. Lawson has noted, the fields of the north Hampshire downs would have been full of spring lambs around Whitsun, the time when the lawcode was issued.[2] The lamb was thus a symbol of hope, but it was also a symbol of the Apocalypse, and we might sense a degree of inevitability through Aethelred's actions in 1008.

76. The *Agnus Dei* (Lamb of God) coin, probably issued in 1009 to accompany the Enham lawcode.

Was the 'immense raiding army' expected in England? From a modern worldview, the lawcode of 1008 would suggest hopelessness, but the context is somewhat more realistic in the milieu of the defence of the kingdom. The lawcode should be classed alongside the ship-building and armour-making: as a new army was created for their defence, a new Christian people were declared by the lawcode. This was all perfectly logical in terms of an early medieval worldview. Before being too quick to make anachronistic judgement, we should bear in mind that, within living memory, with the British army trapped in northern France by a German army poised to launch the invasion of Britain, King George VI called for a National Day of Prayer in May 1940; the spirits may well have been staunchly alike, even if the similarities stop here.

It may have been logical for the English to have expected yet another Viking onslaught when there was a lull in the wars after the giving of tribute in 1007. This allowed the building of ships, which the Anglo-Saxon Chronicle records for 1008. As has been shown in the previous chapter, Aethelred was making use of a policy to buy time in order to strengthen the kingdom's defences. It may also be asked whether Aethelred knew that Thorkell's army was the force which was due to arrive. The coincidence of the construction of ships during 1008 and their deployment in 1009, in anticipation of an army which arrived in that same year, would seem to suggest that each side had some idea of what the other was doing. Thorkell could not raise such an army in Denmark, which presumably included some of the same Vikings who had left England in peace in 1007, without attracting some attention, especially if his force had been recruited from across Scandinavia. King Aethelred's construction of more ships than 'had been in England in any king's time' and his gathering of them at the Kentish port of Sandwich suggests a strategic plan that involved more than waiting for the other side to act. We might surmise that he knew that a large force was being gathered on the other side of the North Sea. Such a plan would have allowed the English force to strike against their attackers when they were approaching the kingdom (or even if they gathered in Normandy) rather than when they had landed. This was surely a major leap forward in terms of strategy.

However, the grand strategy faced a major setback before the Viking force had even reached the kingdom. With so many ships and their crews gathered in one place, tension was bound to be enormous. A noble from Sussex, Wulfnoth *Cild* ('Child') was accused of crimes, now unknown, by the brother of Eadric *Streona*, a certain Brihtric. We hear little else of either party beside their appearance in this fateful annal, although we may be able to see something of their respective alliances. Wulfnoth may have been the father of Godwine, later Earl of Wessex, who is mentioned in the will of the *Aetheling* Athelstan as a recipient of some of the *aetheling's* estate.[3] Brihtric, on the other hand, is associated by the chronicler with all that was bad (or yet to be condemned) in the kingdom, as he was tainted by his kinship to Eadric *Streona*. Nonetheless, the familial alliances and regional rivalries seem highly appropriate; Athelstan and later Edmund, the elder sons of King Aethelred, were cultivating alliances with the seemingly disaffected nobility of the kingdom, largely in the east Midlands, but presumably the geographical interests went deeper into the English kingdom.

We do not know the crimes of which Wulfnoth *Cild* was accused. The chronicler's silence on the issue leaves us to assume that they are yet more false accusations by the bad advisors of the king, but Wulfnoth's reaction suggests that the charges were serious. The twenty ships which he 'enticed' to him are an indication of the close bonds among the kin groups. If a force of 200 ships was gathered at Sandwich, then twenty ships represented a tenth of the forces available to the nobility of the kingdom here (some 1,000 to 1,500 men?); this was more than a simple renegade action. His ravaging of the south coast – presumably Sussex, Hampshire and Dorset – may well have been politically inspired as, if his own patrimony was in Sussex, there seems to be little other explanation for these actions. Nicholas Higham has suggested that because the areas which provided Wulfnoth's vessels (the 300-hide ship sokes) and supporters were probably around coastal Sussex, his ship crews were experienced sailors. Higham argues that if by contrast the crews of the eighty ships taken by Brihtric in pursuit of Wulfnoth's men were from the landlocked west Midlands, they would therefore have had less experience of handling ships at sea, and so were at a disadvantage.[4] Before Brihtric was able to reach Wulfnoth's fleet, there was a storm in the English Channel, which resulted in the wrecking of most of Brihtric's ships. Wulfnoth's ships were able to withstand this storm; perhaps they were better sailors. Alternatively, perhaps, having been at sea for a longer time, they had been able to reach a port, such as Bosham in Sussex or the ports around Hampshire, or had simply managed to drag the ships far enough onto a beach to be out of harm's way. It is possible that Brihtric was fielding the whole force of his brother's Mercian ealdormanry, but as eighty ships would have required about 24,000 hides, this seems to have been even more than the augmented Mercia was capable of providing on the basis of the 1008 ship soke. Even Wulfnoth's twenty ships would have required some 6,000 hides, more than a couple of shires, suggesting that Wulfnoth was fielding a force greater than his patrimony. What was at stake here was presumably more than simply a familial conflict between the kin of Eadric and the supporters of the *aethelings*, even if such tensions may have been at its heart. When the survivors of the storm were able to reach land, Wulfnoth's force found it an easy task to destroy their ships. We do not hear what happened to Wulfnoth, or indeed Brihtric, after this, but Wulfnoth's probable son, Godwine (later to be Earl Godwine), was able to remain in Sussex, and so a royally enforced reconciliation was a possibility. However, the destruction of a large part of a national fleet was hardly a minor undertaking, and Wulfnoth's exile may have ensued,[5] thus providing fertile ground for the cultivation of resentments in the following years.

Once the debacle had ended, with half of the royal fleet destroyed and the rest retreating to the less exposed and more defensible port of London, the expected Danish invasion force arrived in English waters. This was to prove, as Keynes has described it, 'one of the most

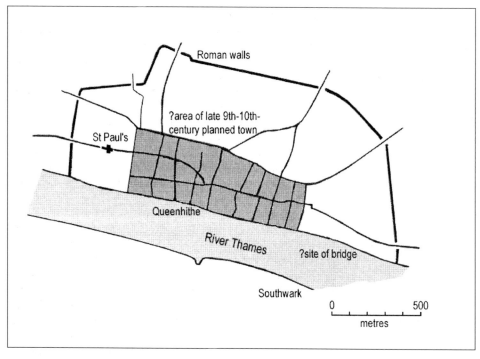

Roman walls

?area of late 9th-10th-
century planned town

St Paul's

Queenhithe

River Thames

?site of bridge

Southwark

0   500

metres

77. The key strategic point to Aethelred's kingdom? A map of London in the eleventh century, this
shows the defences of the former Roman city and the importance of Thames waterfront.

catastrophic events of the reign'.[6] However, the operations against Thorkell's invading army
were logical and suggest that a certain amount of strategic planning was still undertaken by
Aethelred and his advisors. Retreating with the remnants of the royal fleet to London was
to prove a sensible precaution, even if the Abingdon chronicler implies that this was royal
cowardice in the face of Wulfnoth's treachery, which 'carelessly wasted the nation's efforts'.
The Viking force arrived in Sandwich, perhaps, as John of Worcester's version of the
Chronicle records, having just made rendezvous with the other Viking commanders,
Hemming and Eilaf.[7] Thorkell may have believed that Sandwich was still the English base,
and it was fortunate for Aethelred that he had retreated to a more defensible site. Subsequent
Viking attacks were launched upon Canterbury, which managed to buy a truce for itself,
and upon southern England – Hampshire, Berkshire and Sussex. London, by contrast, was
able to stand firm in defence, presumably because of the presence of much of the royal fleet
in the Thames, which would have prevented the Vikings from moving too far upstream.
The strategic key to the kingdom had perceptibly shifted from the area of the old kingdom
of Wessex to the Thames Valley region and London. On many occasions in the following
years, the control of this growing city became the surest means of holding the kingdom.
The old Roman city may have been no larger than many of the other large towns in
England, but its central position in regard to the south and the Midlands, and its links to
the European continent made it a nodal point in Aethelred's kingdom (see chapter 1).
'Praise God', wrote the Abingdon chronicler, some six or seven years later, London 'yet
stands safely, and [the Vikings] always suffered harm there.'[8]

The war against Thorkell's army was not so one-sided as the chronicler seems to imply, as
Aethelred was yet able to call out a national force to counter the Vikings, and the entry for 1009

suggests that the English came in full strength when summoned. The chronicler's reference to 'a certain occasion' when the king had surrounded the Vikings who were vulnerable in returning to their ships implies that the pursuit of the Viking army was a constant activity – a particular near success was one event among many. The chronicler names Eadric *Streona* as the agent of treachery, as he apparently prevented a successful fulfilment of English victory. This is a record which may be taken with a pinch of salt. The chronicler refers to Eadric's action here as being 'just as it ever was'. In fact, this was the first recorded apparently malevolent action on the part of Eadric in preventing English victory against the Vikings; blaming Eadric was presumably more appropriate in such a literary context than blaming the fortunes of war.

The availability of information about the actions of the enemy may seem somewhat strange to our minds in an era of military secrecy; the Vikings' apparent capacity to anticipate English plans, such as the 'warning' that the English had mustered a *fyrd* against them in London, fits neatly into the Chronicle's milieu of the English side being rife with treachery. However, as we have seen, early medieval warfare was an affair of display and ritual; for the English force, their key purpose was to ensure that the enemy could be brought to fight. For Thorkell's Vikings, their aim was to make sure that they were not forced to fight. Undertaking such raids upon the countryside was a risky strategy for the Vikings, as the army could not move in one large formation while involved in destroying crops and plundering the countryside; in order to ravage lands efficiently, the Viking army was exposed to attack by the enemy, who, the Chronicle concedes, kept a close tail upon them.[9] One might question how effective these Viking actions actually may have been in ensuring that the army was well-fed and survived, as their attacks upon estates could not be as effective as they might have hoped. Thorkell's men were slowly destroying the infrastructure of the southern English countryside, and presumably also undermining Aethelred's authority, but they were in dangerous territory, far from their ships, and, perhaps as a result of the previous year's military reforms, the tenacious King Aethelred was able to keep his defence force together well into the winter months. The Danes retreated to Kent in order to repair their ships in the spring of 1009. As this was more usually a time at which to commence a campaign, it may not have demonstrated a position of strength, but instead that the campaigning of the previous months had taken its toll. The strategy in 1010 was to try to bring the English to battle in East Anglia rather than in the south of the kingdom. For the Vikings, this was a far riskier strategy than that employed in 1009, and their reluctance to go further south than the Thames valley may well reflect the dangers of their position.

RESISTANCE IN EAST ANGLIA

The Vikings therefore arrived in East Anglia, where the Anglo-Saxon Chronicle tells us that they had heard that Ulfcetel, the successful English leader of 1004 (see chapter 9), was waiting with his force. The East Anglians, the Chronicle records, 'fled' in the face of the Vikings. The chronicler criticises sparingly, naming only the instigator of the flight. This suggests that here events were accepted as part of the fortunes of war rather than perceived as treachery. However, the men of Cambridgeshire still managed to withstand the Vikings 'firmly', providing a staunch defence, even if it was a defence which was not successful, leading to many casualties. For three months, from May until August, the Vikings were in East Anglia, during which time they 'ravaged and burnt the land, and even went into the wild fens, and slew men and cattle, and burned throughout the fens, and burned down Thetford and Cambridge'. Terrible as these actions were for the inhabitants, and especially for the newly established fenland monasteries whose lands presumably suffered here, the Vikings' residence in East Anglia for some three months suggests that an English strategy of

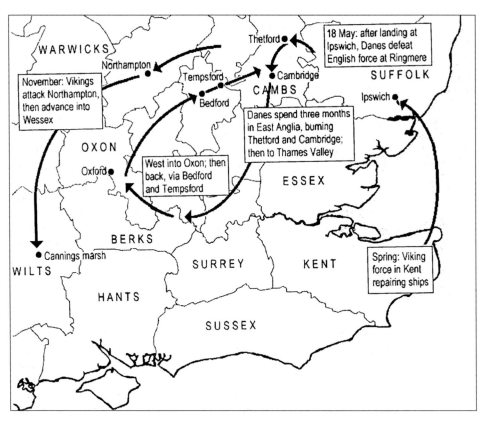

Map labels:

WARWICKS

Thetford ●

18 May: after landing at Ipswich, Danes defeat English force at Ringmere

Northampton ▲

November: Vikings attack Northampton, then advance into Wessex

Tempsford ●

● Cambridge

CAMBS

SUFFOLK

Bedford

Ipswich ●

Danes spend three months in East Anglia, burning Thetford and Cambridge; then to Thames Valley

OXON

Oxford ●

West into Oxon; then back, via Bedford and Tempsford

ESSEX

BERKS

● Cannings marsh

WILTS

SURREY

KENT

Spring: Viking force in Kent repairing ships

HANTS

SUSSEX

78. The movements of Thorkel's Viking army in and around East Anglia and English responses in 1010.

containment was at hand. Although the fenland monasteries had benefited from the patronage of the tenth-century monastic reform movement and their estates had riches to yield, three months in the East Anglian fens were hardly the ideal site of military opportunity in the height of the campaigning season. An important aspect of the historical geography of East Anglia may have been how difficult it was to advance westward into the east Midlands due to the presence of the fenlands as a very effective strategic barrier to movement. The Abingdon chronicler may well have focused upon events in this region because of the eastern English viewpoint from which he wrote.[10]

It was probably in late August, however, that the Vikings presented a real threat once more to the West Saxon kingdom. They advanced south to the Thames valley into Oxfordshire, and then north again to Buckinghamshire. Up until now, Aethelred had been relatively effective in keeping the Vikings at the margins of the kingdom, but the English army went home. This may seem to have been a foolhardy decision, but they had been away from their homes since being called out in the previous winter. If three months had passed since the Vikings had arrived in East Anglia on 18 May, late August was rather close to harvest time. Even if traditional historical interpretations of the Anglo-Saxon army with large bodies of poorly trained peasants in its ranks have given way to a picture of a force of well-armed nobles,[11] men of lesser status were presumably needed in order to campaign – to drive the carts, arrange the supplies of food and pitch camps. To such men, as well as their lords, harvests in their own lands took priority over military service.

It may have been in anticipation of this disbandment of the army that the Vikings advanced south, 'and ever burned as they went'. Bedford and Tempsford both fell to the onslaught. The Chronicle entry is somewhat hazy on its precise chronology here, actually implying that the English army returned home as a result of the Viking advance out of East Anglia, but the comment that 'it was then that the *fyrd* should have gone out a second time, in case [the Vikings] should intend to go inland', suggests that the Viking attacks south were indeed a result of the English disbandment in late August.

A national army could not be collected on a second occasion, so the kingdom was compelled to rely on local forces to defend individual shires. This could be an effective policy when Viking attacks were sporadic but it was not such a good strategy here. In the end, the Chronicle recalled bitterly that 'no shire would help the next'. What had gone wrong? In 1010, very little: few mistakes actually seem to have been made under the circumstances. The national army had been kept out on campaign for longer than under any other Anglo-Saxon king – longer, even, than Harold's famous coast watch of 1066 – and to an extent Aethelred had been successful as he had managed to limit Viking devastation to the East Anglian fenlands. It was only upon the unavoidable disbandment of the English force that the Vikings actually gained a freer rein with which to move into the English kingdom.

THE DEATH OF AN ARCHBISHOP

Even by the end of 1010 Aethelred had not yet sued for peace. The kingdom had endured a great deal and, the Chronicle remarked as it listed all the shires which the Vikings had 'overrun', peace was made too late. Tribute was paid (the Chronicle, for once, does not say how much) but, while it prevented the Viking army from operating as a whole, the English forces were in disarray and may have been unable to prevent the small troops of Vikings from peeling off and indulging in attacks of private enterprise through the kingdom. While this was obviously breaking the spirit of a peace agreement, the agreement itself may have remained intact. Peace was technically not broken until 8 September, when the Viking army, or at least a substantial part of it, besieged Canterbury for three weeks (or possibly less, as the Chronicle may include their activities inside the city in that timescale). Canterbury was the cradle of English Christianity, the place to which St Augustine had introduced the Roman religion into the Kentish kingdom at the end of the sixth century. As the seat of the primate of all England, Canterbury was a powerful city with both religious and economic influence, as well as deep significance for the English people.

The Chronicle records that the city was betrayed by an Englishman, a certain Abbot Aelmaer, 'whose life Archbishop Aelfheah [of Canterbury] had saved', although it fails to inform us of the details of either case. Such treachery by a man of God, whether real or an exaggerated interpretation, was of Biblical proportions. All the religious men and women of the town, of whom there must have been many,[12] were taken by the Vikings while they searched the town. For what, the chronicler does not say, but we might assume that it was a search for precious goods. This was hardly a friendly action, but by now, the beginning of the eleventh century, the Vikings were at least generally more willing to respect the lives of Churchmen and women than their ninth-century ancestors may have been.[13] When the Viking force left Canterbury, the archbishop was the only important person whom they took with them; the Bishop of Rochester, the Abbess of Minster in Thanet,[14] a king's reeve and the now disreputable Abbot Aelmaer, were allowed to escape by the Vikings. There is little sign that these people, or indeed the larger mass of lesser Church people, were ransomed as the tribute paid to the Vikings was in the following year – unless, of course, Thorkell's men managed to find enough wealth in the town to ransom the lives of these. The archbishop himself, we are told, refused to be ransomed; a decision which may have been instrumental in his martyrdom.

123

79. The shires which the Anglo-Saxon Chronicle records as having been 'overrun'by the Vikings in 1011.

1012 saw the death of the unfortunate archbishop at the hands of the Vikings, probably in Southwark or Greenwich, as Aethelred's councillors (as well as, probably, the king himself) were in London itself, upon the north bank of the Thames. The archbishop's death is often held up as an unparalleled example of Viking savagery and it is almost theatrical: the Vikings are very drunk from wine 'brought from the south' and like savages they throw cattle bones at him until he is finally killed by the 'head' (the flat side?)[15] of an axe upon his skull, an image that reinforces a popular conception of the Vikings as the untamed, violent renegades of their day.

However, terrible though it was, the story burgeoning with every step as the martyr's remains were carried toward the minster church of St Paul's, Archbishop Aelfheah's death stands as a singular atrocity in the history of the Vikings in England. It was such that Thorkell changed sides, taking forty-five ships with him to work for King Aethelred. A sense of Christian morality may have been at play here, perhaps highlighting divisions between the Viking leaders in the large army that Thorkell had gathered; if the archbishop had been killed in anger at an assembly, then it may have been more a result of disagreements between Viking leaders than the archbishop's refusal to be ransomed. The final factor at work in breaking up the Viking force was not ideological, but was an offer that might be able to break through most social bonds, which Aethelred ensured he employed at just the right time. A large amount of money – £48,000, according to the Abingdon manuscript – was offered to Thorkell to make use of his military expertise and his ships. The English king had bought the services of a powerful ally and in the years to come he was going to need him.

11

THE FINAL YEARS OF
AETHELRED'S KINGDOM

The purchase of the services of some forty-five ships under the command of the Danish Viking, Thorkell, may show some prescience on the part of Aethelred and his advisors in 1012. In the following year, a new Viking army arrived in England. This army brought the final affliction to the English kingdom. If Thorkell's appearance had brought the kingdom to its knees, then it was Swein and his son, Cnut, who were to make it collapse.

The arrival of a large army under Swein in 1013 is unsurprising, however. If Aethelred had bought the services of a part of Thorkell's army as the Chronicle's reference to his forty-five ships tells us, then, it may follow that there were also a number of mercenary Vikings in the North Sea who were willing to take the services of a new master. This meant a ready-made army for Swein, should he have been willing to employ them. We might wonder whether some of the same Vikings who had fought for Thorkell from 1009 to 1012 would now confront some of their own comrades who were by this time in the pay of King Aethelred. However tempting it may be to read a deep sense of drama and possible tragedy into such situations, including the reported animosity between Thorkell and Swein, it should not necessarily be assumed that the two Viking warlords were propelled by mutual loathing. Swein's invasion of England, as Simon Keynes has suggested, was probably motivated less by revenge, whether against Thorkell or Aethelred, than by the seizure of an important opportunity to finally conquer the kingdom of the English.[1] Swein's final conquest was less a saga, therefore, than a political act that was undertaken for sensible reasons.

These pragmatic conditions, under which different groups were willing to ally with others and then move back again are characteristic of the later years of King Aethelred's reign. Loyalty and treason were only effective so long as normal conditions of government applied. In the last years, outside southern England at least, it is reasonable to assume that much of royal authority may have broken down.[2] In such an environment, nobles were likely to revert to the alliances which they knew – those of kinship and locality – rather than maintain their obligations to a less visible royal presence. Pragmatism could be a rational master to follow. For Aethelred, such 'treason' could be disappointing, even disastrous, but it cannot have been wholly unexpected. In the final years of his reign, King Aethelred simply proceeded with his appointed task of governing an ever-decreasing realm;

the king could still muster his reserves of energy and surprise onlookers. As Janet Nelson commented regarding the reign of the ninth-century Frankish ruler, Louis the Pious, historians have a habit of interpreting 'last years' of a reign from the perspective of the ruler's demise. In the cases of Louis the Pious, King Henry II, and even Queen Victoria, the rulers did not know when that end was to come and until death came, they continued to make policy decisions and take initiatives 'with one foot in the grave'.[3] Aethelred may have known that he was ill, and by then, comparatively old, in 1015, but in 1013 and upon his return from exile in 1014, his rule was nonetheless active, an example of tenacious perseverance in holding on to the throne.

London to Normandy

Swein did not experience an irresistible sweep to power in the English kingdom then. He had to fight hard in order to gain any advantage in the face of the alliance of Aethelred and Thorkell. Swein began his campaign in the same manner as Thorkell some four years earlier, with a landing at Sandwich. The Abingdon chronicler's comment that he 'then went very quickly round East Anglia' is probably intended to show the speed with which Swein could strike wherever he wished in the kingdom. To an extent, the Chronicle is probably correct. However, the account may also show the degree to which the south of the kingdom had

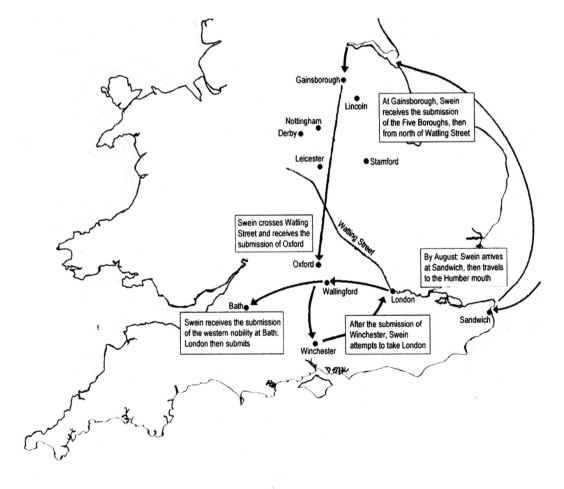

80. The movements of the Viking army of King Swein Forkbeard in 1013.

become a dangerous area for the Vikings if the defences of the kingdom had been consolidated in a similar manner to their employment during the campaigns against Thorkell. It would have been logical for some or all of the combined fleets of Aethelred and Thorkell to then have been moored at Sandwich, the traditional gathering point for the defensive fleets of the English kingdom at times of crisis. There may be little other explanation for Swein's rapid move to East Anglia.

Therefore, it may well have been for such reasons of accident rather than design that the 1013 Danish conquest of England began in the north and east Midlands. The landing in Sandwich, which would have taken Swein straight into the heart of the English kingdom, was abortive, then. However, if an invasion based upon the north of the kingdom was only a secondary plan, then it was an effective basis from which Swein could work. The area of Lindsey and the Five Boroughs was the first to submit to Swein. This is traditionally presumed to have been a result of the supposed Danish 'ancestry' of the area's inhabitants,[4] but in view of the extent to which ethnicity could be an identity 'created' by its users, the submission of the area is more likely to have been a result of political conditions. Loyalty only operated so long as it could be reciprocated with tangible rewards. If the king was unable to provide protection for his subjects living on the peripheries of the kingdom, then that political relationship had already broken down before the 'treachery' came into operation. After all, through royal pragmatism, English defences were concentrated in Wessex and the south of England.

Curiously, there is less historical condemnation of the submission of the southern English to Swein than of the northern towns, as if somehow the northerners could make a decision whereas the south was presented with a *fait accompli*. The Abingdon chronicler is unsympathetic. He refers to the northerners who submitted to Swein as the *Here* – meaning the 'army', the term once used to refer to the Danish army of the ninth century. The use of this term invokes a sense of 'otherness', as if to imply that their immediate submission to a Danish king was because they were themselves Danes, and were simply satisfying their natural inclinations. However, hostages were still taken by Swein, whom Swein entrusted to his son, Cnut, with the important task of their care. The presence of the hostages in this process implies a genuine submission of the northern shires and not just rapid 'treachery'. Swein was being systematic in his conquest of the English kingdom.

Matthew Innes has suggested that as Swein crossed into southern England, he used Watling Street as a 'political and ethnic marker';[5] this was the exploitation, even the creation of differences between the regions of the kingdom. Swein 'wrought the worst evil that any force could do'. He was embarking upon a campaign of making the kingdom give allegiance and hostages to him, town by town: Oxford, followed by Winchester, fell to Swein, evidently even without a fight. English royal authority now had to contract to a small core – that of London. The former principal city of the Roman province of Britain was ideally suited to controlling the English kingdom from the south and, as we have seen in the previous chapter, it was proving an important strategic point. While London remained in Aethelred's hands, Swein's task in becoming king of the English was difficult. Swein realised this, as the Chronicle records the drowning of a number of Swein's army, 'because they gave no thought for a bridge'.

There may have been more than impatience behind this. Swein's force was arriving from Winchester in the south and an attack on London from the north side of the Thames, where the city itself lay, would have limited the effectiveness of Thorkell's riverborne fleet by placing the city between Swein and the river. Bridges across the Thames from the first bridge west of London, at Staines, onwards were presumably defended. In order to avoid these, an attempt to ford the river may have been necessary, even if the river took its toll

81. The remains of the *burh* at Wallingford.

82. the River Thames in full flood at Wallingford, now in Oxfordshire, but formerly in Berkshire. It was here that Swein crossed the Thames after an attack on London.

on some of Swein's men. The attempted attack failed as the people of London 'defended with full force', a point which the Abingdon chronicler attributes to the presence of King Aethelred and Thorkell within the city.

Swein's response was to consolidate his position in Wessex by advancing westwards, presumably while Aethelred and Thorkell could not move west out of London. At the *burh* of Wallingford, Swein's force crossed the River Thames again, presumably receiving the submission of the citizens at the same time, as the river crossing was well defended by the fortification and we could not expect a crossing to have taken place without the submission of the *burh*. From Wallingford, Swein travelled west to Bath, the site of the imperial coronation of King Edgar, where he was given submission and yet more hostages by Aethelmaer, Ealdorman of the Western Provinces, who had succeeded his father, Aethelweard 'the chronicler', to the ealdormanry some years earlier.

At this point, when Swein moved northwards again to meet with the ships held by his son, he was acclaimed 'full king'. What did the Chronicle mean by this? Presumably, as we later learn Swein's position, he was acclaimed by the men of his Viking army at Gainsborough in Lincolnshire, one of the Five Boroughs. This does not appear to have been a seizure of only the northern part of the kingdom. In view of the collapse of English authority in many southern towns with the exception of London, Swein was king of the whole of the English people, although naturally we might expect his authority to have been stronger in the more distant regions of the English kingdom, outside Wessex, where Aethelred's royal authority had not been so well-established. The title 'full king' implies that there was no indication of any treaty to share power, and although the Abingdon chronicler continues to refer to Aethelred as 'the king', for the time being he had become a political irrelevance.

London, the key to the kingdom, submitted to Swein, giving hostages, 'for fear that he might destroy them utterly', but Thorkell's fleet appears to have remained in Aethelred's service, or at least friendly to him, as the Chronicle records that the king was 'for a time with the fleet which lay in the Thames'. This may seem somewhat incongruous in view of the fact that Thorkell's fleet, moored at Greenwich, demanded supplies and money, and yet 'ravaged as often as they pleased'. For one matter, Thorkell's fleet had probably not been fully paid for their services (a failure which is probably understandable, given the circumstances for the kingdom). But why, in this case, should they have been willing for Aethelred to be with them? A possible answer is that Aethelred had now become an effective outlaw – a malign authority within the English kingdom, and therefore if Thorkell's contract with the English people had ended by default, Aethelred was now on the same level.

Aethelred was therefore not safe in England. From the Thames, he took refuge on the Isle of Wight, making use of the same natural defences of the island to protect his position as Vikings had in 1006. Aethelred may have been using the island as a staging post on his infamous exile to Normandy. However, we might wonder why he then spent Christmas upon the Island if the situation were so dire: would it not have been better to have gone immediately to Normandy, under the circumstances? Practically speaking, yes. But politically, Aethelred may still have wished to demonstrate his position as a king of Wessex. The Isle of Wight was an ideal place from which to do this, and it may hardly have been insignificant that Aethelred was now in the place of the Vikings who had received the West Saxon Christmas food rents from the Isle of Wight while Aethelred had been in Shropshire in 1006.

The Christmas festival ended, Aethelred finally left Wessex to join his family in exile, at the court of the Norman Duke, Richard II. While King Swein of Denmark and England was upon the English throne, Aethelred's reign was over.

THREE KINGS OF ENGLAND

Unfortunately for Swein, however, he was not to remain long upon the English throne. The Abingdon Chronicle records the 'happy event of Swein's death' upon 3 February 1014, with some satisfaction. Following this, the councillors, or at least 'those who were in England' (presumably others had followed Aethelred, or had gone elsewhere into exile) sent messengers to the king to inform him that no lord 'was more beloved to them than their natural lord'; in the spring, the king returned to his kingdom. What had changed in the meantime, between the acclamation of Swein and his untimely death?

An allegation could of course be made that foul deeds had been perpetrated against Swein, as although regicide could be viewed with horror when an anointed king was the victim, Swein had not gone through a coronation ceremony.[6] However, in terms of our extant sources, we can only remark upon the general shift in mood for the return of the 'natural' (i.e. English) lord to the kingdom. It is likely that there never had been a change of mood; at least not amongst those close to the West Saxon dominated region of southern England, as well as amongst those kin-groups close to the West Saxon royal family, including the favoured region of Mercia. Their allegiance to King Swein had presumably been temporary, necessitated by political circumstance. In his famous apocalyptic *Sermon of the Wolf to the English*, Wulfstan, the Archbishop of York and Bishop of Worcester, had written in disgust at the exile of Aethelred, anointed king of the English, implying that he was writing in the early months of 1014.[7] Even the pessimistic tones of the Anglo-Saxon Chronicle subside slightly when it refers to the return of Aethelred to England, with the promise to be a 'loyal lord' and 'amend each of the matters which they had all despised'.[8] 'All' Danish kings were to be exiled from England. A new order had been declared, with an irrevocable agreement between the king and his people, or so it seemed.

In northern England and the east Midlands, there were other ideas. Gainsborough and the area of the Five Boroughs had achieved a level of political influence that may have been unprecedented. It is therefore hardly surprising that the people of Lindsey should have come to an agreement with Swein's son, Cnut, accepting him as Swein's successor in England. This was pure political opportunism. Sigeferth and Morcar, two of the leading men of the Five Boroughs, from a well-established and powerful family in the eastern Midlands,[9] were instrumental in creating the links with the Vikings, as Cnut married their kinswoman, Aelfgifu of Northampton. This was a mutually convenient relationship; it allowed the men of Lindsey to counter the growing influence of the ealdormanry of Mercia within the kingdom.[10] Although the regional rivalries within the kingdom had changed somewhat since the fearful days of the death of Edgar in 975, the principles of familial rivalries remained and once more they were dramatically manifesting themselves at this time of crisis. Given the opportunity, powerful families were ready to evolve their political allegiances to suit their requirements. As we have seen, such actions were not 'treachery' but a wholly understandable response to the contraction of the sphere of royal influence back into southern England. In absence of such West Saxon royal authority, it was hardly surprising that the men of Lindsey should have lent their support to Cnut.

However, yet again, fortune was on the side of King Aethelred, as upon his return to the kingdom he was quick to act against those whom he must have perceived as traitors. Building upon the momentum of rising popular support already gained by his return to Wessex, King Aethelred launched a surprise attack that caught the men of Lindsey and the Viking force before they had fully prepared for their own offensive. Aethelred's assault on Lindsey could have been intended to demonstrate what he perceived as the illegality of supporting Swein and Cnut's seizures of the English throne. As we have seen on previous occasions, Aethelred could be an active king when the occasion required, and the Chronicle points out that he attacked Lindsey with full force, killing every person who could be found. Even allowing for exaggeration, this was the wrath of the righteous descending with fury and Cnut's response demonstrates the effectiveness of King Aethelred's action.

In the face of the assault from the south, Cnut quickly retreated by sea, leaving the northern forces in the lurch, but taking the valuable hostages with him. These, Cnut dropped off in Sandwich, minus their hands, ears and noses. It was a drastic action, but nonetheless a brutal public demonstration of Cnut's political will, and their survival meant that they would provide a permanent visual reminder of what Cnut perceived as the bad faith of the hostage grantors.[11]

From this perspective, we can see that the situation in 1014 must have presented a dilemma for the citizens of Winchester, London, Oxford and Bath, and any other towns which had sent hostages to Swein in 1013. We should not overlook the sadness which the decision to fight against Cnut must have entailed for the nobles of the kingdom; hostages were probably adolescent sons and their mutilation would have been a terrible occasion, traumatising many of the West Saxon and Mercian nobility for a generation to come. Nonetheless, the decision which the southerners and Mercians took to fight against Cnut was legally justifiable; the hostages and submission had been given to Swein, not to his son. Political realism was the mother of necessity, and the level of the support given to Aethelred's kingship is demonstrated by the fact that the Anglo-Saxon nobility was able to make this decision in the dire circumstances of that moment.

The payment of some '£21,000' to the army 'which lay at Greenwich' is presented by the Abingdon chronicler as an additional evil for the English kingdom. This is the first we hear of Thorkell's army since its ravaging of the area around the Thames with Aethelred's connivance at the end of the previous year. Presumably they had remained at Greenwich since, but while the English payment is presented as a bribe for enforced peacemaking, its context suggests its military importance. While King Aethelred was in Lindsey, ravaging by fire and sword, Cnut was at large, and we may remark upon the strategic significance of the position of Thorkell's ships. Cnut may have landed the unfortunate hostages at Sandwich, but the position of Thorkell's army ensured that Cnut was not able to travel up the Thames to reach London. Therefore, although the payment of £21,000 is often interpreted as a misfortune of 1014 (along with a flood of Biblical proportions on Michaelmas eve), it was nonetheless a reasonable payment for a very valuable service.

FEAR, LOATHING AND RIVALRY

If the events of 1014 were to herald a new beginning in the English kingdom, any celebrations were to be short-lived. The following year is marked in the Anglo-Saxon Chronicle by a heightened sense of suspicions, counter-suspicions and perceived treachery, from protagonists who included those very close to King Aethelred.

Even the most naïvely optimistic could hardly have expected there to have been no repercussions in the political fallout from the previous year. However, as Sigeferth and Morcar, two of the important nobles from the Five Boroughs of the Danelaw, made their way to a national assembly at Oxford, we might wonder whether they assumed that they were to be the beneficiaries of a royal pardon. Although attendance at assemblies could be under penalty of outlawry and attendees may have had little choice in the matter, magnanimity may have been hoped for; while King Aethelred may have been strenuous in his

83. St Michael's church tower, Oxford. Sited along the town walls, this may have formed part of the town's fortification in the late Anglo-Saxon period (probably eleventh century).

pursuit of those who offended him, he could also be magnanimous: the act of granting forgiveness on occasions was, after all, a political ritual.[12] Unfortunately for Sigeferth and Morcar, the unpredictability of royal anger was also part of that ritual. However, the chronicler's by now staunchly entrenched bias against Eadric meant that the fate of the two 'chief thegns', Sigeferth and Morcar, was attributed to Eadric's treacherous hands. They were 'enticed' into Eadric's chamber and, while inside, 'basely killed'. The Chronicle gives little more detail, but squarely lays the blame for the death at the feet of Eadric; the depiction of the act taking place in Eadric's chamber also suggests that the assembly was under the auspices of his authority.

In the absence of any other evidence, Eadric's complicity in the murder can only be accepted with reservations, but in view of Sigeferth and Morcar's transgressions, he may have been acting with royal approval, if not indeed authority, as executioner. If it was at least believed amongst contemporaries that Eadric had had Sigeferth and Morcar killed, there was a background to their long-standing rivalry, which was focused upon the rise of northern Mercian political influence during the later tenth century. King Aethelred's order that the widow of Sigeferth be seized and brought to the West Saxon Mercian abbey of Malmesbury may indicate that he intended to give Eadric authority over the family lands in the east Midlands. When added to those held in Mercia by Eadric,[13] this may well have augmented the ealdorman's power.

However, Aethelred's son, Edmund (later 'Ironside') had other ideas. The problem that faced so many medieval rulers – that of the adult son chafing for power – was finally manifesting itself in dramatic terms at the end of Aethelred's life. Before the king or Eadric could do anything, the *aetheling* Edmund seized Sigeferth's wife for himself. This was no romantic gesture to save her from a cloistered life, but was done in order for Edmund to consolidate a powerbase in the east Midlands where his support seems to have been strongest (and with this in mind, it is notable that Edmund had not followed his father into exile in 1013).[14] The will of Edmund's elder brother, the *aetheling* Athelstan, made and ratified around midsummer 1014, had reflected the close relationship between the two sons of Aethelred's first marriage and the nobility of the east Midlands. Athelstan had gone to some lengths in order to make sure that his father would agree to his wishes; there is uncertainty in the language used in the will, regarding his father's permission to make bequests, suggesting that there was a real sense of fear that the king would not allow the document to be ratified.[15]

Here then we see the emergence of a polarised factionalism within the English kingdom. As the eldest surviving royal son, Edmund Ironside naturally saw himself as the successor to Aethelred, and yet the Ealdorman Eadric may have seen his position threatened.

It is finally here, in 1015, when we see the structure of patronage and kinship bonds breaking apart the kingdom. Up to now, there had always been some way of bringing the disparate factions back together under royal authority, but in 1015, a crucial element was missing. The king himself lay ill, at an otherwise unremarkable manor in Cosham, southern Hampshire. From this, the picture of the lazy, inactive king has emerged over the years: historical myth is much more concerned with sinfulness and sloth than genuine illness, and so the Aethelred of later historiography was not seen as ill, but lazy. Be that as it may, a long, evidently debilitating illness for the king was probably the worst possible fate. If the kingdom relied upon the presence and personality of the king to bring the factions together then under any conditions, let alone the destabilising conditions of 1015–16, those factions were bound to reign uncontrolled. Not only this, but Cnut also returned to England, to receive the vital support of Ealdorman Eadric, no less.

Eadric is often blamed for his work as a traitor (not least with Henry of Huntingdon's gruesome image of Eadric's head impaled at Tower Hill in 1017[16]), but it is in recent years that historians have come to appreciate the difficulties of his position. In supporting Cnut, we may agree that he was advancing his own interests, but support for Cnut was also justifiable in the fact that the leading men of the kingdom had chosen him as a successor to Swein.[17] Under the circumstances of King Aethelred's illness and Edmund's rebellion, this was understandable.

Edmund Ironside's position was equally tenable. If his interests were based in the east Midlands, he held them in common with a disaffected faction of the English nobility who had suffered while Eadric's family and associates had gained importance in the years since 1006.[18] Moreover, Edmund and, earlier, his elder brother, Athelstan, may even have felt their positions to be threatened by the emergence of Edward and Alfred, the sons from Aethelred's marriage to Emma. As Stafford has observed, bearing in mind the circumstances of King Aethelred's own ascent to the throne in 978, any misgivings held by the elder sons of the king may have been justified: Queen Emma was the political equal of Edgar's queen, Aelfthryth; during the first decades of the eleventh century, Emma was active in promoting the interests of her sons, just as Aelfthryth had been, and the young Edward's role in bringing Aethelred back from Normandy could hardly have assuaged Edmund's concerns.[19]

The Chronicle records that Eadric and Edmund met in 1015, but separated before battle could be joined against the Vikings and 'retreated from their enemies'. While the implication was that Eadric had forced the English army to break up through his wish to 'betray' Edmund, it could also be suggested that it may actually have been a meeting to negotiate their own positions within the kingdom. In view of the threat to 'English' security, such an activity may appear somewhat disingenuous but we should remember that Eadric and Edmund may have perceived each other as no less of a threat than the Danes. To these people, family and local interests were far more important than the 'national' picture which, in common with the Abingdon chronicler, we are too often ready to see as all-important. Therefore, with neither Eadric or Edmund willing or even able to come to a consensus, a 'national' army simply could not exist.

Eadric's readiness to join with Cnut's force could not have been as much of a surprise as the chronicler implies, and with Edmund having rebelled by going against his father's wishes, those who fought with Eadric and Cnut could hardly have been traitors, either. Equally, as Edmund Ironside, in conjunction with Earl Uhtred, charged into the west Midlands to attack Shropshire, we could suggest that this was also justified. As Ann Williams has observed, Shropshire and western Mercia contained the lands of Eadric's kin and so striking these lands was a priority if Edmund perceived Eadric, not Cnut, to be his main political adversary.[20] Although the Abingdon chronicler expresses some surprise that Edmund and Uhtred did not fight against Cnut, the fact that Cnut and, presumably, Eadric with him were forced to return to ravage the Northumbrian lands of Uhtred in retaliation is an indication of the effectiveness of this policy. Uhtred was forced to return and the factional balance was disturbed as he was forced to submit to Cnut, giving hostages. Again, here Eadric is portrayed as the evil advisor, as Cnut killed Uhtred 'on the advice of Ealdorman Eadric', a killing infamous for sparking off a longstanding feud.[21] Such an image downgrades the strength of Eadric's own position, however; the ealdorman's influence came through the authority which he held, not through mere whisperings and intrigue in dark corners of the court. Eadric remained a powerful political player in his own right; just one example among the many powerful families who had dominated, and were yet to dominate, the affairs of the English kingdom throughout the tenth and eleventh centuries.

In the meantime, King Aethelred had returned to London in the early spring of 1016, after what we might suppose had been an uncomfortable winter. While London was to be where the king died, his presence was also a last political act. In the city where the king had spent his last years, he was still needed with his own army. But there was to be no glorious last charge. Under threat of treachery, after leading out a force from London, the king returned to the city. Was this cowardice or the action of an exhausted man? Illness is likely to have played more of a role in Aethelred's decision than cowardice, but there were practical reasons in avoiding capture; as a captive, the king could have been forced to declare a successor. Moreover, London had been shown to be the centre of the kingdom, a stronghold for the king and the remnants of royal authority.

It was here that Aethelred died, on St George's Day, 23 April 1016. John of Worcester recorded the king's burial in St Paul's Church,[22] while the Abingdon chronicler conceded a last judgement that gave some grudging credit to Aethelred's political abilities: Aethelred had 'held his kingdom with great hardship and troubles as long as his life lasted'. The king, who had reigned for some thirty-eight years, was dead and the kingdom was now in turmoil. There was more yet to come.

12
AFTERMATH

It may be indicative of the political abilities of Edmund Ironside that he was able to move quickly following the death of his father. The Anglo-Saxon Chronicle records that Edmund gained the support of 'all' the king's councillors in London. Despite Edmund's earlier misgivings about the possibility of a repeat of the circumstances that brought his father to power, there may have been a relatively uncomplicated succession; the younger *aethelings*, Edward and Alfred, were by now in exile in Normandy, although their mother, Queen Emma (who was also Edmund's step-mother), remained in London. We should remember that up until Aethelred's death, Edmund had been cast as the rebellious son; under such circumstances, Edmund may not necessarily have been able to count upon the support of those southern English nobility who had remained loyal to Aethelred. Therefore, Edmund's accession to the throne, or at least his assumption of royal power, was quite remarkable. Of course, it was hardly illogical, either. For one matter, the dying Aethelred may have been instrumental in designating Edmund as his successor. King Edmund now came to embody the interests of many of the southern English nobility and their support may not have been given unreservedly. Edmund had been chosen as king, but the kingdom which he ruled had not yet emerged from the circumstances of the last years of Aethelred's reign.

Edmund rallied the West Saxon forces at Penselwood, near Gillingham, on the border between Dorset, Somerset and Wiltshire. Here, there may have been an important gathering point in the West Saxon kingdom; after all, Edmund was invoking royal rights for his kingdom, perhaps in the same manner as King Alfred called his forces to 'Ecgbert's Stone' in the same area in 878, before reclaiming his kingdom at the Battle of Edington.[1] In 1016, the Anglo-Saxon Chronicle records that Edmund 'seized [*gerad*] Wessex'. This was a key point, showing the importance of gaining the support of the people of Wessex, who are recorded as submitting to him. Indeed, the language used by the Chronicle for Edmund's 'seizure' of Wessex is similar to that used to describe Cnut's earlier receipt of submission.

In this sense, with Edmund's concentration upon control of Wessex and the south, the English kingdom had already been divided before the infamous agreement made between Cnut and Edmund after the Battle of Ashingdon. The arrangements made in that peace agreement were simply a recognition of political circumstances that existed *de facto* – Cnut, with the support of some of the nobility of the northern Danelaw, was exercising those rights of kingship which he must have seen as his since 1014. Although of course both Edmund and Cnut were each engaged in trying to oust the other's position, and the three major battles of 1016 –

84. Penselwood, the ancient woodland which has demarcated the division between eastern and western Wessex. Close to the original gathering point for the armies of King Alfred in the defence of Wessex in 878 and perhaps emblematic in the new King Edmund's evocation of West Saxon kingship, Penselwood saw the first major battle between Cnut and Edmund Ironside, both contenders for the English throne. Neither here nor at Sherston (Wiltshire) was a decisive result achieved for either side.

Penselwood, Sherston (Wiltshire) and Ashingdon (Essex) – were part of this process, the resulting peace agreement in late October was a mutual recognition of the fact that their positions were then relatively evenly matched. Making peace was a means of establishing this.

However, what may have made a difference to the eventual political balance was again Mercia. As was the case with the last months of Aethelred's reign, the kingship of Edmund is characterised by the activities of Ealdorman Eadric. While the position from which Eadric operated has already been addressed as a necessary antidote to the chronicler's obvious vitriol against Eadric, Eadric's return to the side of King Edmund seems to have allowed a change in the political circumstances. It was with Eadric's force that the English army encountered Cnut at Ashingdon, and it was, so the chronicler relates, Eadric and the *Magonsaete* (from north-western Mercia) who were the first to desert the battlefield. Was this simply the fortunes of war or a deliberate act of treachery on the part of Eadric? The chronicler seems to have thought the latter, as he relates that 'nothing more ill-advised was ever advised' when Edmund allowed the infamous ealdorman to enter his service. From a twenty-first-century perspective, we might be quick to agree; but the flight of the *Magonsaete* took place as a result of the more usual regional interests. Edmund had been forced to acknowledge this regional power which Eadric exercised, and Eadric was evidently able to recognise that fact. Again, Eadric was thinking first of his own kindred and lands, just as was the case with so many other English nobles; the only difference here was that Eadric could actually act decisively upon this.

As the chronicler laments, Ashingdon may have seen a betrayal for 'all the people of England', but as King Edmund's power and influence were already limited, we should not necessarily read into this a 'national' tragedy. But it was still a military defeat; even a disaster. Many of those who had once served King Aethelred died at Ashingdon: the Bishop of Dorchester, the Abbot of Ramsey, Ealdorman Aelfric of Hampshire, Ealdorman Godwine of Lindsey (who had presumably been in a difficult position if fighting for King Edmund) and Ulfcetel of East Anglia.

This victory allowed Cnut to translate his position as a king in northern England into rule over Mercia. Edmund would now rule over southern England only, but we should

85. The Anglo-Saxon minster church at Deerhurst, Gloucestershire. It was near here that the peace agreement was made between Cnut and Edmund Ironside after the Battle of Ashingdon.

86. A detail of King Cnut, as portrayed in the New Minster *Liber Vitae* (the book of life), with his wife, Aethelred's widow, Queen Emma (Aelfgifu), on the occasion of presenting a gold cross to the New Minster (after British Library Stowe MS 944). Cnut portrayed himself as a legitimate English monarch, and was willing to make use of the church of the West Saxon royal family to do so.

remember that only sixty years earlier, during the first years of the reign of Edmund's grand-father, Edgar, that the kingdom had last been divided. The unity of the kingdom was only effected when it was politically convenient, and here division seemed the sensible option. John of Worcester's version of the Chronicle gives a more specific version of the division, with Wessex, East Anglia, Essex and London to Edmund and the rest ('the northern parts') being taken by Cnut.[2] John relates that the peace was made at Alney, near Deerhurst, in northern Gloucestershire, upon an island in the Severn; although Gloucestershire could hardly be described as 'West Saxon', it may have represented a middle point of neutral ground between the territories of the respective kings. According to John's account, the Crown was to be retained by Edmund, but this may have represented the letter, not the reality of the agreement. Cnut, the former 'sea-king' and landless warrior with a massive fleet, was now established in England; he had been acclaimed king following the death of his father in 1014, and if he did not hold the English Crown, he was still a king in deed and we might wonder as to the nature of the rights which he may have been intending to assert.

Edmund's reign was to last only another month. On 30 November, he died in London; we do not know the reason, and while obvious speculations are of poison or murder, Cnut's assumption of power as a legitimate ruler is more worthy of consideration. By now, it was winter and this was hardly a favourable time to begin a military campaign. However, as a result of the deaths in battle of the English nobility in 1016, this time there was to be no major resis-tance against Cnut. As a result of the circumstances of a major battle followed by the death of the English king within a short time, Cnut had a favourable window of opportunity. By having already established a powerbase within the English regions amongst the families of the Danelaw, Cnut may have overcome many of those difficulties which normally faced Wessex-based monarchs. Furthermore, the wholesale replacement of the ealdormen with a new group of earls who owed their allegiance to Cnut allowed the reduction of any potential threat.

However, it is a testament to the years of effective rule during the reign of King Aethelred that the English political machinery was still in operation during the reigns of Edmund and Cnut. While only two charters of uncertain degrees of trustworthiness survive from the reign of Edmund,[3] suggesting that the *witan* were not meeting as often as they might (or at least did not prioritise the granting of land), the systems of taxation and law still remained in place and the Anglo-Saxon Chronicle records a levy of £72,000 for 1018. If this figure reflects the proportions of money taken, it was by far the highest level of army taxation – part of which went to pay off Cnut's force and part may have been intended to finance a planned conquest of Denmark. In 1019, Cnut's brother, Harald, died, allowing Cnut to return to Denmark to take over the kingdom. For the first time a 'North Sea Empire' was in existence.

The man who began as a Danish Viking leader had now become an English king, who, conversely, seized territory in Scandinavia. In terms of success and failure in kingship, the apparent contrast could hardly be greater; the contraction of the English kingdom under Aethelred 'the Unready' compares unfavourably with the achievements of Cnut 'the Great'. This is, of course, understandable. However, it was the English base of the kingdom that allowed Cnut to manifest himself as a Danish ruler. The legacy of King Aethelred played a part in this, ensuring that the kingdom was in an effective position to continue with relative prosperity and the exercise of God's law for an English people with strong royal jurisdiction – the 'idea' of 'England' was still a strong political force. Aethelred had endured a quarter of a century of major Viking attacks and exercised English kingship in the process, dealing with issues of patronage and legitimacy in a similar manner to his tenth-century predecessors. Therefore, it is not with the demise of King Aethelred during a period of crisis, but instead with the continuation of the Old English state during the eleventh century, that a consideration of the reign of King Aethelred can justifiably end.

Notes

Abbreviations used:

Anglo-Norman Studies R.A. Brown (ed. to vol.11, subsequently ed. M. Chibnall), *Proceedings of the Battle Conference on Anglo-Norman Studies* 1978 etc. (Woodbridge, 1979 etc.) (cited by volume number, conference and publication years)

EHD 1 D. Whitelock (ed.), *English Historical Documents*, vol.1: *c.500–1042* (London, 2nd ed., 1979)

Sawyer P.H. Sawyer (ed.), *Anglo-Saxon Charters: An Annotated List and Bibliography* (London, 1968); revised edn ed. S. Kelly available on the British Academy-Royal Historical Society Anglo-Saxon Charters website <www.trin.cam.ac.uk/chartwww>

Introduction: Reputations

1. *The Saga of Gunnlaug Serpent's Tongue*, in *English and Norse Documents Relating to the Reign of Ethelred the Unready*, ed. M.A. Ashdown (Cambridge, 1930), pp.190–5.

2. R.G. Poole, 'Verses and Prose in *Gunnlaugs Saga Ormstungu*', in *The Sagas of the Icelanders: A Book of Essays*, ed. J. Tucker (New York and London, 1989), pp.169–72 of 160–84. J. Jesch, 'Skaldic Verse in Scandinavian England', in *Vikings and the Danelaw: Select Papers from the Proceedings of the Thirteenth Viking Congress*, ed. J. Graham-Campbell, R. Hall, J. Jesch and D.N. Parsons (Oxford, 2001), p. 317 of pp.313–25

3. See the citation of Óttarr's *Hofudlausn* in R.G. Poole, 'In Search of the *Partar*', *Scandinavian Studies* 52 (1980), pp.264–77.

4. C. Plummer, *Two of the Anglo-Saxon Chronicles Parallel* (Oxford, 2 vols, 1892–99), vol.2, p.169, cited in Ashdown, *English and Norse Documents*, p.237.

5. Ashdown, *English and Norse Documents*, p.237. See also F. Barlow, *Edward the Confessor* (London, 1970), pp.6–7.

6. William of Malmesbury, *Gesta Regum Anglorum: The History of the English Kings*, vol.1, ed. R.A.B. Mynors with R.M. Thomson and M. Winterbottom (Oxford, 1998), pp.272–3.

7. J.R.R. Tolkien, *The Two Towers* (London, 3rd ed., 1974), p.164.

8. F.M. Stenton, *Anglo-Saxon England* (Oxford, 3rd ed., 1971), p.394.

9. Einhard, *The Life of Charlemagne*, in *Charlemagne's Courtier: the Complete Einhard*, ed. P.E. Dutton (Ontario, 1998), pp.16–17.

10. S.D. Keynes, 'A Tale of Two Kings: Alfred the Great and Æthelred the Unready', *Transactions of the Royal Historical Society* 5th series, 36 (1986), p.201 of pp.195–207.

11. The 'Abingdon' title actually comes from a manuscript which later used the annals for 980–1016.

12. S.D. Keynes, 'The Declining Reputation of Æthelred the Unready', in *Ethelred the Unready: Papers from the Millenary Conference*, ed. D. Hill (Oxford, 1978), p.239

of pp.227–53; William of Malmesbury, *Gesta Regum*, pp.276–7.

13. A. Campbell (ed.), *The Chronicle of Æthelweard* (Edinburgh, 1962), p.34.

14. A. Campbell, *Chronicle of Æthelweard*, p.xiii, n.2.

1: Kings, Kingship and the Kingdom of the English

1. J. Campbell, 'Observations on English Government from the Tenth Century to the Twelfth Century', *Transactions of the Royal Historical Society* 5th series 25 (1975), pp.39–54; 'The Late Anglo-Saxon State: A Maximum View', *Proceedings of the British Academy* 87 (1995 for 1994), pp.39–65; 'Some Agents and Agencies of the Late Anglo-Saxon State' in *Domesday Studies*, ed. J.C. Holt (Woodbridge, 1987), pp.201–218.

2. However, for the implementation of English political identity, see P. Wormald, '*Engla-Lond*: The Making of an Allegiance', *Journal of Historical Sociology* 7 (1994), pp.1–24.

3. See, for example, A. Williams, '*Princeps Merciorum Gentis*: The Family, Career and Connections of Ælfhere, Ealdorman of Mercia 956–83', *Anglo-Saxon England* 10 (1982), pp.143–72; *Land, Power and Politics: The Family and Career of Odda of Deerhurst* (Deerhurst, 1997); C. Hart, 'Athelstan "Half King" and his Family', *Anglo-Saxon England* 2 (1973), pp.115–44; C. Insley, 'One Wedding and Three Funerals: Politics and Kinship in Early Eleventh-Century Mercia', *Midland History* 25 (2000), pp.28–42 (I am grateful to Charles Insley for providing me with a copy of this paper before it went to press); R. Fletcher, *Bloodfeud: Murder and Revenge in Anglo-Saxon England* (London, 2002).

4. Wormald, '*Engla Lond*'.

5. See generally P. Stafford, *Unification and Conquest: A Political and Social History of England in the Tenth and Eleventh Centuries* (London, 1989), pp.162–79.

6. Anglo-Saxon Chronicle MS 'A' for 855. For a discussion of this, see E. John, 'The Point of Woden', *Anglo-Saxon Studies in Archaeology and History* 5 (1992), pp.127–34.

7. R.N. Quirk, 'Winchester New Minster and its Tenth-Century Tower', *Journal of the British Archaeological Association* 3rd series, 24 (1961), pp.38–9 of pp.16–54.

8. S. Trafford, 'Ethnicity, Migration Theory, and the Historiography of the Scandinavian Settlement of England', in *Cultures in Contact: Scandinavian Settlement in England in the Ninth and Tenth Centuries*, ed. D.M. Hadley and J.D. Richards (Turnhout, Belgium, 2000), pp.17–39. See also other papers in the same volume and D.M. Hadley, '"And they Proceeded to Plough and to Support Themselves": the Scandinavian Settlement of England', *Anglo-Norman Studies* 19 (1997 for 1996), pp.69–96; '"Cockle amongst the Wheat": The Scandinavian Settlement of England', in *Social Identity in Early Medieval Britain*, ed. W.O. Frazer and A. Tyrell (London, 2000), pp.111–35.

9. See, for example, Stafford, *Unification and Conquest*, p.157. For the *ealdormanries*, see Appendix 2.

10. M. Innes, 'Danelaw Identities: Ethnicity, Regionalism, and Political Allegiance', in *Cultures in Contact*, ed. Hadley and Richards, pp.78–83 of 65–88.

11. M. Locherbie-Cameron, 'The Men Named in the Poem', in *The Battle of Maldon, A.D.991*, ed. D. Scragg (Oxford, 1991), p.242 of pp.238–49.

12. D. Whitelock, 'The Dealings of the Kings of England with Northumbria', in *The Anglo-Saxons: Studies in Some Aspects of Their History and Culture Presented to Bruce Dickins*, ed. P. Clemoes (London, 1959), p.87 of pp.70–88; E. John, 'War and Society in the Tenth Century: The Maldon Campaign', *Transactions of the Royal Historical Society* 5th series, 27 (1977), p.188 of pp.173–95.

13. Wulfstan of Winchester, *Life of St Æthelwold*, ed. M. Lapidge and M. Winterbottom (Oxford, 1991), pp.22–5.

14. Stafford, *Unification and Conquest*, p.157. For one example of the development of the sphere of influence of the influential Midlands thegn, Wulfric 'Spott', see P.H. Sawyer (ed.), *Charters of Burton Abbey* (Oxford, 1979), pp.xxxviii–xlvii.

15. Translated in S.D. Keynes and M. Lapidge (eds), *Alfred the Great: Asser's Life of King Alfred and other Contemporary Sources* (Harmondsworth, 1983), pp.171–2 and notes, pp.311–13; for recent discussions, see R. Lavelle, 'Towards a Political Contextualization of Peacemaking and Peace Agreements in Anglo-Saxon England', in *Peace and Negotiation: Strategies for Co-existence in the Middle Ages and the Renaissance*, ed. D. Wolfthal (Turnhout, Belgium, 2000), pp.48–52 of 39–55; P.J.E. Kershaw, 'The Alfred-Guthrum Treaty: Scripting Accommodation and Interaction in Viking-Age England', in *Cultures in Contact*, ed. Hadley and Richards, pp.43–64.

16. For an introduction to these events, see R. Lavelle, 'Æthelwold of Wessex: "King of the Pagans"', *Osprey Military Journal* 2:6 (2000), pp.15–24; J. Campbell, 'What is not known about Edward the Elder', in *Edward the Elder, 899–924*, ed. N.J. Higham and D.H. Hill, (London, 2001), pp.12–23.

17. For suggested connections during the tenth century, see L. Abrams, 'The Anglo-Saxons and the Christianization of Scandinavia', *Anglo-Saxon England* 24 (1995), pp.213–49.

18. A.J. Robertson (ed.), *The Laws of the Kings of England from Edmund to Henry I* (Cambridge, 1925), pp.71–9.

19. See C.N.L. Brooke with G. Keir, *London, 800–1216: The Shaping of a City* (London, 1975), pp.258–75; for a summary of more recent research see A. Vince, 'London', in *The Blackwell Encyclopedia of Anglo-Saxon England*, ed. M. Lapidge, J. Blair, S.D. Keynes and D.G. Scragg (Oxford, 1999), pp.295–6.

20. See, for example, J.L. Nelson, 'The Political Ideas of Alfred of Wessex', in *Kings and Kingship in Medieval Europe*, ed. A. Duggan (London, 1993), pp.125–58; M. Wood, 'The Making of King Aethelstan's Empire: An English Charlemagne', in *Ideal and Reality in Frankish and Anglo-Saxon Society*, ed. P. Wormald, D. Bullough, and R. Collins (Oxford, 1983), pp.250–72.

21. For a contextualisation of Edmund's martyrdom, see I. McDougall, 'Serious Entertainments: An Examination of a Peculiar Type of Viking Atrocity', *Anglo-Saxon England* 22 (1993), pp.201–25.

22. See K. Leyser, 'The Ottonians and Wessex', in his *Communications and Power in Medieval Europe*, ed. T. Reuter (London, 1994), vol.1, pp.73–104.

23. Anglo-Saxon Chronicle 'C' MS for 982.

24. Rodulfus Glaber, *The Five Books of the Histories and the Life of St William*, ed. J. France, N. Bulst and P. Reynolds (Oxford, 1989); N.J. Higham, *The Death of Anglo-Saxon England* (Stroud, 1997), pp.31–2.

25. For an introduction to the Carolingian dynasty in the tenth century, which does not see an inevitable decline before 987, see R. McKitterick, *Frankish Kingdoms under the Carolingians, 751–987* (London, 1983), pp.305–36.

26. See the wills of King Eadred (Sawyer no.1515 [A.D.951x55]; *EHD* 1, pp.554–6) and the *aetheling* Athelstan (Sawyer no.1503 [A.D.1014]; *EHD* 1, pp.593–6).

27. P. Wormald, '*On þa Wæpnedhealfe*: Kingship and Royal Property from Æthelwulf to Edward the Elder', in *Edward the Elder, 899–924*, ed. N.J. Higham and D.H. Hill, (London, 2001), pp.264–79; R. Lavelle, *Royal Estates in Anglo-Saxon Wessex* (University of Southampton, PhD thesis, 2001).

28. Lavelle, *Royal Estates*.

29. Wormald, '*On pa Wæpnedhealfe*'; Keynes, *Alfred the Great*, pp.313–26.

30. P. Stafford, 'The Reign of Æthelred II: A Study in the Limitations on Royal Policy and Action', in *Ethelred the Unready*, ed. Hill, pp.19–21 of pp.15–46. See also her 'The "Farm of One Night" and the Organization of King Edward's Estates in Domesday', *Economic History Review* 33 (1980), pp. 491–502.

31. For a translation of *Rectitudines Singularum Personarum*, see D.C. Douglas (ed.) *English Historical Documents*, vol.2: 1042–1189 (London, 2nd ed., 1981), pp.875–9; for *Gerefa*, see P.V. Addyman, 'Archaeology and Anglo-Saxon Society', in *Problems in Economic and Social Archaeology*, ed. G. de G. Sieveking, I.H. Longworth and K.E. Wilson

(London, 1976), pp.318–19 of 309–22. See P.D.A. Harvey, '*Rectitudines Singularum Personarum* and *Gerefa*', *English Historical Review* 108 (1993), pp.1–22.

32. Sawyer no.359 (A.D. 900); Robertson, *Anglo-Saxon Charters*, pp.206–7. See R.P. Abels, *Alfred the Great: War, Kingship and Culture in Anglo-Saxon England* (London, 1998), pp.43–4.

33. J.A. Simpson and E.S.C. Weiner, *The Oxford English Dictionary* (Oxford, 2nd edn 20 vols, 1989), vol.5, pp.733–5.

34. See D.H. Hill, *An Atlas of Anglo-Saxon England* (Oxford, 1981), pp.85 and 87–91, for an initial illustration.

2: THE YOUNG *AETHELING* AND HIS FAMILY

1. *EHD* 1, p.228.

2. See, for example, *The Life of St Dunstan*, in *EHD* 1, p.902; *King Edgar's Establishment of Monasteries*, in *EHD* 1, p.920.

3. Wulfstan of Winchester, *The Life of St Æthelwold*, ed. M. Lapidge and M. Winterbottom (Oxford, 1991), pp.30–1 (for Aelfric's abbreviation, see a translation in *EHD* 1, p.907).

4. For example: Wulfstan, *Life of St Æthelwold*, pp.43–45; Aelfric, *Life of St Æthelwold*; *Life of St Oswald*, in *The Historians of the Church of York and its Archbishops*, ed. J. Raine (London, 3 vols, 1879–94), vol.1, pp.425–7; *Life of St Dunstan*, in *EHD* 1, p.902; *King Edgar's Establishment of Monasteries*, in *EHD* 1, pp.920–23.

5. T. Symons (ed.), *Regularis Concordia Anglicae Nationis Monachorum: the Monastic Agreement of the Monks and Nuns of the English Nation* (London, 1953), ch.3 (p.2). For the position of the King's wife in this, see P.A. Stafford, *Queen Emma and Queen Edith: Queenship and Women's Power in Eleventh-Century England* (Oxford, 1997), pp.62–4.

6. W.A. Chaney, *The Cult of Kingship in Anglo-Saxon England: the Transition from Paganism to Christianity* (Manchester, 1970), pp.251–2.

7. See, for example, R. Hamer, *A Choice of Anglo-Saxon Verse* (London, 1970), pp.25–9.

8. J.L. Nelson, 'The Second English *Ordo*', in her *Politics and Ritual in Early Medieval Europe* (London, 1986), p.367 of pp.361–74.

9. For the consecration and its attribution to Aelfthryth, see Nelson, 'Second English *Ordo*', pp.372–4.

10. Sawyer no.745, cited in Stafford, *Emma and Edith*, p.201, n.28.

11. See above, p.18.

12. T. Reuter, *Germany in the Middle Ages, 800–1056* (London, 1991), pp.148–9. See also the royal banquet in the *Life of St Oswald*, p.438.

13. R.R. Darlington, P. McGurk and J. Bray (eds), *The Chronicle of John of Worcester*, vol.2, *The Annals from 450 to 1066* (Oxford, 1995), for 973 (pp.422–5).

14. Translated in *EHD* 1, pp.434–7.

15. J. Barrow, 'Chester's Earliest Regatta? Edgar's Dee-Rowing Revisited', *Early Medieval Europe* 10 (2001), pp.81–93; D.E. Thornton, 'Edgar and the Eight Kings, A.D. 973: *Textus et Dramatis Personae*', *Early Medieval Europe* 10, pp.49–79; *Early Medieval Europe*.

For meetings on board ships, see R.G. Poole, *Viking Poems on War and Peace* (Toronto and London, 1991), p.73.

16. Sawyer, no. 566 (A.D. 955).

17. Whitelock, *EHD* 1, pp.226, n.3.

18. A. Murray, *Suicide in the Middle Ages*, vol.2, *The Curse on Self-Murder* (Oxford, 2000), pp.565–7.

19. M. Dolley, 'An Introduction to the Coinage of Aethelred', in *Ethelred the Unready*, ed. Hill, pp.117–18 of 115–33.

20. S. Jayakumar, 'Some "Foreign Policies" of Edgar "the Peaceable"', *Haskins Society Journal* 10 (forthcoming).

21. D.J. Schove, *A Chronology of Comets and Eclipses, AD 1–1000* (Woodbridge, 1986), p.297; I am grateful to Owen Brazell for correspondence on this and other astronomical phenomena during the reign of King Aethelred.

22. B. Yorke, 'Æthelwold and the Politics of the Tenth Century', in *Bishop Æthelwold: His Career and Influence*, ed. Yorke (Woodbridge, 1988), pp.81–6 of 65–88.

23. S.D. Keynes, *The Diplomas of King Æthelred 'The Unready', 978–1016: A Study in their use as Historical Evidence* (Cambridge, 1980), p.163.

24. See P. Stafford's citation of the *Life of St Wulfhilde*, in *Queens, Concubines and Dowagers: The King's Wife in the Early Middle Ages* (London, 1983), p.32.

25. For the use of repudiation in 'serial monogamy', see Stafford, *Queens, Concubines and Dowagers*, pp.74–5.

26. Keynes, *Diplomas*, p.164, citing S 745 (A.D. 966). Yorke, 'Æthelwold', pp.82–3, also considers this in terms of showing Aelfthryth's legitimacy.

27. Keynes, *Diplomas*, pp.130–4.

28. A. Williams, 'Some Notes and Considerations on Problems Connected with the English Royal Succession, 860–1066', *Anglo-Norman Studies* 1 (1979 for 1978), p.156 of pp.144–67, citing Chaney, *Cult of Kingship*, p.25.

29. See also Edmund Ironside's concerns in chapter 11 below; he had been born to a reigning King (Aethelred), yet he still feared being denied the kingdom.

30. For an introduction to William's early years, see D. Bates, *William the Conqueror* (Stroud, 2nd edn, 2001), pp.36–40; for William's establishment of his military reputation, see J. Gillingham, 'William the Bastard at War', in *Studies in Medieval History presented to R.. Allen Brown*, ed. C. Harper-Bill, C. Holdsworth and J.L. Nelson (Woodbridge, 1989), pp.141–58.

31. A point which should be suggested only in these endnotes, due to the questionable derivation of the bones of 'Edward the Martyr' is that the body's skull was of an elongated shape, from premature fusion of the sagittal suture. Such a condition could result from a hyperactive thyroid gland. This was a detail pointed out to me by Stephany Leach from reference to T.E.A. Stowell's article below (n.42). If these were indeed Edward's bones (it must be stressed that there is some question about this), it is possible that such a medical condition may give some explanation for Edward's bad temper.

32. Barbara Yorke, for one, suggests that some details may be 'derived from an informed source', even if

Byrhtferth has some obvious biases; 'Edward, King and Martyr: A Saxon Murder Mystery', in *Studies in the Early History of Shaftesbury Abbey*, ed. L. Keen (Dorchester, 1999), pp.101–2 of 99–116.

33. Keynes, *Diplomas*, pp.166–7.

34. However, cf D.J.V. Fisher, 'The Anti-Monastic Reaction in the Reign of Edward the Martyr', *Cambridge Historical Journal* 10 (1950–2), p.268 of pp.254–70, who considers this to be inaccurate.

35. Fisher, 'Anti-Monastic Reaction', p.255.

36. See Hart, 'Æthelstan "Half-King"', pp.134–5.

37. Yorke, 'Æthelwold', p.66. For Dunstan's archiepiscopal career, see N.P. Brooks, *The Early History of the Church of Canterbury: Christ Church from 597 to 1066* (Leicester, 1984), pp.243–50.

38. *EHD* 1, p.912.

39. Noted by Whitelock, *EHD* 1, p.914, n.8.

40. *Life of St Oswald*, p.446.

41. A. Williams, '*Princeps Merciorum Gentis*: the Family, Career and Connections of Ælfhere, Ealdorman of Mercia', *Anglo-Saxon England* 10 (1982) pp.165–9.

42. T.E.A. Stowell, 'The Bones of Edward the Martyr', *The Criminologist* 5 (1970), p.119 of pp.97–119.

43. See the Anglo-Saxon Chronicle MS 'E' for 1087 (William I) and 1100 (William II).

44. See J. Bond, 'Forests, Chases, Warrens and Parks in Medieval Wessex', in *The Medieval Landscape of Wessex*, ed. M. Aston and C. Lewis (Oxford, 1994), pp.115–58, especially 121–3.

45. Lavelle, *Royal Estates*.

46. I am grateful to Stephany Leach for her examination of Stowell's article, and the insights that current forensic archaeology can cast upon what may be a number of post-mortem fractures.

47. S.D. Keynes, 'King Alfred the Great and Shaftesbury Abbey', in *Studies in the Early History of Shaftesbury Abbey*, ed. Keen, p.55 of pp.17–72.

48. Anglo-Saxon Chronicle 'D' MS for 979.

49. D.W. Rollason, 'The Cults of Murdered Royal Saints in Anglo-Saxon England', *Anglo-Saxon England* 11 (1983), pp.18–22 of 1–22.

50. Yorke, 'Edward', pp.100–1.

51. Below, p.83–5.

52. Keynes, *Diplomas* p.174, n.82.

53. Keynes, p.175, *Diplomas* n.83, citing Sawyer no.835.

54. Keynes, *Diplomas*, p.175, n.84.

55. Stafford, 'Reign of Æthelred II', especially pp.17 and 24–6.

56. Anglo-Saxon Chronicle for 899/900; see Lavelle, 'Æthelwold of Wessex'; Campbell, 'What is Not Known about the Reign of Edward the Elder'.

57. Brooks, *Early History*, p.250.

58. Keynes, *Diplomas*, pp.176–86.

59. William of Malmesbury, *Life of Dunstan*, in *Memorials of St Dunstan*, ed. W. Stubbs (London, 1874), pp.313–14, cited by Keynes, *Diplomas*, pp.180–1.

60. Stafford, 'Reign of Æthelred II', p.27.

61. Osbern, *Life of Dunstan*, in *Memorials of St Dunstan*, ed. Stubbs, p.117.

3: THE BEGINNING OF THE SECOND VIKING AGE

1. Keynes, 'Tale of Two Kings', p.201.

2. However, for the attribution of Halley's Comet to 995, see below, p.94.

3. For example, John, 'War and Society', p.173.

4. Goda may appear as a *Minister* (a thegn or servant) in the witness list to S 838 (A.D. 981), a West Country charter.

5. S.D. Keynes, 'The Historical Context of the Battle of Maldon', in *Battle of Maldon*, ed. Scragg, p.86 of pp.81–113.

6. On the basis of a victory by Byrhtnoth in the twelfth-century *Liber Eliensis* (translated by A. Kennedy, 'Byrhtnoth's Obits and Twelfth-Century Accounts of the Battle of Maldon', in *Battle of Maldon*, ed. Scragg, pp.66–8 of 59–78) and the *Life of St Oswald's* rhetorical flourishes of English resistance (*EHD*, p.917), John also suggests that the Vikings had been defeated at Maldon in 988 as well as in 991 ('War and Society', pp.185–9; *Reassessing Anglo-Saxon England* (Manchester, 1996), pp.143–4). If we accept that the *Life of St Oswald* is simply exaggerating Byrhtnoth's achievement with a posthumous glow, then this leaves only the *Liber Eliensis* to indicate a battle at Maldon in 988. However, despite a eulogy of Ealdorman Byrhtnoth's status of near-hagiographical proportions, John is probably right to place the Maldon battle in the context of a wider campaign in 991, discussed here in chapter 5.

7. John, 'War and Society', pp.173–4.

8. N.J. Higham, *The Death of Anglo-Saxon England* (Stroud, 1997), p.19.

9. Keynes, 'Historical Context', pp.85–6; For attacks on Wales, see D.E. Thornton, 'Maredidd ab Owain (d. 999): the Most Famous King of the Welsh', *Welsh History Review* 18 (1996–97), pp. 572–3 of 567–91.

10. D. Ó Corráin, 'Ireland, Wales, Man, and the Hebrides', in *The Oxford Illustrated History of the Vikings* (Oxford, 1997), pp.100–1 of pp.83–109. For the economic context, see P. Holm, 'The Slave Trade of Dublin, Ninth to Twelfth Centuries', *Peritia* 6 (1986), pp.317–45, especially 331–4.

11. Glaber, *Histories*, pp.36–7; see D. Bates, *Normandy before 1066* (London, 1982), especially pp.2–38.

12. *EHD* 1, pp.894–5.

13. P.H. Sawyer, *The Age of the Vikings* (London, 2nd edn, 1971), p.203.

14. John, 'War and Society', p.190.

15. Sawyer no.1515 (A.D. 951 x55); translated in *EHD* 1, pp.554–6.

16. *Chronicle of Æthelweard*, p.54.

17. Sawyer no.832 (A.D. 977); *EHD* 1, pp.566–7.

4: EARLY MEDIEVAL SCANDINAVIA: VIKINGS AND STATES

1. N. Lund, 'Scandinavia, *c.*700–1066', in *The New Cambridge Medieval History*, vol.2, *c.700–c.900*, ed. R. McKitterick (Cambridge, 1995), p.215 of pp.202–27.

2. See generally K. Randsborg, *The Viking Age in Denmark: the Formation of a State* (London, 1980).

3. Adam of Bremen, *History of the Archbishops of Hamburg-Bremen*, ed. F.J. Tschan (New York, 1959), p.57.

4. Lund, 'Scandinavia', p.217; Lund also discusses this in his 'The Danish Empire and the End of the Viking Age' in *The Oxford Illustrated History of the Vikings*, ed. P.H. Sawyer (Oxford, 1997), pp.163–5 of 156–81.

5. Adam of Bremen, *History of the Archbishops*, p.56.

6. Adam of Bremen, *History of the Archbishops*, pp.61–2.

7. Lund, 'Scandinavia', pp.217–18; 'The Danish Empire', pp.164–5.

8. Cf Reuter, *Germany in the Early Middle Ages*, p.165, who largely considers the Danish acceptance of Christianity to have been subject to German imperial ambitions.

9. Lund, 'Scandinavia', p.218.

10. K.J. Krogh, 'The Royal Viking-Age Monuments at Jelling in the Light of Recent Archaeological Excavations', *Acta Archaeologica* 53 (1982), pp.183–216.

11. Lund, 'Scandinavia', p.218.

12. Roesdahl, *Viking Age Denmark*, pp.47–9.

13. Roesdahl, *Viking Age Denmark*, pp.141–6.

14. E. Roesdahl, 'The Danish Geometric Viking Fortresses and their Context', *Anglo-Norman Studies* 11 (1987 for 1986), p.209 of pp.208–26.

15. *Jomsviking Saga*, in *English and Norse Documents*, ed. Ashdown, p.187.

16. P.H. Blair, *Introduction to Anglo-Saxon England* (Cambridge, 1956), p.93. See also E. John, 'War and Society', pp.175–6.

17. See the argument presented by D.M. Wilson, 'Danish Kings and England in the Late Tenth and Early Eleventh Centuries: Economic Interpretations', *Anglo-Norman Studies* 3 (1981 for 1980), pp.188–96.

18. Lund, 'Danish Perspective', pp.134–7.

19. Adam of Bremen, *History of the Archbishops*, p.72.

20. Lund, 'Scandinavia', p.219.

21. However, cf N. Lund, 'The Danish Perspective', in *Battle of Maldon*, ed. Scragg, p.138 of pp.114–42.

22. Thietmar, *Chronicon*, in *Ottonian Germany: the Chronicon of Thietmar of Merseburg*, ed. D.A. Warner (Manchester, 2001), p.168.

23. Saywer, *Age of the Vikings*, pp.117–18; see generally pp.86–119.

24. A. Binns, 'The Ships of the Vikings: Were they "Viking Ships"?', in *Proceedings of the Eighth Viking Congress*, ed. H. Bekker-Nielson (Odense, 1981), pp.287–94.

25. See J. Bill, 'Ships and Seamanship', in *Oxford Illustrated History of the Vikings*, ed. Sawyer, pp.189–90 of 182–201.

26. For discussion of this, see N.A.M. Rodger, 'Cnut's Geld and the Size of Danish Ships', *English Historical Review* 110 (1995), pp.392–403.

27. O. Olsen, *Five Viking Ships at Roskilde Fjord* (Copenhagen, 1990).

28. Bill, 'Ships and Seamanship', pp.191–2.

29. For a preliminary report, see H.M. Myrhøj and M. Gøthche, 'The Roskilde Ships', in *Maritime Archaeology Newsletter* 8 (1997), available at <www.natmus.dk/nmf/nb/8/english/>.

5: ENGLISH AND VIKINGS AT WAR: THE BATTLE OF MALDON

1. R. Woolf, 'The Ideal of Men Dying with their Lord in the *Germania* and in *The Battle of Maldon*', *Anglo-Saxon England* 5 (1976), pp.63–81; R. Frank, 'The Ideal of Men Dying with their Lord in *The Battle of Maldon*: Anachronism or *Nouvelle Vague*?', in *People and Places in Northern Europe, 500–1600: Essays in Honour of Peter Hayes Sawyer*, ed. I. Wood and N. Lund (Woodbridge, 1991), pp.95–106. One source of controversy was the resemblance to the first-century reference by Tacitus that to survive a chief's death on the battlefield led to 'lifelong infamy and shame'; *Germania*, in *Tacitus: The Agricola and the Germania*, ed. H. Mattingley (Harmondsworth, 1970), p.113.

2. D. Scragg, 'The Battle of Maldon', in *Battle of Maldon*, ed. Scragg, p.32 of pp.15–36.

3. Scragg, 'Battle of Maldon', pp.34–5.

4. See Lund, 'Danish Perspective', p.132.

5. Lund, 'Danish Perspective', pp.137–8. For Swein's apparent exile, see Adam of Bremen, *History of the Bishops of Hamburg-Bremen*, pp.77–8.

6. Lund, 'Danish Perspective', p.133, citing Saywer no.939 (A.D. 995 x9); *EHD* 1, pp.579–80.

7. Sawyer, *Age of the Vikings*, p.126.

8. Here a useful argument will be found in G.R. Halsall's chapter 'Into Battle' in his forthcoming study of *Warfare in the Barbarian West*. In the meantime, it is best to refer to the appearance of horses amongst the war-gear (*heregeat* or *heriot*) given to kings by nobles in late Anglo-Saxon wills: this is explicit appearances of war-gear in the wills, and yet the horses included are too often merely dismissed as forms of transport. In Wulfric's will (Sawyer no.1536 (A.D. 1002 x4); D. Whitelock, *Anglo-Saxon Wills* (Cambridge, 1930), pp.46–51), there is mention of four horses 'two saddled and two unsaddled, and the weapons which are due with them'. Equally, Wulfsige's will (Sawyer no.1537 (A.D. 1022 x43); Whitelock, *Anglo-Saxon Wills*, p.74): horses with armour and weapons to the royal lord and his nephews; For Wulfgeat's will (Sawyer no.1534 (A.D. 1000?); Whitelock, *Anglo-Saxon Wills*, pp.54–7) there is distinction between 'horses', 'mares' and 'colts', amongst which is a mention of weapons; selective breeding seems to have been taking place. Thurstan's will (Sawyer no.1531 (A.D. 1043 x45); Whitelock, *Anglo-Saxon Wills*, pp.80–5) may suffer from Dorothy Whitelock's translation: 'two horses *with* trappings and a helmet and a coat of mail' may be better rendered as 'two horses *and* trappings and helmet and mail', which would place the horses in the context of the war-gear, not as a separate entity. Ketel (Sawyer no.1519 (A.D. 1052 x66); Whitelock, *Anglo-Saxon Wills*, pp.88–91) has a great deal of gear associated with the horse included in the midst of a list of weapons, suggesting that the horse and its gear was thought of as a weapon by their Anglo-Saxon users. Just because there was no use of the word *destrier* in Old English did not mean that there was no use of horses on the pre-Conquest battlefield. For

comments on the wills providing evidence of Anglo-Saxon warhorses, see A. Hyland, *The Medieval Warhorse: From Byzantium to the Crusades* (Stroud, 1994), pp.76–9.

9. J.R.R. Tolkien, 'The Homecoming of Beorhtnoth, Beorhthelm's Son', *Essays and Studies of the English Association* new series 6 (1953), pp.1–18. For more recent criticisms of an apparent lack of military equipment, see N.P. Brooks, 'Weapons and Armour', in *Battle of Maldon*, ed. Scragg, pp.208–19.

10. John, 'War and Society', p.190.

11. *EHD* 1, p.917.

12. Anglo-Saxon Chronicle MS 'D' for 1066.

6: RULING THE KINGDOM

1. Keynes has suggested that the years from *c*.993 to 1006 were 'the years of maturity' for King Aethelred; Keynes, p.197.

2. 'The Dane-Geld (980–1016)', in C.R.L. Fletcher and R. Kipling, *A School History of England* (Oxford, 1911); reprinted in R. Kipling, *Rudyard Kipling's verse: Definitive Edition* (London, 1940), pp.712–13.

3. P. Stafford, 'Historical Implications of the Regional Production of Dies under Æthelred II', *British Numismatic Journal* 48 (1980), pp.45–7 of 35–51.

4. J. Gillingham, '"The Most Precious Jewel in the English Crown": Levels of Danegeld and Heregeld in the Early Eleventh Century', *English Historical Review* 104 (1989), pp.373–84; cf M.K. Lawson, 'The Collection of Danegeld and Heregeld in the Reigns of Aethelred II and Cnut', *English Historical Review* 99 (1984), pp.721–38 and Lawson's later response, 'Danegeld and Heregeld Once More', *English Historical Review* 105 (1990), p.951–61.

5. Sawyer no.882 (A.D. 994 x5); *EHD* 1, pp.569–70.

6. N. Lund, 'Peace and Non-Peace in the Viking Age: Ottar in Biarmaland, the Rus in Byzantium, and Danes and Norwegians in England', in *Proceedings of the Tenth Viking Congress: Larkollen, Norway, 1985*, ed. J.E. Knirk (Oslo, 1987), pp.264–8 of pp.255–69.

7. J.A. Green, 'The Last Century of Danegeld', *English Historical Review* 96 (1981), pp.241–58.

8. I am grateful to Richard Abels for discussion on this point.

9. R.P. Abels, 'King Alfred's Peace-Making Strategies with the Vikings', *Haskins Society Journal* 3 (1992), pp.23–34.

10. Sawyer, *Age of the Vikings*, p.118.

11. See N. Hooper, 'Some Observations on the Navy in Late Anglo-Saxon England', in *Studies in Medieval History*, ed. Harper-Bill *et al.*, pp.203–13.

12. M. Dolley, 'An Introduction to the Coinage of Æthelraed II', in *Ethelred the Unready*, ed. Hill, pp.115–33.

13. Dolley, 'Introduction', p.127.

14. For these 'Emergency *Burhs*', see D.H. Hill, 'Trends in the Development of Towns during the Reign of Ethelred II', in *Ethelred the Unready*, ed. Hill, pp.223–5 of 213–26. L. Alcock, *Cadbury Castle, Somerset: the Early Medieval Archaeology* (Cardiff, 1995), pp.44–62.

15. Lund, 'Danish Perspective'.

16. Anderson. 'The Viking Policy of Ethelred the Unready', in *Anglo-Scandinavian England: Norse-English Relations in the Period before the Conquest*, ed. J.D. Niles and M. Amodio (London, 1989) pp.7–10 of 1–11.

17. Sawyer, 'Ethelred II, Olaf Tryggvason, and the Conversion of Norway', in *Anglo-Scandinavian England*, ed. Niles and Amodio, p.17 of pp.17–24.

18. For a discussion of this political manifestation of conversion, see N.J. Higham, *The Convert Kings: Power and Religious Affiliation in Early Anglo-Saxon England* (Manchester, 1997).

19. *EHD* 1, pp.571–80; for the question of 'feudal anarchy', see T.N. Bisson, 'The "Feudal Revolution"', *Past and Present* 142 (1994), pp.6–42 and D. Barthélemy *et al.*, 'Debate: the "Feudal Revolution"', *Past and Present* 152 (1996), pp.196–223 and 155 (1997), pp.177–225.

20. S.D. Keynes, 'Crime and Punishment in the Reign of King Æthelred the Unready', in *People and Places*, ed. Wood and Lund, p.77 of pp.67–81.

21. Keynes, 'Crime and Punishment', pp.72–3.

22. M.P. Richards, 'Anglo-Saxonism in the Old English Laws', in *Anglo-Saxonism and the Construction of Social Identity*, ed. A.J. Frantzen and J.D. Niles (Gainesville, Florida, 1997) p.53 of pp.40–59.

23. P. Wormald, *The Making of English Law: King Alfred to the Twelfth Century*, vol.1, *Legislation and its Limits* (Oxford, 1999), p.328.

24. *III Aethelred* §8 (*EHD* 1, p.441).

25. Wormald, *Making of English Law*, pp.324–5.

26. Wormald, *Making of English Law*, p.329.

27. Keynes, 'Crime and Punishment', pp.77–8.

28. Sawyer no.883 (A.D. 995); *EHD* 1, pp.571–2.

29. Sawyer no.939 (A.D. 995 x9); *EHD* 1, pp.579–80.

30. Sawyer no.877 (A.D. 993 for 996); *EHD* 1, p.575.

31. P.A. Stafford, 'The Laws of Cnut and the History of Royal Promises', *Anglo-Saxon England* 10 (1983), pp.189–90 of 173–90. See P. Wormald, 'Aethelred the Lawmaker', in *Ethelred the Unready*, ed. Hill, p.65 of pp.47–80.

7: FAMILY DYNAMICS

1. Higham, *The Death of Anglo-Saxon England* (Stroud, 1997), pp.26–7.

2. Stafford, *Queen Emma and Queen Edith*, p.85; Barlow, *Edward the Confessor*, p.26; cf P.H. Sawyer, *From Roman Britain to Norman England* (London, 1978), p.126, who notes that Aethelred named his sons after kings of the English rather than following the order of the dynasty.

3. For Aelfgifu's survival into the late 990s, by which time the *aethelings* Eadwig and Edgar were born, see Keynes, *Diplomas*, p.187, n.118, although Stafford, *Queen Emma and Queen Edith*, p.66, n.3, has suggested that Aelfgifu may have been one of two wives before the appearance of Emma.

4. Stafford, *Emma and Edith*, p.216.

5. C.E. Fell (ed.), *Edward King and Martyr* (Leeds, 1971), p.7, cited by Yorke, 'Edward, King and Martyr', p.101.

6. Asser, *Life of Alfred*, in *Alfred the Great*, ed. Keynes

and Lapidge, p.108.

7. Fell (ed.), *Edward King and Martyr*, pp.4–6. See Yorke, 'Edward, King and Martyr', pp.100–1 and C.E. Fell, 'Edward King and Martyr and the Anglo-Saxon Hagiographical Tradition', in *Ethelred the Unready*, pp.1–13, especially p.11.

8. William of Malmesbury, *Gesta Regum*, pp.256–9.

9. As a chivalric tale, see P. Stafford, *Queens, Concubines and Dowagers: The King's Wife in the Early Middle Ages* (London, 1983), p.21. See Sarah Foot's comments on the origins of Wherwell Abbey in her *Veiled Women*, vol.2, *Female Religious Communities in England, 871–1066* (Aldershot, 2000), pp.215–19.

10. Yorke, 'Æthelwold', p.86.

11. For the closeness of this relationship, see Yorke, 'Æthelwold', pp.81–6.

12. R. Deshman, '*Christus Rex et Magi Regis*: Kingship and Christology in Ottonian and Anglo-Saxon Art', *Frümittelalterliche Studien* 10 (1976), p.398 of pp.367–405.

13. P. Stafford, 'The King's Wife in Wessex, 800–1066', *Past and Present* 91 (1981), p.7 of pp.3–27.

14. Sawyer no.1503 (A.D. 1014); *EHD* 1, p.596.

15. Sawyer no.904 (A.D. 1001).

16. *Dene* was bequeathed to Alfred's younger son in his will (Sawyer no.1507; Keynes and Lapidge (eds), *Alfred the Great*, p.175), suggest that it was intended to remain in royal hands.

17. See B. Dickins, 'The Day of the Battle of *Æthelingadene* (ASC 1001 A)', *Leeds Studies in English* 6 (1937), pp.25–7.

18. Land at Beddington in Surrey had been granted to the Bishop of Winchester in the ninth century, who complained when he was forced to lease it back to King Edward the Elder that a lot of effort had to be put into restocking the land. Sawyer no.1444 (A.D. 900 x9); *EHD* 1, pp.543–4.

19. For its strategic importance, see R. Fleming, 'Domesday Estates of the King and the Godwines: a Study in Late Saxon Politics', *Speculum* 58 (1983), p.1001 of pp.987–1007.

20. Keynes, *Diplomas*, p.187, n.117, admits to being 'tempted to suggest' that it was at *Aethelingadene* where Aelfthryth raised the young *aethelings*; it is a reasonable suggestion, in view of the fact that there is an absence of evidence for an 'institutionalised' relationship between queen-mothers and *aethelings*.

21. See, for example, D. Rollason, *Saints and Relics in Anglo-Saxon England* (Oxford, 1989), pp.196–214.

22. For the importance of popular cults, see C. Cubitt, 'Sites and Sanctity: Revisiting the Cult of Murdered and Martyred Anglo-Saxon Royal Saints', *Early Medieval Europe* 9 (2000), pp.53–83.

23. Keynes, 'King Alfred the Great and Shaftesbury Abbey', pp.50–1.

24. S. Ridyard, *The Royal Saints of Anglo-Saxon England: A Study of West Saxon and East Anglian Cults* (Oxford, 1988), pp.154–71. See also Keynes, *Diplomas*, pp.163–74 and for the emphasis on the two phases of Edward's promotion, A. Thacker, 'Saint-Making and Relic Collecting by Oswald and his Communities', in *St Oswald of Worcester: Life and Influence*, ed. N.P. Brooks and C. Cubitt (London,

1996), p.266 of pp.244–68.

25. Rollason, 'Cults of Murdered Royal Saints', pp.17–18.

26. Cubitt, 'Sites and Sanctity', pp.53–83.

27. Barlow, *Edward the Confessor*, p.29, suggests that Edward cannot have been born before 1005, as he does not appear in charter witness lists of 1004. However, should we necessarily assume that it was as easy to bring a newly born son to a meeting of the *witan* in Aethelred's reign as it had been during the reign of Edgar, which is the period of precedence for the recording of the presence of royal infants?

28. Barlow, *Edward the Confessor*, p.26; Sawyer, *Roman Britain to Norman England*, p.126.

29. C. Clark, 'Onomastics', in *The Cambridge History of the English Language*, ed. N. Blake (Cambridge, 1992), pp.551–2, cited in Williams, *Land, Power and Politics*, p.6.

30. E. Searle, 'Emma the Conqueror', in *Studies in Medieval History*, ed. Harper-Bill *et al.*, pp.284–5 of 281–8.

31. The post-1066 Anglo-Saxon Chronicle 'F' MS addition to the 1002 annal names her 'Ymma' (Emma), but in charter witness lists and documents emphasising her 'English' identity, she is known as Aelfgifu; this has led (arguably anachronistically) to her historical identification as Aelfgifu-Emma. See Stafford, *Queen Emma and Queen Edith*, p.ix.

32. This was suggested by C.E. Karkov in her paper 'Emma/Ælfgyfu and the Reader's Desire' at the *International Medieval Congress*, held at the University of Leeds, 11 July, 2001.

33. For the importance of such immunities, see B.H. Rosenwein, *Negotiating Space: Power, Restraint, and the Privileges of Immunity in Early Medieval Europe* (Ithaca, N.Y., 1999).

34. See above, p.44.

35. For friendly relations between Wessex and Mercia, see S.D. Keynes 'King Alfred and the Mercians', in *Kings, Currency and Alliances: History and Coinage of Southern England in the Ninth Century*, ed. M.A.S. Blackburn and D.N. Dumville (Woodbridge, 1998), pp.1–45.

36. For the Pope's reconciliation of England and Normandy in 991, *EHD* 1, pp.894–5. For later relations, see Bates, *Normandy before 1066*, p.37.

37. See Stenton, *Anglo-Saxon England*, p.379; although he admits that this could not have been foreseen, the very fact that this is addressed is a concession to historical determinism.

38. Stafford, *Queen Emma and Queen Edith*, pp.7–8.

8: MILLENNIUM AND APOCALYPSE: THE POLITICS OF FEAR AND AGGRESSION

1. G. Duby, *L'An Mil* (Paris, 1967).

2. R. Landes, 'Between Aristocracy and Heresy: Popular Participation in the Limousin Peace of God', in *The Peace of God: Social Violence and Religious Response in France around the Year 1000*, ed. T. Head and R. Landes (Ithaca, N.Y., 1992) p.188 of pp.184–218.

3. The most comprehensive survey of Anglo-Saxon

cereal diets is an unpublished thesis by Deborah Banham, *The Knowledge and Uses of Food Plants in Anglo-Saxon England* (University of Cambridge PhD thesis, 1990), but see also her entry on 'Food and Drink' in the *Blackwell Encyclopedia of Anglo-Saxon England*, ed. M. Lapidge et al., pp.190–1 and A. Hagen, *A Handbook of Anglo-Saxon Food: Processing and Consumption* (Pinner, 1992).

4. See John France's comments on the millenarianism in Glaber, *Histories*, pp.lxiii–lxx.

5. For France, see generally papers in Head and Landes (eds), *Peace of God*. For millenarianism in an English context, see P. Wormald, 'Archbishop Wulfstan and the Holiness of Society', in *Anglo-Saxon History: Basic Readings*, ed. D.A.E. Pelteret (New York, 2000), pp.191–224; M. Godden, 'Apocalypse and Invasion in Late Anglo-Saxon England', in *From Anglo-Saxon to Early Middle English: Studies presented to E.G. Stanley*, ed. M. Godden, D. Gray and T. Hoad (Oxford, 1994), pp.130–62; P. Stafford, 'Church and Society in the Age of Aelfric', in *The Old English Homily and its Backgrounds*, ed. P.E. Szarmach and B.F. Huppé (Albany, N.Y., 1978), pp.11–42.

6. Sawyer, *The Age of the Vikings*, p.137.

7. E. John, 'War and Society', p.173.

8. A useful methodology for this study is presented by S. Coupland, 'The Rod of God's Wrath or the People of God's Wrath? The Carolingian Theology of the Viking Invasions', *Journal of Ecclesiastical History* 42 (1991), pp.535–54; however, for later Anglo-Saxon England, see Godden, 'Apocalypse and Invasion'.

9. See generally R.I. Page, 'A Most Vile People': Early English Historians on the Vikings (London, 1987).

10. Thietmar, *Chronicon*, p.337.

11. Suggested by Schove, *Chronology of Eclipses and Comets*, pp. xxxii and 297, to have been deliberately misrecorded under the annal for 995.

12. Glaber, *Histories*, pp.110–11.

13. Glaber, *Histories*, p.111.

14. S.D. Keynes, 'The Vikings in England, *c*.790–1016', in *Oxford Illustrated History of the Vikings*, pp.74–5 of 48–82.

15. Lund, 'Danish Perspective', p.140.

16. Whitelock, *EHD* 1, p.222, n.2.

17. This is a theme brought out in Keynes, *Diplomas*.

18. John of Worcester, *Chronicle*, pp.450–1.

19. Sawyer no.898 (A.D. 1001).

20. E.M.C. van Houts (ed.), *The Gesta Normannorum Ducum of William of Jumièges, Orderic Vitalis and Robert of Torigni* (Oxford, 1995), pp.10–15.

21. Bates, *Normandy before 1066*, p.37.

22. J.L. Nelson, 'England and the Continent in the Anglo-Saxon Period', in *England in Europe, 1066–1453*, ed. N. Saul (London, 1994), p.31 of pp.21–35, although Eleanor Searle has noted that Richard II, Duke of Normandy, held land in this region; 'Emma the Conqueror', p.284 and n.16 of pp.281–8.

23. John, 'War and Society', pp.190–1.

24. Cited by M. Magnusson, *Vikings!* (London, 1980), pp.271–2. See also William of Malmesbury, *Gesta Regum*, pp.300–1; Henry of Huntingdon, *Historia*

Anglorum: The History of the English People, ed. D.E. Greenway (Oxford, 1996), pp.340–1.

25. A. Williams, 'Cockles amongst the Wheat: Danes and English in the Western Midlands in the First Half of the Eleventh Century', *Midland History* 11 (1986), p.14 of pp.1–22.

26. Such a calculation can be undertaken with <www.earth.com/calendar>.

27. J. Wilcox, 'The St. Brice's Day Massacre and Archbishop Wulfstan', in *Peace and Negotiation*, ed. Wolfthal, p.84 of pp.79–91.

28. Sawyer no.909 (A.D. 1004); *EHD* 1, pp.590–3.

29. Keynes, *Diplomas*, p.204 suggests that they may also have been mercenaries in employment or paid-off and settled Vikings.

30. J. Blair, *Anglo-Saxon Oxfordshire* (Stroud, 1994), pp.167–8.

31. Blair, *Anglo-Saxon Oxfordshire*, p.168.

32. J. Campbell, 'England, France, Flanders and Germany: Some Comparisons and Connections', in *Ethelred the Unready*, ed. Hill, p.260 of pp.255–70.

33. Stenton, *Anglo-Saxon England*, p.380.

34. Campbell, 'England, France, Flanders and Germany', p.260. Wilcox, 'St. Brice's Day Massacre', pp.85–6, attempts to deconstruct the process from decision-making to massacre. See also Henry of Huntingdon, *Historia Anglorum*, pp.340–1, who refers to 'secret letters' sent to every city.

35. D.M. Metcalf makes a similar point in 'The Ranking of the Boroughs: Numismatic Evidence from the Reign of Æthelred II', in *Ethelred 'The Unready'*, ed. Hill, p.172 of pp.159–212.

36. B. Sawyer and P.H. Sawyer, *Medieval Scandinavia: From Conversion to Reformation* (Minneapolis and London, 1993), pp.100–12.

37. For a consideration of the dynamics at work in the contact between 'popular' and 'formal' religion in late Anglo-Saxon England, see generally K. Jolly, *Popular Religion in Late Saxon England: Elf Charms in Context* (Chapel Hill and London, 1996).

38. See R.I. Moore, *The Formation of a Persecuting Society: Power and Deviance in Western Europe, 950–1250* (Oxford, 1987), especially pp.13–19, although he does not address events in England in this period.

39. However, cf Wilcox, 'St. Brice's Day Massacre', pp.90–1, who suggests that Wulfstan was willing to include 'assimilated Danish people' within his 'protective net of an ordered Christian community', at least in the years that followed 1002.

9: DEFEATS, RESISTANCE... AND FAILURE?

1. William of Jumièges, *Gesta Normannorum Ducum*, pp.15–19.

2. Implied by Van Houts; *Gesta Normannorum Ducum*, p.17, n.3.

3. Stafford, *Queen Emma and Queen Edith*, pp.7–8.

4. Halsall, *Warfare in the Barbarian West*.

5. Campbell, 'Observations on English Government'. See chapter 1, above.

6. Higham, *Death of Anglo-Saxon England*, p.27.

7. Keynes, *Diplomas*, p.208, n.199.

8. See chapter 2, above.

9. Cited by Stafford, *Queen Emma and Queen Edith*, p.92, n.118. The marriage does not seem unlikely, Aethelred similarly used another daughter, Aelfgifu, to draw Uhtred of Northumbria into the royal fold.

10. Cf Keynes, *Diplomas*, pp.199 and 208.

11. Poole, *Viking Poems*, pp.113 and 115.

12. C.J. Morris, *Marriage and Murder in Eleventh-Century Northumbria: a Study of 'De Obsessione Dunelmi'* (York, 1992), contains a translation: pp.1–2 of 1–5. A.J. Reynolds, *Anglo-Saxon Law in the Landscape: An Archaeological Study of the Old English Judicial System* (University of London, PhD thesis, 1999) contains a useful study of executions in later Anglo-Saxon society.

13. Morris, *Marriage and Murder*; Fletcher, *Bloodfeud*. However, for reservations on the nature of 'feud' see G.R. Halsall, 'Reflections on Early Medieval Violence: the Example of the "Blood Feud"', *Memoria y Civilización* 2 (1999), pp.7–29.

14. B. Meehan, 'The Siege of Durham, the Battle of Carham and the Cession of Lothian', *Scottish Historical Review* 55 (1976), pp.1–19; this is in spite of the *De Obsessione's* drastic mistake of ascribing the events of 1006 to 969.

15. For these, see C.P. Lewis, 'The Early Earls of Norman England', *Anglo-Norman Studies* 13 (1991 for 1990), pp.207–23.

16. Uhtred is recorded in the witness lists to Sawyer nos921 (A.D. 1009), 922 (A.D. 1009), 926 (A.D. 1012), 931 (A.D. 1013), 933 (A.D. 1014), 934 (A.D. 1015).

17. Stafford, *Queen Emma and Queen Edith*, p.92, n.118.

18. See Rodger, 'Cnut's Geld and the Size of Ships'.

19. Gillingham, 'William the Bastard at War'; 'Richard I and the Science of War in the Middle Ages', in *War and Government in the Middle Ages*, ed. J. Gillingham and J.C. Holt (Woodbridge, 1984), pp.78–91. See also R.P. Abels, 'English Logistics and Military Administration, 871–1066: the Impact of the Viking Wars', in *Military Aspects of Scandinavian Society in a European Perspective, A.D. 1–1300*, ed. A.N. Jørgensen and B.L. Clausen (Copenhagen, 1997), p.263 of pp.257–65.

20. Abels, 'English Logistics and Military Administration', p.263.

21. For the difficulties of a single operation across a much narrower body of water in 1066, see C. Gillmor, 'Naval Logistics of the Cross-Channel Operation, 1066', *Anglo-Norman Studies* 7 (1985 for 1984), pp.114–28.

22. Keynes, *Diplomas*, pp.210-12; Stafford, 'Reign of Æthelred II', p.33.

23. G.R. Halsall, 'Anthropology and the Study of Pre-Conquest Warfare and Society: The Ritual War in Anglo-Saxon England', in *Weapons and Warfare in Anglo-Saxon England*, ed. S.C. Hawkes (Oxford, 1989), p.166 of pp.155–77.

24. Page, *'A Most Vile People'*, pp.27–8, sees it as an act of daring and heroic behaviour on the part of the Vikings.

25. A.J. Reynolds, *Later Anglo-Saxon England: Life and Landscape* (Stroud, 1999), p.95.

26. Bede, *Ecclesiastical History of the English* People, ed. B.

27. Colgrave (Oxford, 1969), II.9, pp.164-5.

27. Keynes, 'Declining Reputation', p.234, suggests that it is ironic.

28. See generally D.H. Hill and S. Sharp, 'An Anglo-Saxon Beacon System', in *Names, Places and People: An Onomastic Miscellany for John McNeal Dodgson*, ed. A.R. Rumble and A.D. Mills (Stamford, 1997), pp.157–65; Reynolds, *Late Anglo-Saxon England*, pp.92–6.

29. B. Yorke, 'The Bishops of Winchester, the Kings of Wessex and the Development of Winchester in the Ninth and early Tenth centuries', *Proceedings of the Hampshire Field Club and Archaeological Society* 40 (1984), pp.61–70.

30. M. Biddle, 'Seasonal Festivals and Residence: Winchester, Westminster and Gloucester in the Tenth to Twelfth Centuries', *Anglo-Norman Studies* 8 (1986 for 1985), pp.51–72. For a later evolution of the crown-wearing ceremony, see M. Hare, 'Kings Crowns and Festivals: the Origins of Gloucester as a Royal Ceremonial Centre', *Transactions of the Bristol and Gloucestershire Archaeological Society* 115 (1997), pp.41–78. See also B. Kjølbye-Biddle, 'Old Minster, St Swithun's Day 1093', in *Winchester Cathedral: Nine Hundred Years, 1093–1993*, ed. J. Crook (Chichester, 1993), pp.13–20.

31. Lund, 'Peace and Non-Peace in the Viking Age', pp.256 and 258–9.

32. John of Worcester, *Chronicle*, pp.458–9.

33. Williams, 'Cockles amongst the Wheat', p.3.

34. For English raids into Wales in the tenth through to the mid-eleventh century, see Stafford, *Unification and Conquest*, p.120.

35. F. Thorn and C. Thorn (eds), *Domesday Book: Shropshire* (Chichester, 1986), entry nos 4(1):10–12. See generally Stafford 'Farm of One Night' and above pp.22–4.

36. Abels, 'English Logistics and Military Administration', p.262.

37. Hill, 'Trends in the Development of Towns', pp.223–5.

38. Alcock, *Cadbury Castle, Somerset*, pp.44–62.

10: THORKELL'S ARMY

1. Keynes, *Diplomas*, pp.217–19.

2. M.K. Lawson, 'Archbishop Wulfstan and the Homiletic Development in the Laws of Æthelred II and Cnut', *English Historical Review* 107 (1992), p.576 of pp.565–86.

3. Sawyer no.1503 (A.D. 1014).

4. Higham, *Death of Anglo-Saxon England*, pp.50–1.

5. Higham, *Death of Anglo-Saxon England*, p.51, notes the favourable position of Wulfnoth's son, Godwine with Cnut by 1018.

6. Keynes, *Diplomas*, pp.216–17.

7. John of Worcester, *Chronicle*, pp.462–3.

8. Keynes, 'Declining Reputation', p.232, has suggested that the chronicler may even have been writing from London.

9. Gillingham, 'William the Bastard at War'; 'Richard I and the Science of War'.

10. Keynes, 'Declining Reputation', p.232, has consid-

ered a Ramsey location, but his preference for a London author of the Chronicle may not rule out an eastern English interest.

11. For royal armies, see R.P. Abels, *Lordship and Military Obligation in Anglo-Saxon England* (Berkeley, 1988), pp.146–84.

12. There may have been more than 1,000 in a city of 6,000, on the eve of the Norman Conquest; a tentative calculation extrapolated from Brooks, *Early History*, p.32.

13. For the ninth-century Vikings at their most destructive, see N.P. Brooks, 'England in the Ninth Century: The Crucible of Defeat', *Transactions of the Royal Historical Society* 5th series, 29 (1979), pp.1–20.

14. Alternatively, a possible foundation at St Mildred's Church, Canterbury; Brooks, *Early History*, pp.34–5.

15. Whitelock, *EHD* 1, p.245, n.5.

11: THE FINAL YEARS OF AETHELRED'S KINGDOM

1. Keynes, *Diplomas*, p.223.

2. The last charter for anywhere north of 'English' Mercia was granted in 1013 (Sawyer no.931), although of course this may be a result of the survival of evidence.

3. J.L. Nelson, 'The Last Years of Louis the Pious', in *Charlemagne's Heir: New Perspectives on the Reign of Louis the Pious*, ed. P. Godman and R. Collins (Oxford, 1990), p. 147 of pp.147–59.

4. Stenton, *Anglo-Saxon England*, pp.384–5.

5. Innes, 'Danelaw Identities', pp.74–5.

6. John Gillingham remarked on the notable absence in the pre-Conquest English sources of records of the political uses of poisoning, even though it was comparatively common on the European continent; '1066 and the Introduction of Chivalry into England', in *Law and Government in Medieval England and Normandy: Essays presented to James Holt*, ed. G. Garnett and J. Hudson (Cambridge, 1994), p.55 of pp.31–55. However, Gillingham suggests that, in comparison to the Normans, the pre-chivalric English may not have needed recourse to poison when they had such easy access to political violence.

7. *EHD* 1, p.931 of pp.928–34.

8. See Stafford, 'Laws of Cnut and the History of Royal Promises'.

9. Insley, 'One Wedding and Three Funerals'.

10. Insley, 'One Wedding and Three Funerals'.

11. R. Lavelle, *Hostages and Peacemaking in Anglo-Saxon England* (University of York, MA dissertation, 1997). For an example of the survival of such a mutilated hostage, see A. Williams, 'Land and Power in the Eleventh Century: the Estates of Harold Godwineson', *Anglo-Norman Studies* 3 (1981 for 1980), p.182 of pp.171–234; for the use of bodily mutilation in lawcodes, see Keynes, 'Tale of Two Kings', p.212. See also K. O'Brien O'Keefe, 'Body and Law in Late Anglo-Saxon England', *Anglo-Saxon England* 27 (1998), pp.209–32.

12. For the German evidence, where this appears to have been a fine art, see Reuter, *Germany in the Early Middle Ages*, pp.206–8.

13. Williams, 'Cockles amongst the Wheat', p.3.

14. Stafford, 'Aethelred II', p.36; Insley, 'One Wedding and Three Funerals', p.34.

15. See Higham, *Death of Anglo-Saxon England*, pp.41–4, who sees the will as a rallying call to the nobles named by Aethelstan.

16. Henry of Huntingdon, *Historia Anglorum*, pp.362–3. See also A. Campbell (ed.), *Encomium Emmae Reginae* (London, 1949), pp.30–3.

17. Stafford, *Unification and Conquest*, p.68.

18. Keynes, *Diplomas*, pp.211–13.

19. Stafford, 'Æthelred II', p.36.

20. Williams, 'Cockles amongst the Wheat', p.5.

21. See above, chapter 9, n.13.

22. John of Worcester, *Chronicle*, pp.484–5.

AFTERMATH

1. Anglo-Saxon Chronicle for 878; Asser, *Life of Alfred*, in *Alfred the Great*, ed. Keynes and Lapidge, p.84.

2. John of Worcester, *Chronicle*, pp.942–3.

3. Sawyer, nos 947 and 948.

APPENDIX 1: CHRONOLOGY
OF EVENTS

959   Death of King Eadwig; succession of Edgar to the whole English kingdom.

964   Expulsion of secular clerics from Old Minster, Winchester, Chertsey and Cerne Abbas; marriage of King Edgar to Aelfthryth.

966   Date of New Minster refoundation charter: display of West-Saxon royal family (King, Queen and new *aetheling*, Edmund).

969   Edgar orders Thanet to be ravaged.
Death of Edmund *aetheling*.

973   Second coronation of Edgar, alongside Queen Aelfthryth; Edgar rowed along River Dee at Chester by other British kings (or meets them?). Death of King Edgar; succession of Edward.

977   Collapse of upper storey at Calne (Wilts); injuries and deaths of many royal councillors.

978   Murder of King Edward ('the Martyr') at Corfe (Dorset); succession of Aethelred.

979   Consecration of King Aethelred II at Kingston-upon-Thames (Surrey).

980   Southampton, Thanet and Cheshire ravaged by Vikings; approximate date of the building of the geometric fortresses in Denmark.

981   St Petroc's Monastery, Padstow (Cornwall) ravaged; coastal raids on Devon and Cornwall.

982   Ravaging in Portland (Dorset) and west Wales; fire in London; deaths of Ealdormen Aethelmaer of Hampshire and Edwin of Sussex.

984   Death of Bishop Aethelwold.

985   Ealdorman Aelfric of Mercia exiled.

986   Lands of Rochester diocese laid waste by Aethelred.

987   Death of King Harald Bluetooth in Denmark.

988   Battle at Watchet (Somerset); death of Archbishop Dunstan.

991   Ravaging at Folkestone, ?Sandwich, Ipswich and Maldon; death of Ealdorman Byrhtnoth of Essex in battle at Maldon; peace made and £10,000 payment recorded.

992   Attempt to muster a navy from London; Aelfric, Ealdorman of Hampshire gives the game away.

993   Bamburgh sacked; ravaging from the Humber mouth in Lindsey and Northumbria; King Aethelred blinds the son of Ealdorman Aelfric.

994   Attack on London; ravaging on coast and Essex, Kent, Sussex, Hampshire; Vikings winter in Southampton; £16,000 tribute recorded; probable date of peace treaty *II Aethelred* probably composed between King Aethelred and Olaf Tryggvason, Norwegian Viking leader.

995   Approximate date of death of King Eric the Victorious of Sweden; Swein perhaps succeeds to whole Danish kingdom.

997   Ravaging on north Somerset coast (Watchet again), Cornwall, Wales, Devon; attack on *burh* at Lydford and Tavistock Abbey (Devon).

998   Ravaging in Dorset; Vikings encamp on Isle of Wight, receiving supplies from Hampshire and Sussex.

999   Vikings beat Kentish army at Rochester; ravaging of west Kent.

1000   Viking force in Normandy; Aethelred ravages Cumbria, Strathclyde and Isle of Man, and probably also sends a force to attack the Cotentin region of Normandy; approximate date of death of Queen Aelfthryth; also of King Olaf Tryggvason of Norway, at the Battle of the Svöld.

1001   Ravaging 'almost everywhere'; Hampshire *fyrd* beaten at *Aethelingadene* (East and West Dean, Sussex); deaths of two King's high reeves; burning of Teignton; battle at ?Exeter or Pinhoe, burning of Clyst (Devon); encampment on Isle of Wight, burning of Waltham (probably Hants.).

1002   £24,000 tribute recorded; Ealdorman Leofsige of Essex banished for murder of King's high reeve, Aefic; arrival of Queen Emma in England; massacre of Danes in England ordered by King Aethelred on St Brice's Day (13 November).

1003   Exeter stormed and destroyed by Vikings; ravaging and burning of Wilton after Ealdorman Aelfric fails to lead the English army.

1004   Ravaging and burning of Norwich; failed peace and ravaging of Thetford.

1005   Great famine throughout England.

1006   Possible 'coup' in the replacement of royal advisors, including dispossession of Wulfgeat, blinding of Wulfheah and Ufegeat, sons of Ealdorman Aelfhelm, and killing of Ealdorman Aelfheah; ravaging and burning of Sandwich; Viking encampment on Isle of Wight while Aethelred in Shropshire; ravaging in Hampshire and Berkshire; Wallingford burnt; peace and tribute arranged by Aethelred; Uhtred of Bamburgh victorious against the Scots at Durham.

1007   £36,000 tribute recorded.

1008   Military reorganisation in England ordered by King Aethelred.

1009   English fleet brought together at Sandwich; Wulfnoth *Cild* accused of crimes and so ravages south coast; storm destroys eighty English ships in pursuit; Canterbury and eastern England sue for peace with Thorkil ('3,000 pounds'); ravaging in Sussex, Hampshire and Berkshire from Isle of Wight; wintering on the Thames.

1010   Unsuccessful attack on London; burning Oxford; Vikings repairing ships in Kent during spring; Successful resistance at Ringmere by the men of Cambridgeshire; King's son (or brother-in-law), Athelstan killed; ravaging in East Anglia, burning Thetford and Cambridge; burning in Buckinghamshire, Oxfordshire, Northampton and Wiltshire.

1011   Peace agreed in return for tribute and provisions for Vikings; siege and ransacking of Canterbury and capture of Archbishop.

1012   Martyrdom of Aelfheah, Archbishop of

Canterbury; peace and tribute at '48,000 pounds'; forty-five ships under Thorkell sell themselves to Aethelred's service.

1013 Swein returns to England, with his son, Cnut; Swein acclaimed King at Gainsborough; receives submission from Northumbria, Lindsey, Five Boroughs (Lincoln, Nottingham, Derby, Leicester, Stamford), Danes north of Watling Street, Oxford, Winchester; Swein fails to capture London; submission of western nobles at Bath, so subsequent submission of London; exile of the royal family; Thorkell demands tribute and provisions at Greenwich, but ravages anyway.

1014 Death of Swein; acclamation of King Cnut amongst Danes; return of Aethelred; Cnut consolidates his position in Lindsey at Gainsborough; English hostages mutilated at Sandwich; £21,000 recorded as paid to Thorkell's army at Greenwich; many villages suffer flooding at the end of September; Archbishop Wulfstan preaches the *Sermon of the Wolf to the English*.

1015 Assembly at Oxford; Ealdorman Eadric kills English thegns; Edmund (Ironside) the *aetheling* rebels against his father, receiving the submission of the Five Boroughs; Cnut ravages in Dorset, Wiltshire and Somerset; King Aethelred lies ill; Ealdorman Eadric allies with Cnut.

1016 Cnut comes into Mercia, ravaging and burning; Edmund and Earl Uhtred ravage in north-west England; Cnut ravages Buckinghamshire, Bedfordshire, Huntingdonshire, Northamptonshire, fens, Stamford, Lincolnshire, Nottinghamshire, into Northumbria to York; Earl Uhtred submits to Cnut and is murdered.
Death of King Aethelred on St George's day; Edmund Ironside becomes King; battles at Penselwood (Somerset) and Sherston (Wilts); Edmund relieves London and fights Vikings at Brentford; Vikings attack London again and ravage Mercia, returning to Kent; King Edmund meets Ealdorman Eadric at Aylesford (Kent); Danes head into Essex and Mercia.
Battle of Ashingdon: deaths of English nobility; victory for Cnut; peace agreement between Cnut and Edmund at Alney by Deerhurst (Glos.); payment to Danes; separation of kingdom between Wessex and Mercia; London buys peace from Cnut.
Death of King Edmund on St Andrew's day.

1017 Cnut succeeds to whole of England, dividing it into four: he takes Wessex; Thorkell takes East Anglia, Eadric takes Mercia; the Norwegian noble Eric of Hlathir takes Northumbria; Cnut has Eadric killed; Cnut marries Emma.

1018 Payment of '72,000 pounds' recorded.

Ealdormen, AD 965–1016

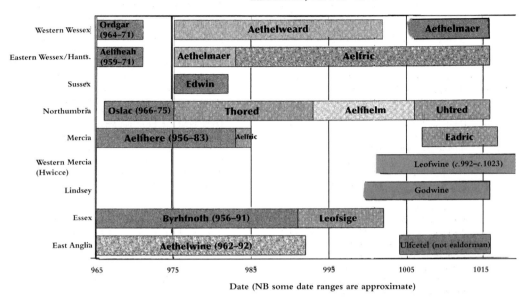

Date (NB some date ranges are approximate)

This diagram is intended to allow comparison of the different ealdormanries and who held particular offices at any one time. A degree of simplification has been necessary in this diagram, as it does not reflect points at which territorial encroachments were made through the augmentation of the ealdorman's authority at the expense of others (most notably, that of Ealdorman Eadric 'Streona' in the early eleventh century). The convoluted politics of early medieval Northumbria, reflected in the changing relationships between the lordship of Bamburgh and the ealdormanries of York and Northumbria probably also require a diagram in itself, and here this diagram may give a false impression of simplicity if it is not approached with reservations. While it is probable that the ealdormanries of Lindsey and Western Mercia were newly created in the 990s, this can really only be suggested through a lack of evidence for these ealdormanries before that decade. The earliest known date of office-holding is reflected through the use of the 'faded' bar diagrams, showing that the precise dates of appointments to new offices are difficult to ascertain. The placement up of one ealdorman immediately before the next may also give a falsely precise impression of immediate successions to offices, and some dates are more approximate than others. Nonetheless, this may aid the visualisation of the changes in office during, and before, the reign of King Aethelred.

Appendix 3: Genealogy of the West-Saxon royal family in the tenth and eleventh centuries

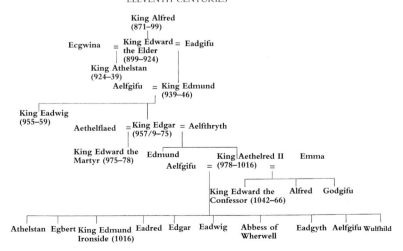

APPENDIX 4: LAW IN ACTION

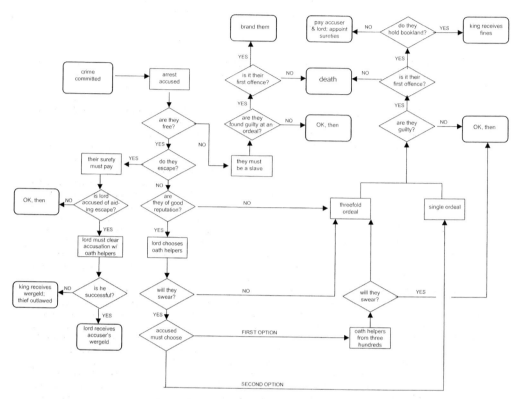

EXTRACT FROM *I AETHELRED* (THE WOODSTOCK LAWCODE)

This is the ordinance which King Aethelred and his councillors have ordained, at Woodstock [Oxfordshire] in Mercia, for the peace of all the people, following English law.

That is, that every freeman shall have a trustworthy surety [*borh*] to hold him to every legal duty, should he be accused.

If, however, he [the accused] should be of bad reputation [*tyhtbysig*], he shall go to the threefold ordeal.

If his lord says that he [the accused] has failed neither in oath nor in ordeal since the assembly at Bromdun, let him [the lord] choose two trustworthy thegns from the hundred, and they shall swear that his oath has never failed nor that he has ever been convicted of theft [literally 'paid thief-geld'] – unless he [the lord] has a reeve who is worthy of doing this [instead].

If the oath is forthcoming, the [accused] man shall choose whichever he will, either the single ordeal or an oath worth a pound [in value, supported by oath helpers] from three hundreds, [if the object is] over 30 pence in value.

If they then dare not give the oath, he [the accused] shall go to the threefold ordeal.

If he is found guilty, on the first occasion he shall give his accuser double value and the lord his wergeld ['man-price'], and he shall appoint trustworthy sureties that henceforth he will desist from every kind of misdeed.

And on the second occasion he shall not make any amends except by his head.

If he should escape and avoid the ordeal, his surety shall pay the value of his goods to the accuser and the wergeld of the accused to the lord who is entitled to the fines incurred by him.

And if the lord should be accused of advising escape and wrongdoing, he [the lord] shall choose five thegns, and shall make himself the sixth, and shall clear himself of the charge.

And if he should succeed in clearing himself, he shall be entitled to the wergeld [from the accuser?].

And if he should fail, the King shall take the wergeld, and the thief [the accused] shall be outlawed by all the people.

And every lord shall be personally [responsible as] surety for his own household men [*hiredmen*].

And if a man is accused and escapes, the lord shall pay his wergeld to the King.

And if the lord should be accused of advising escape, he shall clear himself with [the help of] five thegns, and shall make himself the sixth.

Should he fail to clear himself, he shall pay his [own] wergeld to the King, and the man shall be outlawed.

And the King shall be entitled to all the fines which are incurred by men who hold bookland, and no-one [of these] shall pay the compensation following any charge, unless in the presence of the King's reeve.

And if a slave is found guilty at the ordeal, he shall be branded on the first occasion.

And on the second occasion, he shall not be able to make any amends except by his head.

…

Note: The extract provided here is translated to illustrate the workings of the law. A useful version of the entire lawcode, with parallel Old English text, and an editorial numbering of the clauses, is that of A.J. Robertson, *The Laws of the Kings of England from Edmund to Henry I* (Cambridge, 1925), pp.53–5. For a translation of the lawcode which is suitably attentive to the conditional tenses and provides an alternative numbering system, see P. Wormald, *The Making of English Law: King Alfred to the Twelfth Century*, vol.1, *Legislation and its Limits* (Oxford, 1999), pp.324–5. The interpretations of this lawcode upon a flow diagram have benefited from the useful suggestions of Maria Drummond.

The lawcode promulgated at Woodstock is generally considered to have been a product of the 990s. It was not, contrary to the title given to it by modern legal historians, the first lawcode of Aethelred's reign. However, the first main sections, reproduced here in translation and followed in the flow diagram, may show the workings of the law set to a practical purpose. The lawcode contains clauses for all possible contingencies, which reflect a strong interest by the State in private property. The aim of the lawcode seems to have been to ensure that all men had a surety or guarantor in the form of either their lord or another man. The process of dealing with a slave reflects the fact that the use of sureties and witnesses (oath-helpers) was a luxury available only to those of free status (a *ceorl* or thegn). A slave did not have recourse to law in the same manner as a freeman, and although the lawcode's reliance on the word of social superiors in maintaining innocence may strike us as potentially 'barbaric' (with room for abuse), we should remind ourselves that it is not dissimilar from the importance placed upon having witnesses of good reputation in modern adversarial legal systems. In *I Aethelred*, there were still a number of stages which the accused had to go through. It is probable that the surety and the lord could have been one and the same man, and perhaps in the majority of cases they were, but the 'legalese' of the code ensures that some distinction is made for these cases in which they were not one and the same.

After the justification of the accused's reputation, at least since a previous lawcode had been promulgated at 'Bromdun' (a lawcode which may now be lost), oath-helpers had to be chosen. Providing that they were willing to swear to his innocence, the accused would then be allowed to proceed to the next stage; either the 'simple' or single ordeal or choosing oath-helpers from three hundreds. If they would, or could, testify his innocence, then he was safe. If they would not, or indeed if the first group of oath-helpers would not testify, then the accused had to go to the triple ordeal. This would mean the use of trial by fire, trial by water or the like, relying upon the judgement of God manifested through the person of the King, which, after all, was the important message which lay behind late Anglo-Saxon royal lawmaking.

Elements of the diagram have been simplified to show the process of law, and the reception by the King of the fines from the guilty man's bookland may be additional to all stages of the law rather than simply being a question asked if it were a first offence. However, the diagram still shows the importance of all the contingencies accounted for in the lawcode. For this reason, the language of the code purposefully repeats itself, as Patrick Wormald, has demonstrated, (*Making of English Law*, pp.324–5). The Woodstock lawcode showed a realm that was consolidating by building on past achievement, rather than shoring up a dam of anarchy. It was a product of a kingship with a strong awareness of the importance of legislation.

APPENDIX 5: GLOSSARY

Aetheling: An Old English word meaning 'noble' (of the royal family) or 'prince'.

Anglo-Saxon Chronicle: A set of annals for the English kingdom. Originally begun under the orders of King Alfred, who ensured that the West Saxon kingdom had an 'official' history; by the tenth century there were different versions of the Chronicle in England. Of most interest for the reign of King Aethelred is the Abingdon or 'C' manuscript, which was not written down year-by-year, but reflected a rather personal perspective from around the final year of the reign.

Bookland: Land held by charter or, by the end of the Anglo-Saxon period, understood to be held with the same rights as a charter allowed. Such lands could often be alienated as the holder wished, but they also gave a degree of high status for the holder of the charter.

Burh: An Old English word used to refer to fortifications or a town (presumably fortified). A great deal of work had gone into the administration of the extensive fortifications of the West-Saxon kingdom, as the 'Burghal Hidage', a document from the reign of King Edward the Elder (899–924) reflects. By the time of Aethelred, it was also important to ensure that the local mint was also well protected.

Ceorl: A term for a free peasant landowner, which could be an insult when used to refer to someone of high status (hence 'churlish' in Modern English).

Danelaw: A term used to refer to the region formerly under Scandinavian political control in the late ninth and early tenth centuries, consisting of East Anglia, part of Mercia and much of northern England. The idea of a separate 'Danish' law persisted even when these areas were subsumed under West-Saxon authority.

Ealdorman: An official appointed to administer a region of the kingdom. Ealdormen were tasked with the operation

153

of justice on behalf of the King, but in times of war they commanded local military forces. Although in theory, the King decided upon appointments, the middle years of the tenth century saw the rise of powerful dynasties who ensured that the office could be hereditary.

Fyrd: An Old English word denoting an 'expedition'; this was used to refer to the summoning of a military force, on either a local or national basis. The term's usual implication was defence, used in opposition to the term *Here*, which generally indicated an invading army.

Geld: A term used to refer to taxes or money in general. 'Danegeld' is a post-Conquest word for an additional tax – the '*Heregeld*', or 'army tax' – which could be levied in the English kingdom. All such money was not necessarily used to bribe invading Vikings to leave the English kingdom, as is often assumed.

Shire: A division ('share') of the English kingdom, many of which were used as the bases of English counties. Wessex may have been the first kingdom to use such a system, but shires were imposed upon the rest of the England under West-Saxon control during the tenth century. They formed some of the administrative building blocks of the kingdom.

Thegn: A land-owning noble, owing services (military or otherwise) to his lord. In real terms, a thegn's power and influence could vary significantly.

Witan: Old English term, referring to the 'wise men' or 'counsellors' of the King, advisors on policy and laws. These were the great, the good and probably also the bad of the kingdom: the bishops, ealdormen and other well-placed nobles, who met under the King's jurisdiction at the *witanagemot*, a 'national' assembly which was convened at different sites in southern England.

GUIDE TO FURTHER READING

The Anglo-Saxon Chronicle can be read through various translations; at the time of writing, the most readily available is that of Michael Swanton but another is provided in Dorothy Whitelock's *English Historical Documents*, a volume which is probably the most comprehensive collection of translated sources from the Anglo-Saxon period. Margaret Ashdown's *English and Norse Documents* is useful for translations of Scandinavian sagas and skaldic verse; although such works are of varying degrees of reliability, many provide a different perception of Aethelred's realm within the North Sea. Written for a readership in an established Anglo-Danish court, some three decades after the invasion of England, the *Encomium* of Queen Emma provides a perspective on the last year of Aethelred's reign, the short reign of Edmund Ironside and the first years of Cnut's consolidation of power.

Simon Keynes's *Diplomas of Æthelred 'The Unready'* is a seminal monograph on the subject of King Aethelred himself, but it is also useful because of the picture which it provides on royal government in the tenth century, which allowed Keynes to contextualise King Aethelred for the first time. Keynes's work also provides a full account of Aethelred's reign, from the controversies surrounding his succession to the throne to the final years – an account which makes full use of the charter evidence. An essay by Keynes on the 'Declining Reputation' of Aethelred was published in a volume of conference proceedings edited by David Hill in 1978. Taken as a whole, *Ethelred the Unready* was perhaps the first major revisionist book on the King's reign and, as it includes essays by Pauline Stafford on the King's methods of governance, Patrick Wormald on the laws of Aethelred and David Hill on the urban infrastructure of the kingdom, it remains an essential study.

Sir Frank Stenton's *Anglo-Saxon England* is still perhaps the 'classic' text on early medieval England, and is worth reading for a less than sympathetic view of the 'Decline of the Old English monarchy' under Aethelred. For other general works on later Anglo-Saxon England, a good place to begin is the volume edited by James Campbell, *The Anglo-Saxons*. The variety of scholarship which it contains remains an excellent introduction to the kingdom. Campbell himself has undertaken detailed work on the Old English State in a number of papers which consider the kings' rights and abilities to extract taxation from their subjects. Nicholas Higham's *Death of Anglo-Saxon England* provides a view of the Anglo-Saxon kingdom from the reign of Aethelred to the Norman Conquest, contextualising the events of 978–1016 with some useful insights. Pauline Stafford's *Unification and Conquest* also deals with a number of themes of the later Anglo-Saxon kingdom, and is useful for its view of the relationship between the West-Saxon 'core' of the English kingdom and the different regions. For more detailed texts on the regional importance of specific families, see works by Ann Williams, Charles Insley, Cyril Hart and Richard Fletcher.

The relationship between the English and the Vikings in the period still remains an obvious preoccupation. For the Vikings, see studies by Niels Lund and Peter Sawyer, scholars who have added to the transformation of our understanding of rather more sophisticated states than had hitherto been supposed. Other useful works are by Else Roesdahl and Klavs Randsborg. With regard to the wars of the period, see works by Richard Abels and the volumes on the Battle of Maldon edited by Janet Cooper and Donald Scragg respectively.

BIBLIOGRAPHY

TRANSLATED PRIMARY SOURCES

Adam of Bremen, *History of the Archbishops of Hamburg-Bremen*, ed. F.J. Tschan (New York, 1959)

Anglo-Saxon Chronicle, ed. M.J. Swanton (London, 1996)

Anglo-Saxon Wills, ed. D. Whitelock (Cambridge, 1930)

The Chronicle of John of Worcester, vol.2, *The Annals from 450 to 1066*, ed. R.R. Darlington, P. McGurk and J. Bray (Oxford, 1995)

English and Norse Documents Relating to the Reign of Ethelred the Unready, ed. M.A. Ashdown (Cambridge, 1930)

English Historical Documents, vol.1: *c.500–1042*, ed. D. Whitelock (London, 2nd edn, 1979)

The Gesta Normannorum Ducum of William of Jumièges, Orderic Vitalis and Robert of Torigni, ed. E.M.C. van Houts (Oxford, 1995)

Henry of Huntingdon, *Historia Anglorum: The History of the English People*, ed. D.E. Greenway (Oxford, 1996)

The Laws of the Kings of England from Edmund to Henry I, ed. A.J. Robertson, (Cambridge, 1925)

Thietmar, *Chronicon*, in *Ottonian Germany: the Chronicon of Thietmar of Merseburg*, ed. D.A. Warner (Manchester, 2001)

William of Malmesbury, *Gesta Regum Anglorum: The History of the English Kings*, vol.1, ed. R.A.B. Mynors with R.M. Thomson and M. Winterbottom (Oxford, 1998)

Wulfstan of Winchester, *Life of St Æthelwold*, ed. M. Lapidge and M. Winterbottom (Oxford, 1991)

SECONDARY WORKS

Abels, R.P., *Lordship and Military Obligation in Anglo-Saxon England* (Berkeley, 1988)

Abels, R.P., 'English Logistics and Military Administration, 871–1066: the Impact of the Viking Wars', in *Military Aspects of Scandinavian Society in a European Perspective, A.D. 1–1300*, ed. A.N. Jørgensen and B.L. Clausen (Copenhagen, 1997), pp.257–65

Anderson, O., 'The Viking Policy of Ethelred the Unready', in *Anglo-Scandinavian England: Norse-English Relations in the Period before the Conquest*, ed. J.D. Niles and M. Amodio (London, 1989), pp.1–11

Campbell, J., 'Observations on English Government from the Tenth Century to the Twelfth Century', *Transactions of the Royal Historical Society* 5th series 25 (1975), pp.39–54

Campbell, J., 'Some Agents and Agencies of the Late Anglo-Saxon State' in *Domesday Studies*, ed. J.C. Holt (Woodbridge, 1987), pp.201–218

Campbell, J., 'The Late Anglo-Saxon State: A Maximum View', *Proceedings of the British Academy* 87 (1995 for 1994), pp.39–65

Campbell, J., John, E. and Wormald, P. (eds), *The Anglo-Saxons* (London, 1982)

Cooper, J., (ed.), *The Battle of Maldon: Fiction and Fact* (London, 1993)

Cubitt, C., 'Sites and Sanctity: Revisiting the Cult of Murdered and Martyred Anglo-Saxon Royal Saints', *Early Medieval Europe* 9 (2000), pp.53–83

Fisher, D.J.V., 'The Anti-Monastic Reaction in the Reign of Edward the Martyr', *Cambridge Historical Journal* 10 (1950–2), pp.254–70

Fletcher, R., *Bloodfeud: Murder and Revenge in Anglo-Saxon England* (London, 2002)

Gillingham, J., '"The Most Precious Jewel in the English Crown": Levels of Danegeld and Heregeld in the Early Eleventh Century', *English Historical Review* 104 (1989), pp.373–84

Godden, M., 'Apocalypse and Invasion in Late Anglo-Saxon England', in *From Anglo-Saxon to Early Middle English: Studies presented to E.G. Stanley*, ed. M. Godden, D. Gray and T. Hoad (Oxford, 1994), pp.130–62

Graham-Campbell, J., *The Viking World* (London, 1980)

Hadley, D.M. and Richards, J.D. (eds), *Cultures in Contact: Scandinavian Settlement in England in the Ninth and Tenth Centuries* (Turnhout, Belgium, 2000)

Hart, C., 'Athelstan "Half King" and his Family', *Anglo-Saxon England* 2 (1973), pp.115–44

Higham, N.J., *The Death of Anglo-Saxon England* (Stroud, 1997)

Hill, D.H. (ed.), *Ethelred the Unready: Papers from the Millenary Conference* (Oxford, 1978)

Hill, D.H., *An Atlas of Anglo-Saxon England* (Oxford, 1981)

Hill, D.H. and Rumble, A.R. (eds), *The Defence of Wessex: the Burghal Hidage and Anglo-Saxon Fortifications* (Manchester, 1996)

Hooper, N., 'Some Observations on the Navy in Late Anglo-Saxon England', *Studies in Medieval History presented to R. Allen Brown*, ed. C. Harper-Bill, C. Holdsworth and J.L. Nelson (Woodbridge, 1989), pp.203–13

Insley, C., 'One Wedding and Three Funerals: Politics and Kinship in Early Eleventh Century Mercia', *Midland History* 25 (2000), pp.28–42

John, E., 'War and Society in the Tenth Century: The Maldon Campaign', *Transactions of the Royal Historical Society* 5th series, 27 (1977), pp.173–95

Keynes, S.D., *The Diplomas of King Æthelred 'The Unready', 978–1016: A Study in their use as Historical Evidence* (Cambridge, 1980)

Keynes, S.D., 'A Tale of Two Kings: Alfred the Great and Æthelred the Unready', *Transactions of the Royal Historical Society* 5th series, 36 (1986), pp.195–207

Keynes, S.D., 'Crime and Punishment in the Reign of King Æthelred the Unready', in *People and Places in Northern Europe 500–1600*, ed. I. Wood and N. Lund (Woodbridge, 1996), pp.67–81

Kjølbye-Biddle, B., 'Old Minster, St Swithun's Day 1093', in *Winchester Cathedral: Nine Hundred Years, 1093–1993*, ed. J. Crook (Chichester, 1993), pp.13–20

Krogh, K.J., 'The Royal Viking-Age Monuments at Jelling in the Light of Recent Archaeological Excavations', *Acta Archaeologica* 53 (1982), pp.183–216

Lapidge, M., Blair, J., Keynes, S.D., and Scragg, D.G. (eds), *The Blackwell Encyclopaedia of Anglo-Saxon England* (Oxford, 1999)

Lawson, M.K., 'Danegeld and Heregeld Once More', *English Historical Review* 105 (1990), p.951–61

Lawson, M.K., 'Archbishop Wulfstan and the Homiletic Development in the Laws of Æthelred II and Cnut', *English Historical Review* 107 (1992), pp.565–86

Lawson, M.K., *Cnut: the Danes in England in the Early Eleventh Century* (London, 1993)

Lund, N., 'Peace and Non-Peace in the Viking Age: Ottar in Biarmaland, the Rus in Byzantium, and Danes and Norwegians in England', in *Proceedings of the Tenth Viking Congress: Larkollen, Norway, 1985*, ed. J.E. Knirk (Oslo, 1987), pp.255–69

Lund, N., 'The Armies of Swein Forkbeard and Cnut: *Leding* or *Lið*?', *Anglo-Saxon England* 15 (1986), pp.105–18

Lund, N., 'Scandinavia, *c*.700–1066', in *The New Cambridge Medieval History*, vol.2, *c.700–c.900*, ed. R. McKitterick (Cambridge, 1995), pp.202–27

McDougall, I., 'Serious Entertainments: An Examination of a Peculiar Type of Viking Atrocity', *Anglo-Saxon England* 22 (1993), pp.201–25

Meehan, B., 'The Siege of Durham, the Battle of Carham and the Cession of Lothian', *Scottish Historical Review* 55 (1976), pp.1–19

Morris, C.J., *Marriage and Murder in Eleventh-Century Northumbria: a Study of 'De Obsessione Dunelmi'* (York, 1992)

Nelson, J.L., 'The Second English *Ordo*', in J.L. Nelson, *Politics and Ritual in Early Medieval Europe* (London, 1986), p.367 of pp.361–74

Nelson, J.L., 'England and the Continent in the Anglo-Saxon Period', in *England in Europe, 1066–1453*, ed. N. Saul (London, 1994), pp.21–35

Olsen, O., *Five Viking Ships at Roskilde Fjord* (Copenhagen, 1990)

Page, R.I., *'A Most Vile People': Early English Historians on the Vikings* (London, 1987)

Poole, R.G., *Viking Poems on War and Peace* (Toronto and London, 1991)

Radford, C.A.R., 'Later Pre-Conquest Boroughs and their Defences', *Medieval Archaeology* 14 (1970), pp.83–103

Randsborg, K., *The Viking Age in Denmark: the Formation of a State* (London, 1980)

Reynolds, A.J., *Later Anglo-Saxon England: Life and Landscape* (Stroud, 1999)

Ridyard, S., *The Royal Saints of Anglo-Saxon England: A Study of West Saxon and East Anglian Cults* (Oxford, 1988)

Rodger, N.A.M., 'Cnut's Geld and the Size of Danish Ships', *English Historical Review* 110 (1995), pp.392–403

Roesdahl, E., *Viking Age Denmark* (London, 1982)

Roesdahl, E., 'The Danish Geometric Viking Fortresses and their Context', *Anglo-Norman Studies* 11 (1987 for 1986), pp.208–26

Rollason, D.W., 'The Cults of Murdered Royal Saints in Anglo-Saxon England', *Anglo-Saxon England* 11 (1983), pp.1–22

Sawyer, B., and Sawyer, P.H., *Medieval Scandinavia: From Conversion to Reformation* (Minneapolis and London, 1993)

Sawyer, P.H., *The Age of the Vikings* (London, 2nd edn, 1971)

Sawyer, P.H., 'Ethelred II, Olaf Tryggvason, and the Conversion of Norway', in *Anglo-Scandinavian England: Norse-English Relations in the Period before the Conquest*, ed. J.D. Niles and M. Amodio (London, 1989) pp.17–24

Sawyer, P.H. (ed.), *The Oxford Illustrated History of the Vikings* (Oxford, 1997)

Scragg, D.G. (ed.), *The Battle of Maldon, A.D. 991* (Oxford, 1991)

Stafford, P., 'Church and Society in the Age of Aelfric', in *The Old English Homily and its Backgrounds*, ed. P.E. Szarmach and B.F. Huppé (Albany, N.Y., 1978), pp.11–42

Stafford, P., 'Historical Implications of the Regional Production of Dies under Æthelred II', *British Numismatic Journal* 48 (1980), pp.35–51

Stafford, P., 'The King's Wife in Wessex, 800–1066', *Past and Present* 91 (1981), pp.3–27

Stafford, P., 'The Laws of Cnut and the History of Royal Promises', *Anglo-Saxon England* 10 (1983), pp.173–90

Stafford, P., *Queens, Concubines and Dowagers: The King's Wife in the Early Middle Ages* (London, 1983)

Stafford, P., *Unification and Conquest: A Political and Social History of England in the Tenth and Eleventh Centuries* (London, 1989)

Stafford, P., *Queen Emma and Queen Edith: Queenship and Women's Power in Eleventh-Century England* (Oxford, 1997)

Stenton, F.M., *Anglo-Saxon England* (Oxford, 3rd edn, 1971)

Stowell, T.E.A., 'The Bones of Edward the Martyr', *The Criminologist* 5 (1970), pp.97–119

Thacker, A., 'Saint-Making and Relic Collecting by Oswald and his Communities', in *St Oswald of Worcester: Life and Influence*, ed. N.P. Brooks and C. Cubitt (London, 1996), pp.244–68

Whitelock, D., 'The Dealings of the Kings of England with Northumbria', in *The Anglo-Saxons: Studies in Some Aspects of Their History and Culture Presented to Bruce Dickins*, ed. P. Clemoes (London, 1959), pp.70–88

Wilcox, J., 'The St. Brice's Day Massacre and Archbishop Wulfstan', in *Peace and Negotiation: Strategies for Coexistence in the Middle Ages and the Renaissance*, ed. D. Wolfthal (Turnhout, Belgium, 2000), pp.79–91

Williams, A., 'Some Notes and Considerations on Problems Connected with the English Royal Succession, 860–1066', *Anglo-Norman Studies* 1 (1979 for 1978), pp.144–67

Williams, A., *'Princeps Merciorum Gentis*: The Family, Career and Connections of Ælfhere, Ealdorman of Mercia 956–83', *Anglo-Saxon England* 10 (1982), pp.143–72

Williams, A., 'Cockles amongst the Wheat: Danes and English in the Western Midlands in the First Half of the Eleventh Century', *Midland History* 11 (1986), pp.1–22

Williams, A., *Land, Power and Politics: The Family and Career of Odda of Deerhurst* (Deerhurst, 1997)

Williams, A., *Kingship and Government in Pre-Conquest England, c.500–1066* (Basingstoke, 1999)

Wilson, D.M., 'Danish Kings and England in the Late Tenth and Early Eleventh Centuries: Economic Interpretations', *Anglo-Norman Studies* 3 (1981 for 1980), pp.188–96

Wormald, P., '*Engla-Lond*: The Making of an Allegiance', *Journal of Historical Sociology* 7 (1994), pp.1–24

Wormald, P., *The Making of English Law: King Alfred to the Twelfth Century*, vol.1, *Legislation and its Limits* (Oxford, 1999)

Wormald, P., 'Archbishop Wulfstan and the Holiness of Society', in *Anglo-Saxon History: Basic Readings*, ed. D.A.E. Pelteret (New York, 2000), pp.191–224

Yorke, B., 'Æthelwold and the Politics of the Tenth Century', in *Bishop Æthelwold: His Career and Influence*, ed. B. Yorke (Woodbridge, 1988), pp.65–88

Yorke, B., 'Edward, King and Martyr: A Saxon Murder Mystery', in *Studies in the Early History of Shaftesbury Abbey*, ed. L. Keen (Dorchester, 1999), pp.99–116

LIST OF ILLUSTRATIONS

Thanks are due to the following for permission to reproduce images in this book: Helga Schütze of the Danish National Museum for permission to reproduce photographs taken at the Hobro (Fyrkat) fortress and the Viking Ship Museum at Rosikilde (41, 45, and plates 10, 11 and 14); the trustees of the site of Shaftesbury Abbey, Dorset <www.shaftesburyabbey:co.uk>, for permission to reproduce an image of the modem dedication to Edward the Martyr (29); the British Library for allowing Tempus Publishing to use the image from the Old English Hexateuch (British Library Cotton MS Claudius B.iv) for the cover and plate 9. Professor Barbara Yorke of King Alfred's College, Winchester, for her images of the causeway at Maldon, Essex (49, 50 and plate 17); Ternpus Publishing, for images from their archive (23, 44, 51, 66, 71); Don Lavelle, for the photograph of Athelney and a number of reconstruction drawings and paintings (7, 35, 40, 46, 72; plates 7, 8, 12, 13, 15, 16, 20). All other images used in this book are from the author's own collection.

INDEX